The Selection and Use of Instructional Media

The Selection and Use of Instructional Media

A. J. Romiszowski

KOGAN PAGE

7770985

First published 1974 by
Kogan Page Limited
116a Pentonville Road, London N1 9JN

Setting by Dahling Dahling, London
Printed in Great Britain by
Compton Printing Ltd
Aylesbury, Bucks.

SBN 85038 032 4

Contents

List of Figures

1 A Systematic Approach to Course Design

What are teaching aids?

In order to be quite clear about what we mean by teaching aids, let us start straight away with some definitions. What is a teaching aid? When does it cease to be an aid and become, like the Open University, a teaching system in its own right?

A teaching aid must, as the name suggests, aid the teaching of a topic. This implies two things. First, it does not do the whole job. Parts of the job are performed by other methods (usually a human teacher) and the aid is administered and controlled by the teacher. Secondly, it works. That part of the teaching job entrusted to the aid is performed satisfactorily. We can already see the embryo of a systematic approach to teaching aids. They must obviously be designed for a specific purpose and must then be evaluated to check that they work.

What jobs can teaching aids be expected to do? Teaching involves a number of tasks. The good teacher does much more than merely communicate information. He will follow up the learner's progress, set him tasks to give practice in the use of new information, discuss side issues which arise and attempt to create interest and motivation for the subject. He may use teaching aids to help him in any of these tasks, if by aids we mean such diverse things as diagrams, simulators, prizes and rewards, standardised tests and optional study materials. No teacher relies exclusively on his voice and personality. For the purpose of this book we will limit ourselves to consideration of those teaching aids whose main function is to communicate information.

Learners receive information through the senses, mainly sight and hearing (hence *audio-visual* aids). However, in the training of industrial or craft skills two other senses play

9

almost as important a part: the *sense of touch* and the *kinaesthetic* sense. The latter, the 'sixth' sense, is the one which tells us something is wrong when we try in the dark to climb a stair which is not there. It is the kinaesthetic sense which controls the coordination of physical movements and enables us to reach unerringly for the gear lever or handbrake without the need to look down, or to exert just the right amount of force when tightening a screw. Many of us have learnt to reach for the gear lever; few can tighten a nut to a pre-determined pressure. Both skills have to be learnt by appropriate practice. The use of kinaesthetic sense requires to be practised. This is also true of the other senses. We all have various levels of skill at judging distances which can be improved with practice. Some people have an ear for music, for example, while others are tone deaf. Experiments show that this skill can also be trained. Psychologists talk of sensory, motor and sensory-motor skills, depending on whether learning involves the development of a sense, an action pattern or a combination of senses and actions.

The remaining two senses are little used in teaching. Smell has of course a function in such subjects as chemistry or cookery. Some teachers would still maintain that pain also has a powerful function to perform in education, despite much evidence to the contrary! We will in later chapters confine ourselves to teaching aids which communicate through the first four senses mentioned. Our scope is therefore somewhat wider than that of the normally accepted audio-visual aids. We include the important group of aids which communicate through touch and the kinaesthetic sense: models, training devices and simulators.

However, before we proceed to the 'meat' of this book, let us devote one section to a review of current thinking on the subject of systematic course design in general, and on where the selection of teaching aids fits into the overall picture.

Communication and learning

Various theories or models for communication have been put forward. They are of two main types: *psychological models* which examine the interaction between the learner and his environment (who says what to whom, under what conditions and with what effect); and *engineering models* which explain the process in such terms as 'input', 'output' and 'message' and use analogies to communication in electronic circuits or servo-mechanisms.

An example of the engineering kind of model is represented diagrammatically in Figure 1.1. This is the Shannon-Weaver model suggested in 1949.[1] A message is generated at source and is transmitted by some medium to a receiver at the destination. Any other irrelevant or distracting messages being received are referred to as 'noise' in the communication system. The objective of effective communication is to maintain the maximum 'signal to noise ratio' in the system. So far so good; the question is how to do this. A complex mathematical theory of communication has been developed on the basis of this model and its derivatives. It purports to explain communication in all its forms, human, electrical and so on. It has led to the design and production of machines which learn and machines which teach. The new science of cybernetics is largely concerned with the application of such communication theory to the explanation and simulation of human thought processes. Practical results so far include computers that play chess and learn from their mistakes to play a better game, and complex training devices which adapt the course of training on the basis of the individual learner's error pattern.

One such (now historic) device is SAKI (self adaptive keyboard instructor). This machine is designed to train punch card operators. It presents data to be punched, together with learning prompts in the form of a simulated keyboard where the appropriate key lights up. As learning progresses this aid is gradually withdrawn and the speed at which material is presented increases. An error on any one number, however, modifies the course. That number is again prompted by the re-appearance of the light on the keyboard, more time is

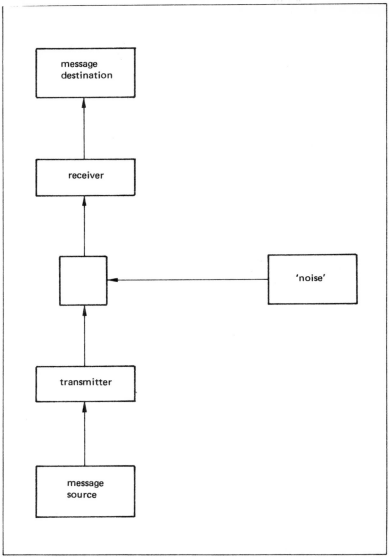

**Figure 1.1 An engineer's model of the communication process
(from C E Shannon and W Weaver,** *The Mathematical Theory of
Communication,* **University of Illinois Press, 1949)**
Any distracting or conflicting messages being received at the destination
are regarded as 'noise' in the communication channel. Efficient communication
aims at reducing 'noise' to a minimum

allowed to punch the number and it appears more often than it used to in the data presented. More help, more time, more practice. What more could a teacher do? Console or encourage perhaps, but the learning proceeds so well in practice that the need for this is minimised. Apart from such devices which are in the main still only used experimentally, the average teacher is likely to feel very little direct impact of cybernetics in the classroom for some time yet. However, the simple concept of signal to noise ratio may prove useful in considering the effects of various teaching procedures.

The second class — psychological models of communication — is concerned with the effect of the message as well as its source and destination. The effect we are particularly interested in is the effect at the destination — what happens to the recipient of our communication. Now we can only tell that the message has had any effect at all if we observe some sort of action or behaviour of the recipient. For example, if we ask someone to close the door we know that if he does this then the message has been received and understood. If we get a flat refusal we are not so sure. He is probably being plain awkward, but he may have misunderstood our message. If we get no response at all, then we do not know whether any message has been received. He may not have heard or he may perhaps be waiting till we say 'please'. We may of course be speaking the wrong language. If our man responds to our message eventually by closing the door, then we may say that he has learnt something, particularly if he persists in this habit of closing the door when we ask him. He may have learnt the meaning of 'close the door' or he may have simply learnt to obey us. We may never know which unless we have more information about the man and his previous background. However, we know for sure that he has learnt something, because his behaviour pattern in a particular situation has changed. Learning can thus be defined as a change in behaviour or as a capacity for new behaviour. We can only establish for certain that learning has taken place if we arrange for the learner to exhibit his new behaviour.

Thus the concept of communication is closely linked to the concept of learning. Our earlier model acknowledged this also. The message is received at the destination and under-

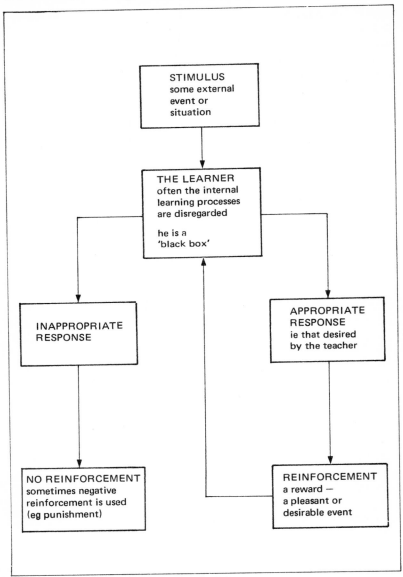

Figure 1.2 A behaviourist learning model
When applied to human learning, the reinforcement takes the form of
knowledge of results. This of course assumes that most responses made
are appropriate, and that the student is motivated and co-operative.

stood. This implies that the meaning was already known or has just been learnt. Now consider our man again, and let us assume he is willing to learn. If we ask him to close the door but he opens the window instead, we would attempt to inform him that this was not the required response. If he does indeed close the door we may congratulate or otherwise reward his efforts. Psychologists refer to this as the *supply of knowledge of results* or *reinforcement*.[2] Communication engineers refer to it as *feedback*. A feedback communication channel is absolutely necessary if a servo-mechanism such as a governor or a thermostat is to function. In the absence of all knowledge of the results learning will not take place. Indeed, performance on a simple task such as drawing lines of a particular length may deteriorate with practice if subjects are blindfolded and are given no indication of their performance.

When we communicate with informed individuals who speak the same language, we simply transmit information or directives. These are understood and are acted upon, if necessary. 'Shut the door, please' will produce a characteristic response. 'My name is John Smith' may produce a snigger or a polite 'hullo'. It is unlikely that next year the hotel manager will greet you with a warm 'Hullo Mr Smith' though of course it happens sometimes. (This is called one-trial learning.) Most learning tasks of any difficulty require more than one trial. One may have to stay at the hotel on the first of every month for a year before the hotel manager remembers one's name. Generally, he will learn the name faster if there are special circumstances which force him to recall it: 'I seem to be missing an ashtray, Mr Smith'.

When attempting to teach, we must arrange appropriate circumstances for practice and recall. We must then also supply feedback to the learner to inform him of his progress. This is the essence of many psychologically based learning models, in particular those belonging to the behaviourist schools. Such a model is represented in Figure 1.2.

Skinner's model

Behaviourists tend to describe their models in terms of *stimulus* and *response* (S — R). Learning has occurred when a specific response is elicited by a specific situation or stimulus with a high degree of probability. The more likely and predictable the response, the more efficient the learning has been. Learning of complex behaviour is regarded as the building up of chains of simple S—R bonds. Professor B F Skinner[3] described the building up of such chains in animals. His techniques of 'shaping' behaviour were then applied (some would say mis-applied) to human learning in the form of the now familiar linear teaching programmes. These attempt to shape human behaviour by presenting a gradual progression of small units of information and related tasks to the learner. At each stage the learner must actively participate by performing the set task. He is then immediately supplied with feedback in the form of the correct answer. In addition, as even pigeons do not learn effectively if allowed to practise incorrect responses, Skinner ensures that the human learner is almost always correct in his responses by the process of reducing the difficulty and supplying extra practice at any points where errors are habitually committed.

The 'skills analysis' approach

Many feel that Skinner's model of human learning is incorrect, or at least incomplete. People do learn from their mistakes if the error of their ways is explained to them. Sometimes they jump a step or two yet come up with what appears to be full understanding. In particular, it is difficult to explain all learning tasks in terms of a chain of S—R bonds built up or 'shaped' one after the other. A step by step procedure such as the solution of a geometry problem or the assembly of a mechanism can be readily described as a series of steps in a chain and may well be learnt by practising each stage and then adding the next one. Such 'progressive-parts' training methods were indeed advocated for industrial procedures by Seymour quite independently of Skinner's work.[4]

Seymour advocates a thorough analysis of the task to be taught before training is commenced, though he is not too clear on how to do this. 'List the knowledge and skills required separately.' How do we recognise which are and which are not necessary? 'By observation and questioning of skilled operators.' This demands certain knowledge and skill on the part of the observer. It is not always easy to tell knowledge and skill elements apart, nor to get any sense out of the skilled operator.

Once the skill elements have been identified, they are described, in sequence on a chart as shown in Figure 1.3. Each of the limbs has its own column, and there are columns for the relevant senses (the choice of columns may vary with the skill being analysed; for example, car-driving skills may require extra columns for the left and right feet). The skills analyst notes down everything that the skilled operator does, in the sequence in which he does it. Thus the vertical edge of the analysis chart may be used as a form of time-scale. Indeed, when repetitive, high-speed skills are being analysed, the time taken to complete each element of the skill is noted and is used as a measure of the difference which exists between the skill level of the new trainee and the experienced operator.

If it is noted that trainees have particular difficulty with only certain elements within the whole task, then special exercises are designed to cope with this difficulty. Then the whole task is practised by the progressive-parts method until proficiency is reached.

In his earlier work, up to the 1950's, Seymour gives no indication of having been influenced by the work of Skinner. Yet the similarities are obvious. Skinner suggests that procedural behaviour may be looked upon as chains of stimulus and response. Seymour breaks down a sequential task into its constituent elements (sequenced in time) and then further analyses the role of each of the limbs (the responses) and how they are controlled by information received by the relevant senses (the stimuli).

In his later book on industrial skills[5] Seymour expands his model to encompass programmed learning. However, he

ITEM	LEFT HAND	RIGHT HAND	VISION	OTHER SENSES	COMMENTS
1. Select leaf			Eyes to pile of leaves, determine leaf for selection and point of grasp.		
		Grasp leaf with T, 1 and 2 move with leaf until nose is visible.			
			Determine position on nose approximately 1" from top of leaf.		
	Grasp selected point with T and 1 on either outer sides of leaf touching stem with tips of both T and 1.				
2. Remove stem		Release hold on leaf and regrasp stem immediately below lefthand T and 1, with fingernails of T and 1 RH. Break stem and commence to draw stem out from leaf, to about 6". Pass hand holding stem behind left hand and continue to draw stem leaving the leaf lightly resting against the back of the LH.			During removal of stem hold leaf in LH at right-angles to body; draw stem with RH towards body until about 6" of stem has been parted from the leaf.
	Hold leaf stationary while stem is being drawn out to 6", rotate hand once in clockwise direction while RH is wrapping leaf around back of hand during the continued drawing out of the stem process. When leaf has passed around heel of hand, and RH starts to draw leaf up back of hand, release hold of nose with T and 1 and lightly hold leaf in hand with 3 and 4 by holding leaf against palm.				
	Grasp leaf lightly as close to stem as possible with T and 1st and 2nd T. Controlling hold by applying sufficient pressure on stem against 1st knuckles of 1 and 2 to enable end of stem to be removed cleanly.	Bring stem between T and 1 LH to cross over 1 and 2 at 1st knuckle joint of LH.	Control passage of stem between fingers of LH.	Kinaesthetic (LH). Sufficient control to hold leaf while end of stem is being removed without holding up normal movement or allowing 'flags' to remain on removed stem.	
3. Place leaf on hand	Rotate hand once in anti-clockwise direction to un-wrap leaf from hand. Reposition T, 1 and 2 on nose of leaf holding leaf on left hand side at nose T on front face of leaf, 1 and 2 on back.	Put aside clean stem in stem bag to RH side.			
		Grasp nose with T on front and 1st and 2nd at back on RH side of leaf at nose. Tear along stem by moving RH across in front of stationary LH quickly, holding nose of leaf firmly during tearing. Hold RH side of leaf lightly between 3 and 4 and palm and grasp nose of LH side of leaf with T on top and 1 and 2 on underside of leaf.	Control RH grasp.	Kinaesthetic (LH). Tension critical to spread leaf fully without tearing.	

Figure 1.3 The form of skills analysis used by W.D. Seymour
(example from *Skills Analysis Training*, Pitman, 1966)

18

sees the relevance of programmed learning as confined to the 'knowledge' content of training, and his own techniques of skills analysis training more relevant to the 'skills' content.

This view would appear to accept only a limited concept of programmed learning — that of a set of written materials structured in small steps, demanding written student responses. We must grant that this is the most commonly held concept of programmed learning — due no doubt to the fact that most published programmes are of this type. However, such programmes are the result of applying Skinner's model to verbal behaviour only. Skinner himself suggests different training structures when dealing with intellectual behaviour or with the shaping of habits and skills.

Indeed, when Skinnerian approaches have been applied to skills training, the resulting course structures have often been indistinguishable from those produced by skills analysis techniques. This is particularly interesting as Seymour would justify his approach by 'communication theory' models of learning, while Skinner would justify his by behaviourist models.

To conclude this section, we see therefore that two of the earlier approaches to the analysis of tasks and the planning of training, based on different theories, converge by giving similar end products. We should add that both these approaches have been widely applied and widely mis-applied. Criticisms of programmed learning (eg on the grounds of neglecting the higher intellectual processes) abound in the press. Similarly John Wellens[6] suggested that the boom in skills analysis training which occurred in British industry in the 1950's and early 1960's was misguided, and the technique was used in many situations where the nature of the training problem did not warrant it.

These mis-applications are not entirely the fault of the originators of the techniques. Skinner never intended the small-step linear programme to be applied to all learning — his disciples did this. Seymour, in his later books, spells out the limitations of applicability of skills analysis, but perhaps too late.

Emergence of an educational technology

We shall be dealing further with the applications and limitations of both these techniques in the last two chapters of this book. For the time being however, we will attempt to present a review of later approaches to the analysis of learning. As we proceed, one thing should become very clear. We are proceeding away from a 'blanket' approach which seeks to use the same technique for all learning, towards a 'horses for courses' approach, where the techniques we use are matched to the characteristics of the problem we face. In fact, we are leaving behind our tendencies to support this or that *theory of learning,* and instead are striving to develop a *theory of instruction.* In so doing, we may of course take notice of existing learning theories (if only to put them in their place) and we would of course take notice of existing research on the learning process (though we may apply novel and more rigorous criteria to assessing the value of this research).

A commonly accepted definition of 'technology' is the systematic application of knowledge (usually scientific knowledge) to achieve a particular practical purpose. Thus construction technology applies what we know about structures, properties of materials, local climatic conditions, social habits and so on, to the systematic design and construction of bridges, buildings, airports etc. Notice that we may draw upon more than one area of knowledge. Notice also that one aspect of a technology (which distinguishes it from an art or a craft) is that as knowledge is applied systematically, we can check back and improve our design as a result of problems which occur in the finished product. For example, for some time now we have had a fairly well-developed knowledge of structures, which enabled us to build bridges which could be guaranteed to carry a certain loading. This differentiated us from the craftsmen of a few centuries ago who were never quite sure whether their stone-arch bridge would stay up when they removed the wooden supports from under the arch. The bridges usually stayed up because, by trial and error over centuries, a set of techniques had been built up which generally produced bridges so solid that they could carry several times the loading required of them. It is amazing how many medieval bridges still withstand the pounding of heavy commercial traffic today. None of the medieval bridge builders could accurately predict the maximum safe loading for their structures. Now we can do this with great precision. However, our own technology is not always perfect. Between the wars, the suspension bridge over the Tacoma Narrows in the USA blew down due to a relatively mild cross wind (about 40 miles per hour), soon after it was built. The designers knew how to allow for the expected vertical loading, but not for the horizontal loading. Now we have learnt to build suspension bridges that are well-ventilated, giving the minimum of resistance to cross winds. By trial and error, a series of rules for the improved design of suspension bridges was devised. However, the present state of development of our technology in respect of the problem of cross winds is probably closer to the state of development of arch-building in the Middle Ages. Nevertheless, we have learnt from previous applications very quickly, and it is unlikely that a brand-new suspension bridge will blow down again.

This digression into bridge-building will, we hope, throw some light on the concept of a 'technology of education'. This current 'in' phrase means different things to different people. At one extreme, educational technology is used to describe the application of hardware, such as filmstrip projectors, videotape recorders, or computers, to education. Such a 'hardware' concept of educational technology is rather limited. It implies the application of the products of other technologies (notably electronics) to education, rather than the 'application of knowledge to the systematic design of education'. Surely it is this latter connotation which is in line with the general definition of 'technology' given earlier. It is this definition of educational technology which we shall adopt. If you like, we are referring to a technology *of* education, rather than technology *in* education.

Do we really have such a technology? Certainly there are areas of knowledge which are, or can be, applied to the design of education. Obvious examples include educational psychology, sociology, comparative education and the history of education. Not so obvious examples would be economics, management sciences and the physical sciences, yet it is these which are currently making themselves felt in proposals for educational reform (eg concepts such as the cost/effectiveness or cost/benefit of a course, or the teacher as a 'manager of resources', or 'individualised, automated instruction' have only recently crept into the jargon of educationalists).

How systematically is our knowledge applied to the design of educational systems? We must assert that in general our level of technological development in education is akin to the medieval bridge builders. The main aim of this chapter is to outline some of the efforts being made to upgrade the level of our technology in just one area of the educational enterprise — the process of instruction. Work such as that of Skinner, Seymour and other early work such as that of Pressey and Bloom laid a foundation upon which a more systematic technology of instructional design is being built. We shall refer to only a few of the contributors to this technology. Our aim here is not to give a full historical account of the development of a technology of education (this would seem premature, although it has been attempted[7]), but rather to outline the main trends and where they are leading.

Gilbert's mathetics

One of the first people to use the term 'technology of education' in the sense defined above, was Tom Gilbert, a disciple of the Skinnerian school. In 1961 he re-organised many of the ideas put forward by other behaviourists and presented them as a set of procedures for the design of instruction. He outlined these in a near-incomprehensible treatise which he entitled *Mathetics* and sub-titled *The Technology of Education*[8]. In this he lays down a set of rules for the analysis of learning tasks, and the construction of appropriate training exercises. His rules are somewhat strict and were originally based more on reasoning than on experimental evidence. Some of his suggestions do however seem to be borne out by subsequent experimentation. In particular his three-class classification of learning tasks into chains, discriminations and generalisations has been of value to trainers.

A *chain* is a series of simple stages which go to make up a procedure. It may be represented by a chain of S—R bonds and may be effectively trained by shaping (à la Skinner) or by Seymour's progressive-parts method. See Figure 1.4. A *discrimination task* is one where several stimuli may occur at any time and the student must respond in a different way to each possible stimulus. An example of a simple discrimination task which most of us learn is to respond correctly to traffic lights. Some of us have learnt it as a sequence and can only mentally recall the exact difference between the meaning of 'Amber' and 'Red and Amber' by reciting to ourselves 'Green, Amber, Red, Red and Amber . . .'. Red and Amber therefore means prepare to go, not prepare to stop . . . or is it the other way round? Gilbert argues that we may have difficulty in responding verbally to this problem, as the way we learnt it originally (as a sequential list) was not appropriate. He argues that discrimination tasks are eventually performed 'all at once' in any order, and so should be taught and practised in this way. Morse code — a very complex discrimination task — is learnt quicker if one attempts as many new letters as possible at one time, rather than learning them one at a time. He illustrates the possibilities of this method by a 4-stage programme to teach the resistor colour code. This compares well in effectiveness with other programmes many times its length. This programme is shown in Figure 1.5. A *generalisation task* involves the student in making generalisations or classifications. Recognising that cows, sheep and goats are all cud-chewing mammals is a generalisation. Gilbert classifies this as a special case of discrimination. One has to discriminate between what goes into the class and what does not. Once again it is more appropriate to learn the whole group at once than to learn them one at a time.

Gilbert suggests an analysis of the performance required in terms of stimulus and response, to identify whether the performance is made up of chains, discriminations or

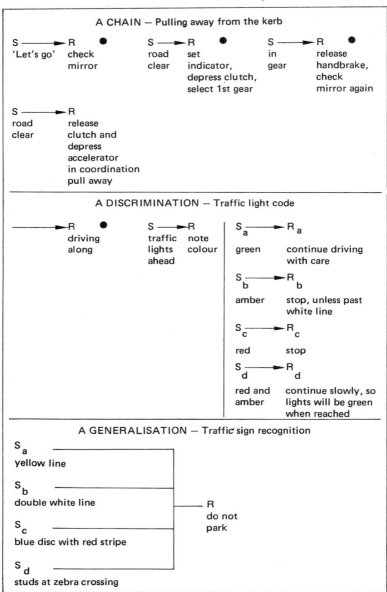

Figure 1.4 The three types of learning task
Gilbert's classification, illustrated by examples from the skill of car driving.

1a. Some electrical resistors have a colour band that tells how much they will resist electric current. On small resistors you can see colours better than numbers. Each colour stands for a number.

THE FIRST THREE COLOUR BANDS ARE READ AS THE NUMBER OF OHMS RESISTANCE

THE FOURTH COLOUR BAND IS READ AS THE PERCENT OF ERROR IN THE RATING

1b. Each of the **First Three Colour Bands** can have one of 10 colours. Read through this list twice. Learn the **Number** for which each **Colour** stands.

a **Five** dollar bill is **Green**	**Zero: Black** nothingness
One Brown penny	a **Red** heart has **Two** parts
a **White** cat has **Nine** lives	**Three Oranges**
Seven Purple seas	a **Four** legged **Yellow** dog
a **Blue** tail fly has **Six** legs	an **Eighty** year old man has **Gray** hair

---

2. List the number for which each **Colour** stands:

Red	White	Purple	Brown	Black
(heart)	(cat)	(seas)	(penny)	(nothingness)

Green	Gray	Blue	Orange	Yellow
(bill)	(hair)	(tail fly)	(oranges)	(dog)

---

3. List the **Number** for which each colour stands:

Black	Brown	Yellow	Gray	Green
White	Purple	Red	Orange	Blue

Figure 1.5 An example of a training exercise for a discrimination task

This exercise uses associations already well established in the (American) student's experience, to help establish the new colour-number associations. Note that all the associations are taught at once. (This example is from a programmed course on Resistor Colour Code by TOR Laboratories Inc 1961.)

generalisations. This 'prescription of the mastery performance' then undergoes several further analyses, in which it is
compared with the performance of typical trainees, the most
common errors they perform, other behaviours they have
previously mastered which are similar and may therefore help
or hinder the acquisition of the new performance, and so on.
It is not our purpose here to give a full description of
mathetical analysis, but the example of the colour code,
illustrated in Figure 1.5 may be examined closer, to illustrate
the general approach:

(a) On observing a master performer we may initially
simply observe that when presented with a small
cylinder with coloured bands (ie a resistor), he says,
or writes down its value.

(b) Closer analysis shows that he does this in several
stages, figure by figure. In S—R notation, this could
appear as follows:

S →	R	•	S →	R	•	S →	R	•	S →	R
First	Write		Second	Write		Third	Add as		Fourth	Interpret
Band	Down		Band	Down		Band	Many Zeros	Band	As the
	Number			Number			As This			Percent
	Appropriate			Appropriate			Colour			of Error
	To The			To The			Stands For			To be
	Colour			Colour						Expected

(c) The mastery performance thus appears to be a
four-stage chain (though only a fairly loose chain —
one could for example note the percentage error
before noting the value if one wished). However, even
a cursory examination of the problems that a new
trainee has with learning this task, shows that the
student's difficulty does not lie in learning that the
first two bands are read as digits, while the third is
read as the number of zeros, but rather in learning
which number is associated with each colour. As a
pre-requisite to performing the whole task, one must

learn the colour code. This is obviously a multiple discrimination:

The Following 10 Stimuli	⎧ Brown is 1 ⎫ Red is 2 Orange is 3 etc ⎭	Should Elicit The Appropriate Number as a Response

(d) To teach this multiple discrimination, Gilbert designed the 3-stage exercise illustrated in Figure 1.5. Several points are worth noting:

1 Three stages are involved in completing the exercise: First, there is a presentation of the colours and numbers (together with a mnemonic which will be discussed later). Secondly, the learner practises supplying the numbers under prompted conditions. Thirdly, the learner practises the total discrimination under the 'real job' conditions. These three stages are named by Gilbert as *demonstration, prompt* and *release* (releasing the behaviour from artificial prompts not present in the final job situation — we might prefer to refer to this stage as 'self-test'). All exercises in a set of mathetical materials should exhibit this 3-stage structure.

2 The mastery performance was defined as reading a resistor value (not painting it on). Therefore the student only practises supplying the value for a given colour (not the colour for a given number). Thus the original S—R pattern is used as the structure for *all three* stages of the learning exercise.

3 In real life any colour band may appear in the first position. One is never expected on the job to list all the number-colour associations in numerical order, nor can one normally predict the order in which colours will appear. Therefore Gilbert

chooses to demonstrate the associations in a random order, and to expect practice from students in other random orders. Otherwise, the learner may end up having to 'run through' the list in his head every time in the way that most of us recall multiplication tables (This is indeed a fine example of inappropriate learning structure, teaching a random-access skill as a sequential skill. The modern 'flash-card' approach is designed to break down the learner's dependence on reciting the multiplication table every time.)

4   Now we come to the 'mnemonic'. The aim is to facilitate learning, as with all mnemonics. However, the structure of this one is particularly interesting. After all there are other learning aids to choose from. Whoever designed the resistor colour code was at least somewhat aware of learning problems and how to deal with them, as he apparently attempted to base the code on the order of colours in a rainbow — Red, Orange, Yellow, Green, Blue, Purple plus the 'dirty' shades (Black and Brown) at one end and the 'clean' shades (Grey and White) at the other. However, that's not particularly easy to remember. Who knows the order of the colours in a rainbow anyway? We need other mnemonics to remember their sequence such as *R*ichard *O*f *Y*ork *G*athers *B*lueberries *V*ainly (V for violet rather than purple).

Gilbert's approach is based on the assumption that meaningful associations already exist in the learner's repertory of behaviour, between the colours and the numbers, only the learner may not be aware of them. To take an example, our student already knows that a heart is red (this behaviour is established and re-inforced by normal convention, by playing cards etc), and most of our students are likely to know from previous learning that a heart has two parts. Using stimulus response notation, our students already have ·

the following two units of behaviour in their repertory:

S →   R   and   S →   R

Red   Colour   Heart   In Two Parts
           of   Structure (called
           Heart   ventricles)

By designing a mnemonic which incorporates both of
these units, Gilbert attempts to 'bridge the gap'
between the colour 'red' and its value 'two'. In effect,
he converts the learning of this single S—R association
into a 2-stage chain, in which the 'prompt word' acts
as both the response of the first stage and the
stimulus of the second, thus:

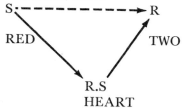

RED   TWO

R.S
HEART

The success of such a technique has been tested over
and over again. It is the method used by professional
'memory men', though of course they select their
own prompt words (or mediators). The success of
Gilbert's programme depends on how well he chooses
the mediators. Do students really know a cat has nine
lives (in Arab countries cats have seven lives)? Why a
yellow dog? Dogs come in a variety of colours. Well,
in the USA (where this example was written) 'yellow
dog' has a slang usage which would render it well
established in the previous behaviour of American
readers. For a British audience, at one time, we might
have selected 'Four Beatles in a Yellow Submarine',
though this has the disadvantage of becoming dated.

Thus a careful analysis of the existing behaviour
repertory of the target audience is required in order to

choose valuable mediating prompts. This analysis may range outside the behaviour directly related to the task being learnt (as in the example above) and it would also include analysis of directly related behaviour (as in the example of using the term 'manual labour' as a prompt in teaching that the French for 'hand' is 'main').

This very brief discussion of mathetics has been introduced as a preview and perhaps to whet the appetite. Further reading may be found in Gilbert's own papers[9] and in several articles[10,11,12]. Many writers of instructional materials have found Gilbert's work stimulating. Although few use his techniques in their totality, many have adopted S–R notation as a technique of analysis, and the 'Demonstrate, Prompt, Release' model as a basis for exercise design. Some have found they can adapt these techniques to deal with almost any instructional task, while others find that the three main behaviour constructs of chain, discrimination and generalisation are insufficient to deal with all forms of learning tasks. Creative behaviour in particular does not seem to be very well described by stimulus-response techniques. Readers who feel this way may find the classification suggested by Robert Gagné more attractive.

Gagné's categories of learning

Robert Gagné suggests a hierarchical list of eight categories of learning[13]. The list is hierarchical in the sense that it proceeds from very simple conditioning-type learning, up to complex learning, such as is involved in problem solving. The list is also hierarchical in the sense that lower levels of learning are prerequisite to higher levels. Figure 1.6 presents the eight categories and illustrates their hierarchical structure. A few words about these categories may help to relate Gagné's work to our earlier discussion.

Gagné distinguishes between 8 different types of learning, as follows:

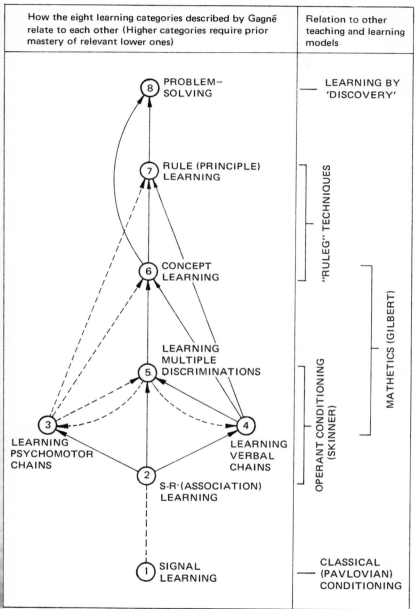

Figure 1.6 Gagné's hierarchy of learning categories

1 Signal learning

This may be equated with the Pavlovian conditioned response. The subject learns that a given event is the signal for another event, as the dinner bell was the signal for Pavlov's dogs' dinner. So he responds to the signal as he would to the event, ie instead of salivating when dinner arrived the dogs did so at the signal. Similarly, a child may learn that its mother's frown is the signal of pain to come, so it responds to the frown as it would to the pain itself.

It is characteristic of this type of learning that the stimulus and the response must be closely associated in time — the stimulus of course *precedes* the response, and it will not produce the desired learning if it takes place too many seconds before the response. (Thus the child will not learn to fear your frown if the frown does not signal any immediate consequences).

2 Stimulus-Response learning

This is differentiated from signal learning in that the response is not a generalised emotional one, but a very precise act. Gagné gives the example of a dog learning to respond to the stimulus of its master's command 'shake hands' by offering its paw, and gives the following characteristics of this type of learning:

(a) The learning is typically *gradual*: some repetition of the association between the stimulus and the response is usually necessary.

(b) The response becomes more and more sure and precise as the repetitions take place (this is what Skinner calls 'shaping').

(c) The controlling stimulus becomes more precise — initially the dog may respond to a variety of commands, but as the training progresses these commands cease to produce a response.

(d) There is reward, or reinforcement, when the animal produces behaviour that is approximately, or exactly what his master requires; and there is no reward when the behaviour is incorrect, or not near enough to being correct.

3 Chaining

Chaining is the type of learning we have already described when discussing Gilbert's work. Characteristics of this type of learning are:

(a) The individual links in the chain must be established first.

(b) Again time is a factor — the events in the chain must occur close together in time.

(c) If both the other two conditions are satisfied, learning a chain is *not* a gradual process, it occurs on a single occasion. In practice the occasion may have to be repeated, because the individual links may not be well enough established.

4 Verbal chaining

Gagné says 'verbal association might well be classified as only a subvariety of chaining ... But because these chains are verbal and because they explain the remarkable versatility of human processes, verbal association has some unique characteristics.' He gives the example of a man learning the French for 'match' (alumette) in the following way: the word 'match' acts as a stimulus for the mental picture of a match. A match 'illuminates'. The syllable 'lum' occurs in il*lum*inate as it does in alumette, so a chain is established. Again we see the similarity to Gilbert's techniques in teaching the colour code.

The conditions for effective learning of verbal chains, according to Gagné, are:

(a) Each link must be established previously — the link in the individual's mind between the word 'match' and the object match must be clear.

(b) 'Response differentiation' must have taken place; ie the individual must know how to say 'alumette' well enough so that the key syllable 'lum' means something to him and can be used as a link with the word 'illuminate'.

(c) A 'coding connection' (Gilbert uses the term mediator) must be established. The mental picture of a flaming match and the word 'illuminate' must be associated. Clearly, people will tend to use different 'coding connections', depending on their previous history; highly verbal people will have more codes available than less verbal people.

5 Discrimination learning

This is the same category as Gilbert's multiple discriminations. The conditions of this type of learning are as follows:

(a) Necessary Ss ⟶ Rs must already be established.

(b) Interference from conflicting stimuli must be reduced to a minimum. That is to say, distinctions must be emphasised; interference is anything which might add to confusion of the stimuli and uncertainty about which of several responses is required.

6 Concept learning

This may be compared to the 'generalisation' of mathetics. In this form of learning a stimulus is *classified* in terms of its abstract properties, as shape, position, number etc. A child learns that a green block A is called a 'cube'. It is then told that block B, which is twice the size of A and red in colour, is also a cube. Concept learning is the type of learning which enables him to identify a cube on the basis of an internalised representation (an idea) which is independent of the dissimi-larities of the two objects — in the Platonic sense, an 'idea of cubeness'. Gagné draws a distinction between a 'concrete concept', which depends on the observable properties of objects, and a 'defined concept', which identifies a class of objects whose common properties are not determinable by observation, but are a matter of verbal definition. (For example, a broom and a screwdriver are both 'tools', but cannot be observed to have much else in common.) Conditions for this type of learning are as follows:

(a) The initial S——R portions of the chain must be learnt.

(b) A *variety* of stimulus situations must be presented, so that the conceptual property common to all of them can be discriminated.

(c) The learning of a new concept may be gradual, because of the need for a variety of stimulus situations.

7 Rule learning

In a formal sense, a rule is a chain of two or more concepts. The simplest type of rule may be 'If A, then B' — eg 'If a (German) feminine noun (concept A) then the feminine article (concept B)'. This may be distinguished from a 'simple verbal fact to be memorised' in that if the rule is correctly learnt, then the learner will be able to apply it in all relevant situations, and he may *not* necessarily be able to state the rule in words. The conditions for this type of learning are as follows:

(a) The concepts to be linked must be clearly established — the learner must know what a 'feminine noun' is and what the 'feminine article' is.

    (b)   A simple process of chaining can then take place.

    (c)   The learning of a rule can take place on a single occasion.

8 Problem-solving

Once a human being has acquired some rules he can combine these rules into a great variety of higher order rules. In doing this he can use what he already knows to *solve problems* which are new to him, (though they may or may not be so to other people). This 'problem-solving' takes place at all levels, from Joe Bloggs working out how to change a tyre without getting his clothes dirty, to Einstein producing the theory of relativity. The conditions of this type of learning are as follows:

    (a)   The learner must be able to identify the essential features of the response that will be the solution *before* he arrives at the solution. Thus Joe Bloggs will identify a solution as correct that gives a reasonable assurance that he won't be covered with mud; Einstein wanted a new statement about the nature of energy which accounted for all that was already known about the nature of energy.

    (b)   Relevant rules are used and recalled.

    (c)   The recalled rules are combined so that a new rule emerges. (Gagné admits little is known about the nature of this 'combining event').

    (d)   Though the overall process of solving a problem may take a very long time, Gagné thinks that the solution is actually arrived at in a 'flash of insight'.

Thus we see that Gagné's model embraces the models of Skinner and of Gilbert, which we presented earlier. It also includes the very primitive type of Pavlovian conditioning which is only of marginal concern to teachers above the kindergarten level. Where it differs is that it extends these models to define categories of higher order learning — the sort of learning that most teachers are particularly concerned about. One very valuable point it makes, over and over again, is to stress just how much success at these higher orders depends on adequate mastery of lower order learning. How this can be used as a method of guiding course exercise design and lesson planning is further expanded in the next chapter.

Does Gagné's model go far enough? Are there still higher orders of learning which it does not cover? Some people feel this is so, though it is surprising that these people have not been able to define such categories clearly nor clearly describe the probable conditions for learning them. Before we come back to this point, let us follow up a development related to course design which has occurred parallel with the birth of the models described so far.

The emergence of behavioural objectives

At about the same time that Gilbert was working on his treatise, another American psychologist, Bob Mager, was writing a book in praise of behavioural objectives[14]. It is based on the simple inference that if one defines learning as a change in behaviour, then the teacher may be wise to define the aims or objectives of his lesson in terms of the behaviour patterns he wishes to establish. This is useful, because it implies a student-orientated, learning-orientated approach, rather than one based on subject matter coverage. It is also useful because once an objective is defined in behavioural terms (ie the student should be able to perform tasks A, B and C), then it is simplicity itself to design an appropriate test situation to evaluate the method of teaching: we simply get the student to attempt A, B and C. Of course, the crunch is to have the objectives defined in behavioural terms. It is not as easy as it sounds, especially in traditional schoolroom subjects which are sometimes taught more through tradition, than for any practical end purpose. The problem perhaps is not so much in stating an objective as in stating the right one. We shall come back to this later on.

The essential ingredients in a behavioural objective, according to Mager, are:

1. A statement of what the student should be able to *do* at the end of the learning session (the terminal behaviour).

2. The *conditions* under which he should be able to exhibit the terminal behaviour.

3. The *standard* to which he should be able to perform (the criteria).

For example: 'The student (1) should be able to find the square root of any number (2) using tables of square roots or logarithm tables and (3) getting the answer correct to 3 significant figures 9 times out of 10.'

Mager popularised the precise statement of objectives for programmed instruction. Later his approach became more widely applied to the design of any form of instructional material. After all, as Mager put it, 'if you don't know where you're heading you'll probably end up someplace else.' However, the concept of objectives stated in performance terms is of a much earlier date. The term has of course always been used in the context of education, but often in a general sense, such as 'to provide equal opportunities for all' or 'to create an environment for self-development'. Gradually it became usual to discriminate between such general *aims* and more detailed *objectives*. It also became usual to think of these categories of objectives:

Cognitive Objectives — what the student should know or be able to do.

Affective Objectives — what the student should feel and should be prepared to do.

Psychomotor Objectives — physical skills that the student should develop.

One person who used these three categories and then developed sub-divisions was B S Bloom. Bloom's taxonomy of the cognitive objectives of education published in 1956[15] became (and still is) a standard handbook for many concerned with curriculum planning and instructional design. Much later (in 1964), the second volume, giving a suggested classification of affective objectives, was published[16]. Psychomotor objectives have not yet been dealt with so thoroughly. The table in Figure 1.7 describes the categories of objectives in the cognitive and affective domains, suggested by Bloom.

Notice again that these are arranged as hierarchy in which the lower levels are prerequisites to the higher levels. To this extent the categories of Bloom's taxonomy are similar to Gagné's categories of learning tasks. Indeed, as far as the cognitive domain is concerned, the similarity is very pronounced, as can be seen by examining a few examples of the application of Bloom's taxonomy.

1 Knowledge

This is considered the lowest level of cognitive objective. To demonstrate the attainment of objectives at this level, students would be expected to do such tasks as: *name* the parts of an object; *point out* a certain object; *state* a definition; *recognise* a phenomenon when he sees it. (Gagné would classify most of these as examples of stimulus-response learning or as learning of verbal chains.)

2 Comprehension

Bloom identifies this level by signs of 'understanding' on the part of the student — such signs as: *selecting* an example of a particular phenomenon; *giving reasons for* a phenomenon; *classifying* an object into a category; *contrasting* two objects/phenomena. (These seem to be examples of multiple discrimination and simple concept learning in Gagné's terms.)

Cognitive Objectives	Affective Objectives
1 The lowest level in this taxonomy begins with the student's recall and recognition of **Knowledge.**	1 The lowest level begins with the student merely **Receiving** stimuli and passively attending to it. It extends to his more actively attending to it,
2 It extends through his **Comprehension** of the knowledge.	2 then his **Responding** to stimuli on request, willingly responding and taking satisfaction in responding
3 To his skill in the **Application** of the knowledge that he comprehends.	3 to his **Valuing** the phenomena or activity so that he voluntarily responds and seeks out further ways to take part in what is going on.
4 The next levels progress from his ability to make an **Analysis** of the situations involving the knowledge, to his skill in the **Synthesis** of it into new organizations.	4 The next stage is his **Conceptualization** of each of the values to which he is responding by identifying characteristics or forming judgements.
5 The highest level lies in his skill in **Evaluation,** so that he can judge the value of the knowledge in realizing specific objectives.	5 The highest level in the taxonomy is the student's **Organization** of the values into a system which is a **Characterization** of himself.

Figure 1.7 Cognitive and Affective Objectives — the Main Categories (from D R Kartwohl, B S Bloom et al, *Taxonomy of Educational Objectives Handbook 12 – Affective Domain,* **Longmans, 1964)**

3 Application

This level is characterised by the student's ability to apply theoretical statements and generalisations to real situations, for example: *calculate* a mathematical result; *perform* a task; *use* a particular set of rules and procedures; *predict* the result of a proposed course of action. (There seems to be much in common here with what Gagné terms 'rule-following'.)

4 Analysis

Being able to *compare* and *contrast* alternatives; *justify* the adoption of certain procedures; *break down* a problem into its components.

5 Synthesis

Being able to *select* among alternative courses of action; *organise* the components of a problem; *derive* a solution to a problem. (Analysis and Synthesis are both involved in Gagné's description of problem-solving activity.)

6 Evaluation

This is, according to Bloom, the highest level of cognitive objective. It is characterised by such activity as being able to *judge* the value of a particular block of knowledge; *argue* for or against a proposal; *defend* or *criticise* a particular viewpoint. (Although some evaluation is involved in problem-solving, Bloom's concept of evaluation seems to go further into the realms of intellectual activity than does Gagne's classification of learning categories.)

There are, however, some important differences between Bloom's and Gagné's classifications:

(a) If you look at Figure 1.7, it is quite obvious that Bloom is suggesting a continuum in the development of a set of objectives from the simple and concrete to the complex and abstract (note the parallel here with well-used instructional cliches). The six levels are like milestones on the way to perfect accomplishment, rather than watertight categories. Gagné's hierarchy on the other hand has specific and exclusive characteristics defined for each category of learning, particularly at the lower levels.

(b) Bloom's taxonomy merely sets out to classify objectives, and, by stating them in terms of observable student behaviour, to indicate appropriate types of test questions. It does not attempt to formulate general rules about how one should teach in order to achieve particular objectives. Gagné's hierarchy, on the other hand, was constructed with this latter aim in mind. Each learning category is not only associated with particular conditions for testing but also with conditions for learning (both external — how the teacher should plan the instructional event and internal — the state of readiness of the learner).

There have been several other attempts to build up a comprehensive model for preparing objectives, eg Miller[17] and for the classification of types of learning, eg Merrill[18]. However, Gagné's and Bloom's approaches seem to be the most widely adopted, and serve to illustrate the current trend among instructional designers to

1   be careful about specifying the objectives of instruction,

2   be careful to design tests which really measure what they set out to, and

3   be careful to design learning activities tailored to the achievement of the specified objectives.

The emergence of the systems approach

What happens when you put the theoretical ideas just discussed into practice? Very soon, two questions assume great importance:

1 How do we know we have the right objectives specified?

2 How do we measure the success of our course?

1 Valid objectives

Taking the first question and re-phrasing it we might ask — where do course objectives come from? Several answers are possible:

(a) A need for certain knowledge or skills is dictated by the trainee's future job.

(b) Certain knowledge or skills are held to be desirable by the society in which the trainee lives.

(c) The trainee himself is interested in attaining certain knowledge or skills.

(d) The teacher has personal interests or preferences which he intends to transmit if at all possible.

The first two summarise the vocational and non-vocational objectives of a course, the third to a large extent governs whether students will partake in the course and what they will gain from it. The last is the inevitable 'noise' in the communication channel, generally held to be of supreme value in non-vocational instruction (education??) and often a problem in vocational instruction (training??).

Thus, to be sure that we specify the right set of

objectives for a given course (the valid objectives) we should first

(a) analyse the job for which the trainee is being prepared and/or

(b) analyse the needs of the society in which he lives, and definitely

(c) analyse and take note of the objectives which trainees set up for themselves, and finally

(d) analyse one's own motives and the motives of others involved in implementing the course.

Discrepancies between any of these categories of objectives and those set up (or discernible in retrospect) for your course are going to lead to inefficiency (high cost), ineffectiveness (high dropout), lack of relevance (student revolt) and so on. Similarly there may be conflicts of objectives within or between categories which must be resolved.

We are implying the need therefore for a very thorough analysis of the whole system in which the course, the trainees and the teachers operate — a systems analysis.

2 Course evaluation
The success of a course is similarly judged by various criteria. As before:

(a) Can students do the job for which they have been trained? (are cognitive and psychomotor objectives met)

(b) Do students fit into the society and can they operate in it? (cognitive, psychomotor and affective)

(c) Are students satisfied with the course? (affective)

(d) Are teachers satisfied with the course? (a reflection one hopes of the above three sets of objectives being met).

But there are many other criteria. Just a few of these are:

(e) Is the cost of the course acceptable?

(f) Is the course structure in line with our philosophical or political viewpoint?

(g) How does this course compare with other alternative courses?

(h) Does the course use all resources efficiently (teachers, time, media, buildings, environment as well as money)?

(i) What are the organisational problems associated with this course structure?

and in general terms:

(j) What can we learn which will enable us to *improve this course*?

(k) What can we learn which will enable us to *improve our general course-design procedures*?

These last two avenues of evaluation summarise the *development* and the *research* aspects of evaluation. They imply that there is feedback from course evaluation to course design, and maybe even to the objectives of our course. They imply that defects in original analysis and course design will be identified and corrected. If you like, they imply a self-correcting system of control, as one finds in self-regulating systems in nature (animal's temperature control) or in engineering (the governor on a steam engine).

This concept of self-regulation is one of the key

concepts in the educational technologist's approach to course design — an approach now commonly named 'the Systems Approach'. Although its techniques may only bear a slight resemblance to those used in engineering system design and the scientific basis of educational systems may be much less developed than in the case of natural systems such as animal nervous systems, the systems approach to education involves the following three basic types of activity common to all systems approaches:

1 Systems analysis

— of system needs (job and task analysis, society's needs, students' aims).

— of system resources (manpower, space, time, materials, money, students' existing abilities).

— leading to a statement of the problem (usually in terms of overall objectives).

2 Design (synthesis) of a solution

— identification of whether the problem is entirely a training problem (other strategies may involve job redesign, redesign of society, change in selection procedures etc).

— if a training problem, identification of precise course objectives.

— deriving instructional tactics (use may be made here of models such as Gilbert's, Bloom's or Gagné's)

— planning of available resources (this involves selection of presentation media)

— preparation of materials, organisational structure, etc.

3 Implementation/evaluation

This usually follows two distinct stages:

— small-scale try-out concentrating on the instructional effectiveness of materials, efficiency of organisation, etc (this is variously called developmental testing, validation, or more recently *formative* evaluation, as it helps to establish the form of the system's components).

— large-scale try-out which, in addition to following up the above factors in the wider context, concerns itself with the value of the course to the organisation, the community and the individual. (As this is in a way the summing-up of an existing implemented system, it is sometimes referred to as *summative* evaluation. However, this distinction between formative and summative evaluation refers mainly to the use made of the information gathered — ie does it lead to changes in the system — rather than to the stage at which the information is gathered.)

These three overall stages in the application of a systems approach to course design may be variously broken down into subsidiary procedures. Different people specify different procedures often illustrating the sequence of procedures by some sort of flow diagram. Two such flow charts are illustrated in Figures 1.8 and 1.9. Although extremely helpful in illustrating the authors' overall approaches, such flow charts are a trifle misleading in that they imply a fixed sequence of procedures. Although some overall sequence is generally followed the intelligent use of a systems approach involves the user in analysis, synthesis and evaluation at all stages of course design. It is not the sequence of the procedures, or the exact methods by which each procedure is carried out that makes the systems approach work, but the intelligence and experience of the course designer (or more commonly the course design team) in performing the procedures and drawing the correct conclusions.

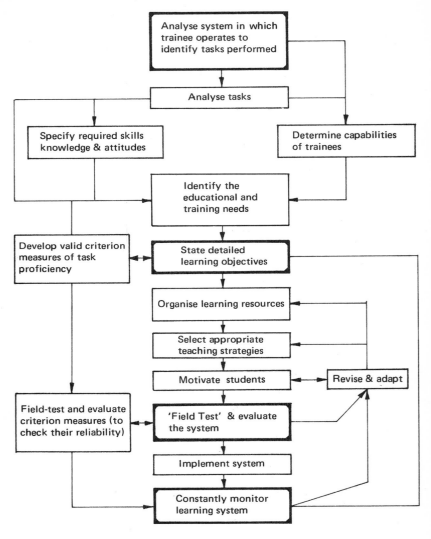

**Figure 1.8 The design and development of a learning system
(Programmed Instruction Centre, Middlesex Polytechnic at Enfield)**

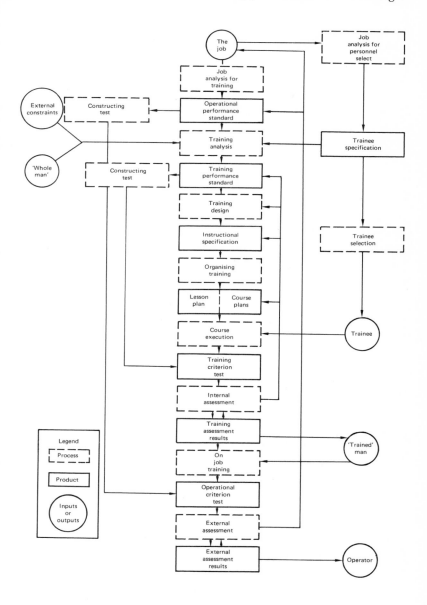

**Figure 1.9 A model of a training system
as used for training design in the Royal Navy**

Further reading on the systems approach may be found in several books listed in the bibliography. The aim of this short résumé is simply to illustrate how various strands of theoretical investigation into learning and instruction now seem to be coming together into a systematic approach to the diagnosis of learning needs and the prescription of appropriate instructional solutions.

The selection of instructional media

The selection of media for the presentation of instruction is now seen as only one stage in an overall systems approach. It is an important stage, but it is by no means the first stage of instructional design. Decisions at this stage depend very much on the results of earlier stages. The main categories of factors that may influence the choice of media are:

1   Task factors — the type of objectives, and hence the type of learning activities which should be provided for the learner.

2   Learner factors — some learners may learn better from certain media than from others (not very much is known about such factors, though they do seem to exist).

3   Economics/availability factors — this may limit our choice in practice. Although certain rules may be laid down here, they are mostly truisms and in reality each new course has its own problems in this category.

The next chapter is concerned mainly with the first category — how task analysis and theoretical models of instruction may be used to guide the selection and use of instructional media. However, the other two categories of factors are also considered, as far as this seems relevant. Later chapters look at specific classes of media in more detail from the point of view of all the factors concerned.

References

1. C E Shannon and W Weaver, *The Mathematical Theory of Communication*, University of Illinois Press, 1949.

2. E L Thorndike, 'The Law of Effect', *American Journal of Psychology*, No 39, 1927.

3. B F Skinner, *Cumulative Record*, Methuen, 1961.

4. W D Seymour, *Industrial Training for Manual Operations*, Pitman, London, 1954.

5. W D Seymour, *Industrial Skills*, Pitman, 1966.

6. J Wellens, 'Editorial', *Industrial Training International*, Vol 3, No 3, 1968.

7. P Saettler, *A History of Instructional Technology*, McGraw, 1968.

8. T F Gilbert, 'Mathetics — The Technology of Education', *Journal of Mathetics*, Nos 1 and 2, 1961. Also re-published as a pamphlet by Longmac, 13, Wisteria Road, London, 1969.

9. Ibid.

10. J H Harless, 'The Two Meanings of Mathetics' in D Unwin and J Leedham (eds), *Aspects of Educational Technology*, Vol 1, Methuen, 1967.

11. M T McGaulley, 'Mathetics in Industrial and Vocational Training' in D Unwin and J Leedham (eds), *Aspects of Educational Technology*, Vol 1, Methuen, 1967.

12. I K Davies, 'Mathetics' in I K Davies and J Hartley (eds), *Contributions to an Educational Technology*, Butterworth, 1972.

13. R M Gagné, *The Conditions of Learning*, Holt, Rinehart, Winston, 1967. (Second revised edition 1970.)

14. R F Mager, *Preparing Instructional Objectives*, Fearon, 1962.

15. B S Bloom et al, *Taxonomy of Educational Objectives Handbook I — The Cognitive Domain*, Longmans, 1956.

16. D R Kartwohl, B S Bloom et al, *Taxonomy of Educational Objectives Handbook 2 — Affective Domain*, Longmans, 1964.

17. R B Miller, *Task Description and Analysis* in R M Gagné (ed), *Psychological Principles in System Development*, Holt, Rinehart, Winston, 1962.

18. M D Merrill, 'Necessary Psychological Conditions for defining Instructional Outcomes', *Educational Technology*, August 1971. See also R D Tennyson and M D Merrill, 'Hierarchical Models in the Development of a Theory of Instruction', *Educational Technology*, September 1971.

Further Reading

Educational Technology
General/Introductory/Reference Books

E W H Briault, *Learning and Teaching Tomorrow*, NCET Occasional Paper No 2, Councils and Education Press, 1969. 16pp.

M Eraut and G Squires, *Annotated Select Bibliography of Educational Technology*, NCET, 1971. 100pp.

N L Gage (ed), *Handbook of Research on Teaching*, Rand McNally, Chicago, 1963. 1218pp.

R F Mager and K M Beach Jr, *Developing Vocational Instruction*, Fearon, 1967. 83pp.

National Council for Educational Technology, *Towards More Effective Learning*, Councils and Education Press, 1969. 87pp.

W K Richmond, *The Teaching Revolution*, Methuen, 1967. 220pp.

J Robinson and N Barnes (eds), *New Media and Methods in Industrial Training*, BBC Publications, 1968. 221pp.

G Taylor (ed), *The Teacher as Manager — A symposium*, NCET, Councils and Education Press, 1970. 166pp.

Theoretical Approaches to Learning/Teaching

R M Beard, *An Outline of Piaget's Developmental Psychology for Students and Teachers*, Routledge and Kegan Paul, 1970. 128pp.

R Borger and A E Seaborne, *The Psychology of Learning*, Penguin, 1966. 249pp.

J S Bruner, *Towards a Theory of Instruction*, Norton, 1966. 176pp.

B F Skinner, *The Technology of Teaching*, Appleton-Century-Crofts, 1968. 271pp.

K U Smith and M F Smith, *Cybernetic Principles of Learning and Educational Design*, Holt, Rinehart, Winston, 1966. 529pp.

Systems Approach, Cybernetics and the Management of Learning
S Beer, *Decision and Control*, Wiley, 1966.

I K Davies, *The Management of Learning*, McGraw-Hill, 1971. 256pp.

R M Gagné (ed), *Psychological Principles in System Development*, Holt, Rinehart, Winston, 1962. 560pp.

A J Romiszowski (ed), *The Systems Approach to Education and Training; Conference Proceedings*, Kogan Page, 1970. 95pp.

R G Smith, *The Design of Instructional Systems*, Human Resources Research Office, Washington DC, 1966. 85pp.

G Taylor (ed), *The Teacher as Manager — A Symposium*, NCET, Councils and Education Press, 1970. 166pp.

C A Thomas (ed), *Pre-structured Instruction*, RAF School of Education, RAF, Upwood, Huntingdon. 91pp.

Validation and Evaluation
R F Mager, *Developing Attitude towards Instruction*, Fearon, 1969. 104pp.

A O Martin, *Assessing Training Effectiveness*, Department of Employment and Productivity, London, 1968. 34pp.

P E Vernon, *The Measurement of Abilities*, University of London Press, 1956. 276pp.

Journals In Educational Technology
A — V Communications Review. Quarterly Research Journal. £5.60 per annum. Department of Audio-Visual Instruction, Washington DC, USA.

Educational Technology. L Lipsitz, 456 Sylvan Avenue, Engelwood Cliffs, New Jersey 07632.

Journal of Educational Technology. Editor N Mackenzie. Official journal of the National Council for Educational Technology. Three times a year. £3.50 per annum. Councils and Education Press, 10 Queen Anne Street, London W1.

Journal of Educational Psychology. American Psychological Association, 1200 Seventeenth Street, NW Washington DC 20036.

NSPI Journal. Ten issues a year. National Society for Programmed Instruction, Trinity University, 715 Stadium Drive, San Antonio, Texas.

Programmed Learning and Educational Technology. Official journal of the Association for Programmed Learning and Educational Technology. Sweet and Maxwell, 11 New Fetter Lane, London EC4.

Recall — Review of Educational Cybernetics and Applied Linguistics. Editor K Bung. Three times a year. £1.20 per annum. Longmac, Research Publications Services, 11 Nelson Road, London SE10.

Visual Education. Editor C Webb. Official magazine of the National Committee for Audio-Visual Aids in Education. Eleven times a year. £2.40 per annum. NCAVAE, 33 Queen Anne Street, London W1M 0AL.

2 The Selection of Media

Factors affecting media choice

Let us first consider briefly the factors which might affect decisions about the choice of particular media. Some of these are illustrated in Figure 2.1. Firstly, a choice of a particular instructional method will often dictate or at least limit, our choice of presentation media. For example, if it is necessary to use a method involving group discussion and the sharing of experiences, then obviously a one-direction medium of presentation such as a tape recorder or television, would not be suitable, as it limits the opportunity for feedback and exchange of ideas. Secondly, the type of learning task facing the student will also eventually influence the media choice, because it dictates or limits, the choice of suitable methods of instruction. For example, the training of some supervisory and personnel management skills is often achieved by group discussion, where individual managers share experiences with others. This may be built round a standard case study which is filmed. However, the necessary group discussion element in this type of training will influence the methods chosen and therefore dictate the appropriate media. Thirdly, the special characteristics of some students will directly influence the media to be chosen. For example, it would be unrealistic to attempt to instruct a group of slow readers using printed material, as you would be introducing other problems into the learning process. And finally, we should not overlook the practical constraints, both administrative and economic, which may limit the choice of methods and media. It appears reasonable, therefore, that before we make any decision about appropriate media we should first of all make appropriate decisions about the instructional methods to be

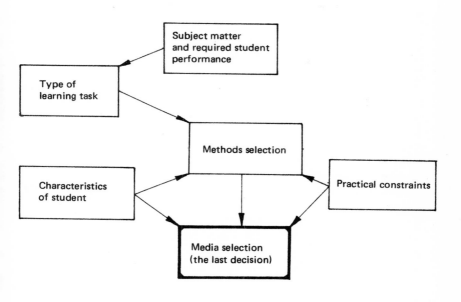

Figure 2.1 Factors influencing media selection

employed; and to make these decisions we should consider the students, the type of learning concerned and any practical constraints which happen to exist.

Perhaps we should add one further factor to our list — the teacher. You may like using an overhead projector or you may hate it. If you do happen to have a particular aversion or phobia for a certain medium of instruction, then you are unlikely to use it well. Whatever the theoretical benefits of the device, they are likely to be wiped out if the skills to use the device are lacking. And it is not only a question of skills. Attitudes count too. In most of the long-term evaluation studies of the use of such 'automated' media as programmed instruction or broadcast television, it has been found that the way the medium is integrated into the course and the feelings of the teaching staff have been among the most important factors affecting the success of the experiment. Thus, while we hope that the teacher has an open mind towards the use of alternative media, we also hope that when faced with equally appropriate alternatives, he will follow his instinct and 'do his own thing'. Blatant disregard for important characteristics of the learning situation (whether task factors, learner characteristics or practical constraints) will inevitably lead to poor course design. But it is no good having a perfect design if you are unable or unwilling to implement it.

Purpose of this chapter

Teachers' skills and attitudes are probably outside the scope of this book, but let's follow them up as an example of media selection. One indirect objective of this book is certainly that the reader should form favourable attitudes towards the systematic use of media (ie should attempt to apply the principles outlined and seek out more information about them). However we must be realistic. Books impart information but information by itself is seldom sufficient to change attitudes (consider traffic infringements, industrial accidents, wars). However, the print medium, though not the best for achieving *affective* objectives, is often very good at achieving *cognitive* objectives. Thus we might expect this book to be more successful at teaching already interested readers to plan and implement lessons in a systematic manner.

How could we test the attainment of such an objective? — by comparing teacher performance before and after on standardised lesson-preparation exercises. What follows in this chapter has been tested in this way and found to work quite well[1]. How could we test for the affective objectives? — by following up the performance of readers for a lengthy period of time both before and after exposure to the book. This is quite impractical, so one relies on snippets of feedback such as the comments of one's own students, readers' letters, etc. Such feedback, though imperfect, is still useful, and is always welcome. Please write!

The structure of the rest of this chapter will be made up in part of algorithms, check lists and decision tables, which are designed to serve as job aids for the systematic selection of media. It is hoped that these will be useful to the reader in the practical lesson-design situation for long after the book has been read. Readers are encouraged to choose their own lesson topic and try the job aids out on that as they read this chapter. A fairly practical topic should be chosen initially.

Optional and essential media characteristics

Before we launch into the body of this chapter, we should consider the range of media at our disposal, and some of their general characteristics. Figure 2.2 presents a classification of some of the media. Although a large number are shown, this is by no means a comprehensive list. However, sufficient are included to illustrate the general characteristics that may be used to classify them.

First, we may classify them according to the sensory channels they use. This is illustrated by the four vertical columns on Figure 2.2.

Secondly, we may classify them according to a variety of other factors. Figure 2.2 uses the factor of teacher control to spread the media out along a vertical axis ranging from media which are completely under the control of the

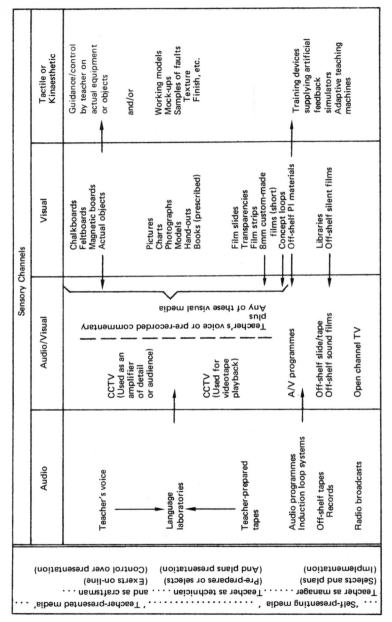

Figure 2.2 A classification of presentation media

teacher (in respect of content, rate of presentation, sequence etc), to those where the teacher's role is minimal and his control restricted to 'managerial' decisions (ie whether to use or not to use).

Two important points emerge from this classification:

1   The 'sensory channel' classification is fairly precise. Most people would agree where to place a given medium in this classification. The 'teacher control' classification is much less precise. Certain films for example, being short and in clearly defined sections, are more under the teacher's control than others (in the sense that the teacher may think of many ways of showing the film, altering the sequence of parts, stopping for a discussion, etc).

2   The 'teacher control' factor is but one of a large number of similar factors that one might have used for classifying the media. Examples of other factors which are particularly important to consider are: large groups, small groups or individual study; fixed or variable rates of presentation; suitability for stable subject matter or for subject matter which often changes.

This classification is not therefore particularly useful as it stands. One would require a multi-dimensional classification and even if one could devise such a comprehensive classification, different people would no doubt wish to place particular media in different positions.

The sole purpose of presenting Figure 2.2 here is to illustrate that the choice of media is a complex decision, influenced by a variety of factors, and therefore no quick and easy all-embracing rule is likely to be developed. Also it illustrates that the search for a classification or taxonomy of media is a counter-productive exercise, if approached in terms of the normal 'labels' attached to media (ie film, TV, concept loop). If we need further evidence of this, we need only look at the results of half a century of media research.

Whenever media are compared we usually get 'no significant difference' results. Peggie Campeau[2] suggests that this may well be due to the 'blanket' nature of the research. One medium favours the achievement of some of the course objectives while the other favours the achievement of others. Thus existing differences cancel out in the overall experiment. Another reason may be that the subject matter chosen for experiments may pre-judge the result. Naturally you compare two media on a topic where both have a reasonable chance of success. No one would set up a comparison of a printed book and a tape recording for a course on bird-song recognition. One medium is obviously inappropriate. So you choose an experimental topic which does not seem to favour either medium particularly, and are then surprised when no significant differences are found in the experimental results.

The 'mythology' of media must be stripped away. A particular medium, be it reality, book or BBC broadcast, is no more than a particular form of 'packaging' for a set of instructional stimuli. The quality of the packaging should not be neglected (ask any ad-man), but what really matters is the functional aspect of the package. Can the package hold the contents — is the medium capable of presenting the instructional stimuli required for learning? Can it arrange for the students to engage in the required learning activity? Very often, no one medium is capable of presenting *all* the required stimuli, so we are led to prescribe a 'multi-media package'. However, the only scientific justification for a multi-media approach is that one medium either is not capable of presenting all the required learning stimuli, or is not capable of eliciting all the required student responses.

The theory that presenting the same information in several media enhances the learning process, though widely held, is little supported by experimental results. Similarly, experiments on the quality of a presentation (eg should we use colour or black and white TV) give inconclusive results when performed under controlled conditions. The trend of media research so far appears to lead to the conclusion that (as far as cognitive objectives are concerned) learning is influenced by the quality of the presentation only to the extent that the quality influences the clarity of the message.

Having said that, however, who would deny that they get more pleasure (and perhaps spend more time) watching colour TV than black and white TV. The completely unexpected speed with which colour television has become established cannot be simply explained as 'keeping up with the Joneses'. Pressures have built up which are causing the BBC to go for colour in their schools broadcasting several years earlier than planned. Furthermore, who would deny that a multi-media presentation, if well put together, is more enjoyable than a presentation using only one medium throughout. It would seem therefore that design factors which influence the quality of the 'package' may have a very important role in helping to ensure that learners participate in the presentation, and thus may help to achieve the course objectives in the open, non-experimental, situation (particularly the affective objectives).

It seems appropriate therefore to think in terms of two classes of media characteristics:

1   *Essential media characteristics.* These are the ones which control the *clarity* of the message. For example the demonstration of a high-speed manual skill demands a moving visual presentation for clarity (it may even demand a slow-motion movie presentation). Learning a foreign vocabulary requires print (to recognise the words) and audio media (to pronounce them).

2   *Optional media characteristics.* These are the characteristics which will improve the *quality* of the presentation. There are several considerations which might influence one's choice, for example:

(a)   Choosing media which are attractive to the learner (eg use of colour, dramatisation, animation, cartoons, illustration etc).

(b)   Choosing media which fit the learner's study

habits (it appears that some learn better from print, others from the spoken word). As we know so little about learner preferences, this may best be arranged by incorporating alternatives and giving the learner a choice.

(c) Choosing media which fit the teacher's teaching habits, skills and preferences.

(d) Choosing media for a particular application where there is some evidence from previous research that marginal improvements in learning efficiency will result.

Is not this classification open to the same criticism as we have just levelled at traditional media classifications? Will there not be just as much difference in the way people classify a particular media characteristic as optional or essential?
We think not. Not if one limits one's essential media characteristics to those which either:

(a) are dictated by the nature of the learning task, and can be identified by a systematic analysis of the course objectives, or

(b) are indicated by the conclusive results of experiments.

There will still be scope for a lot of individual difference in the relative importance that one assigns to optional media characteristics. And a very healthy state of affairs this is too. For one thing, we still know very little about how people learn from different media, and variety of approaches coupled with evaluation of results may help us to extend our knowledge. Also, the interaction between individual learner differences, individual teacher differences and individual media producer differences are so complex that we are never likely to know all the answers anyway. As research progresses and basic principles are more strongly established, a few currently optional media characteristics may be 'promoted' to the rank of essential characteristics, but it is unlikely that we shall ever reach the stage where a particular instructional problem would dictate a unique course design.

Our approach in this chapter will now be to apply a systematic procedure of media selection. We will be concerned more with first identifying essential media characteristics rather than with a search for the 'ideal medium'. This will limit our choice considerably. Then we will proceed to eliminate from this short list any media which are impractical, unavailable, or do not conform to those optional media characteristics which we love most dearly. In this way we will progressively limit our choice more and more closely: 'selection by rejection' will be our motto.

Procedure for lesson design

The overall procedure suggested is shown schematically in Figure 2.3. It is based on an application of the systems approach. Figure 2.3 has been drawn to concentrate on the stages of course design and media selection. The initial task analysis stages which lead up to the statement of behavioural objectives have been omitted (they were described in the previous chapter) and the implementation and evaluation stages have been merely hinted at (stages 9 and 10). Let us now look more closely at each stage in the procedure.

1 Define behavioural objectives for each topic
We are going to select media for each objective in turn. A one-hour lesson may contain one, five, ten or perhaps twenty quite distinct behavioural objectives. It is highly probable that different objectives will require different instructional methods which in turn will demand different media characteristics. This approach to the problem at the 'object-ives level' is suggested by the work of Gagné[3], Briggs[4],[5]

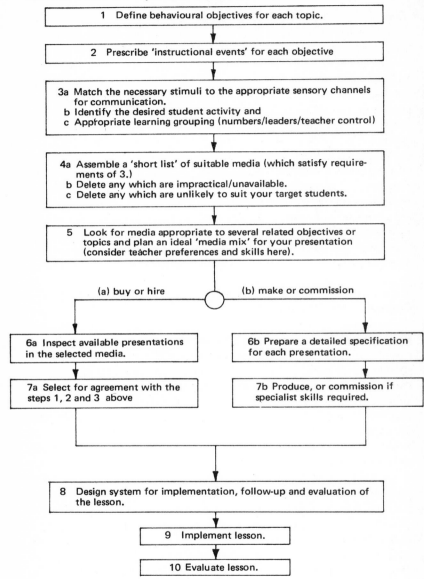

Figure 2.3 Procedure for lesson design (emphasis on media selection)

and others. It differs from the more traditional approaches which select methods and media at the lesson or even the course level.

2 Prescribe the 'instructional events' for each objective

The term 'instructional event' is used here rather than 'teaching method' because it illustrates the 'micro' level at which we are operating. Teaching methods are made up of instructional events. For example, a classroom demonstration of how a particular mechanism works might involve (a) showing the mechanism (presenting the stimulus); (b) directing attention to the relevant parts; (c) explaining their function; (d) encouraging students to apply previously learnt general principles; (e) questioning students; (f) providing feedback to students, and so on. This particular example calls for both visual and verbal media (whether the verbal should be written or spoken is not clear from our analysis so far, and may well be optional). Gagné suggested that different media may not be equally good at performing different instructional functions. Some of his suggestions are summarised in Figure 2.4. This figure is presented only as a general outline. It is not to be used as a job aid, since it is not precise enough for this purpose. For example, if we examine his first instructional function 'presenting the stimulus', then surely we will agree that still pictures are good at presenting certain visual stimuli, moving pictures may be equivalent and in some cases better, but neither will communicate an audio stimulus if this is necessary.

We suggest therefore that the instructional events which you plan should be expressed in terms of stimulus and response. Gilbert's model as presented in the last chapter is useful here, as are Gagné's categories of learning. One may also use Bloom's taxonomy to define the instructional events.

3 Identify essential media characteristics

This is how we fix the *essential* media characteristics:

Functions	Media						
	Objects; Demonstration	Oral Communication	Printed Media	Still Pictures	Moving Pictures	Sound Movies	Teaching Machines
Presenting the stimulus	Yes	Limited	Limited	Yes	Yes	Yes	Yes
Directing attention and other activity	No	Yes	Yes	No	No	Yes	Yes
Providing a model of expected performance	Limited	Yes	Yes	Limited	Limited	Yes	Yes
Furnishing external prompts	Limited	Yes	Yes	Limited	Limited	Yes	Yes
Guiding thinking	No	Yes	Yes	No	No	Yes	Yes
Inducing transfer	Limited	Yes	Limited	Limited	Limited	Limited	Limited
Assessing attainments	No	Yes	Yes	No	No	Yes	Yes
Providing feedback	Limited	Yes	Yes	No	Limited	Yes	Yes

Figure 2.4 Instructional functions of various media as suggested by Gagné (1965)

(a)   The type of responses required of the students (ie discriminating, manipulating, identifying, deducing etc) suggest certain practice exercises which in turn dictate certain media characteristics.

(b)   The type of stimuli required to communicate the message clearly are identified, and dictate the sensory channels which our presentation use.

(c)   The student group size and geographical scatter may be fixed factors, or may be variable in certain situations. Certain instructional events may demand large or small groups for efficiency. Others may suggest individual study. Nevertheless, once the audience group size and their geographical scatter is fixed (whether by the course designer or by external constraints) certain essential media characteristics are also fixed.

As job aids for fixing the essential media characteristics, a series of algorithms have been prepared:

—   Figure 2.5 aids the matching of the type of responses required by the learning task to appropriate media characteristics.

—   Figures 2.6 and 2.7 aid the matching of visual and audio requirements of the stimuli to appropriate media characteristics.

—   Figure 2.8 matches group size and type of learning task to appropriate media. This differs from the other three in that it is not really an algorithm. The relation between the learning task and group size is not precise. Similarly, the division into large, medium and small groups at 50 and 10 members is quite arbitrary (though supported by some empirical research). Thus Figure 2.8 gives general indications on the selection of appropriate media characteristics. One could argue that only in certain cases are the suggested media characteristics essential (ie when we have extremely large or very small groups) while in other 'transitional' cases, the chart only suggests options.

4 Assemble 'short-list' of suitable media.
It is at this stage that one 'exercises one's options'.

(a) The first short-list includes all the media which satisfy the essential media characteristics identified in stage 3.

(b) Delete any which are impractical or unobtainable, or otherwise unsuitable due to environmental constraints. Figure 2.9 may be used as a job aid at this stage.

(c) Delete any which are unlikely to suit your students, whether due to their learning habits, past experiences or psychological characteristics. This is probably the most difficult to do. We often know so little about our students. Sometimes, however, we know with a fair level of confidence that, for example, our students are happier studying individually at home or in the library, than in formal groups, or we may know that a previous teacher used so much TV (and used it badly) that the group is heartily sick of it. Psychological characteristics are more difficult still, for not only must we know what the research findings are (precious few valid studies exist anyway), but also we must be able to recognise these characteristics in our students. There are some indications from research that 'realism' pays off more with low IQ groups than with high IQ groups; that being able to touch and manipulate objects is more important for students with poor mechanical ability, and so on. However, these differences (although they have led to statistically significant results in experiments) are not usually

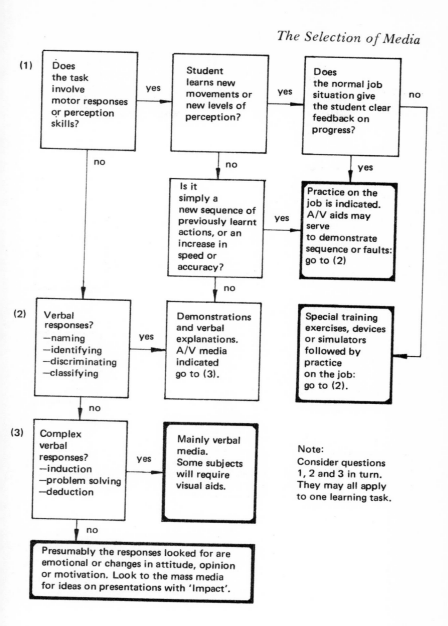

Figure 2.5 Decisions for the matching of learning task to media characteristics

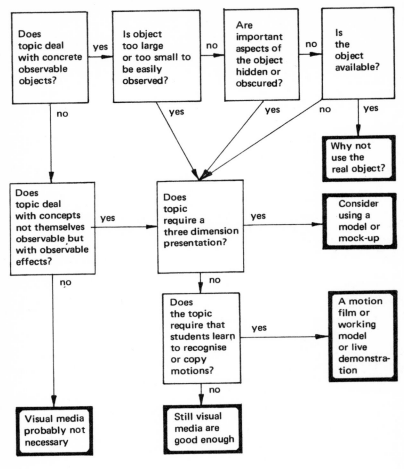

Figure 2.6 Decisions for selecting visual media

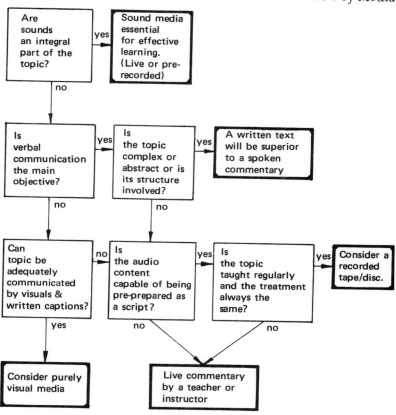

Figure 2.7 Decisions for selecting verbal and sound media

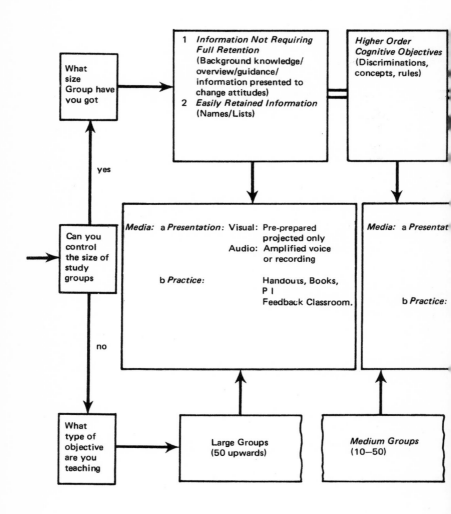

Figure 2.8 Decisions for matching group size to media characteristics

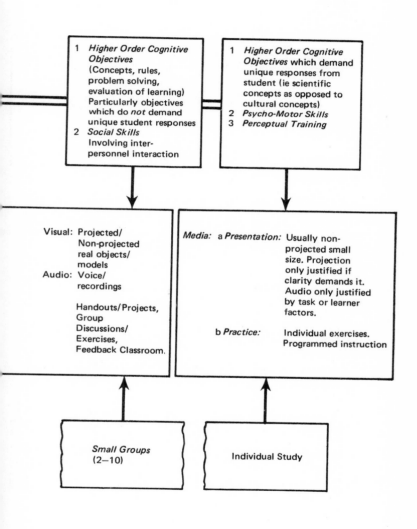

When more than one media option seems appropriate the alternatives should be considered in the light of the following questions, and the most practicable chosen.

Any option which gives one or more 'No' answers, should be avoided. If no options seem appropriate, consider how you could modify either the media or the environment to eliminate the objections.

Negative considerations

		Yes	No
1	Can it be obtained or made at an economical price, relative to the importance of the topic being taught?		
2	Is there enough space to use it effectively?		
3	Will it operate in the conditions of the training area (temperature, humidity, power sources, transportability)?		
4	Is it student-proof (withstands careless handling, not prone to vanish)?		
5	Is it capable of being maintained, and repaired by the user?		
6	Will it have a reasonable working life (bearing in mind the cost), before it is rendered obsolete by changes in the subject?		

Figure 2.9 Practical and environmental constraints

very large, and not always easy to identify in our student group. Furthermore, any group is likely to have a spread of IQ, of mechanical abilities, spatial abilities, reading ages or what have you. Unless we develop individualised course materials, with alternative sets of materials (using alternative media and having alternative contents) we cannot hope to deal effectively with individual differences. Although we may well subscribe to this ideal of individualised instruction, in practice we often have to compromise, developing one set of materials which will suit most of our students reasonably, but few of them perfectly.

To illustrate the variety of inter-related factors which might influence our decisions, let us consider just one decision which might be called for in a hypothetical course. Suppose we wished to teach the working of a mechanism (perhaps the internal combustion engine). Suppose we have identified that visual stimuli are essential. Suppose furthermore that we may practicably make available a set of still diagrams (overhead projector transparencies) or a movie film, or a working (but simplified) model. As the cost increases considerably for each of these options, we wish to assess whether we will get away with the still pictures, or whether the more expensive options are worth considering. Figure 2.10 presents a set of considerations which should be weighed up in making our decision. The first ten considerations are concerned with the learning task, the next ten are concerned with student factors.

Try for yourself the internal combustion engine example. See how closely you agree with our rating (there is no reason why you should agree exactly, as some of the questions call for value judgments).

Our rating on the first ten are: A — 6; B — 4; C — 3. In other words the task factors favour a working model over a still or moving visual.

Let us consider the learner factors for two distinct target groups — (1) undergraduate engineering students (highly selected, above average IQ, proven learning skills, probably

Keep a score of the letters A, B, and C for those questions where you answer YES. Select the high scoring medium.

A . . .Model; B . . .Still Visual; C . . .Movie Film.

Note Questions 1 — 7 relate to real objects only. They may be skipped if you are attempting to visually explain an abstract concept etc.

1 Complex shape or inside details which should be studied?	A: C.
2 Many inter-related parts, the relative position being of importance to the learner?	A: B.
3 Are the functions of the parts to be studied?	A: C.
4 Are the relative sizes important to learner?	A: B.
5 Is it so complex that detailed breakdown and analysis is required to fully understand it?	A: B.
6 Is the motion of the object or its parts to be studied?	A: C.
7 Is the sequence of operation to be studied?	A: B.
8 Is the purpose to demonstrate the performance of a manipulative or motor skill?	C.
9 Will student apply what he learns in an identical situation?	A: C.
10 Will student apply what he learns as general principles in a number of similar situations?	B.

11 Are students of above average IQ?	B.
12 Average or below average IQ?	A: C.
13 Do students need motivation?	C.
14 Are they already well motivated?	B.
15 Do they already have experience of the topic?	B.
16 Do they lack relevant experience?	C.
17 Do your students learn well from verbal or from visual material?	B: C.
18 Do they need to handle or operate equipment to ensure efficient learning?	A.
19 Do they have good mechanical ability?	B: C.
20 Do they have poor mechanical ability?	A.

Figure 2.10 Optional media characteristics: model, still visual or film — check list

well motivated as they selected this course of study); and (2) people preparing for car mechanics questions to be set as part of a car driving test (a common practice in some European countries). They probably have a wide range of IQ's, little previous mechanical experience, low motivation in most cases.

Our ratings on the last ten questions are:

Group 1: A — O; B — 4; C — 2

Group 2: A — 2; B — 1; C — 2

thus giving us total ratings as follows:

Group 1: A — 6; B — 8; C — 5

Group 2: A — 8; B — 5; C — 5

It seems the more expensive media choices may be a waste of money for Group 1, but certainly the expense of a model may pay off for Group 2.

This example is presented here purely to illustrate that weighing up the final choice of media is complex and is in part subjective. This is the area of optional media characteristics.

5 Plan final 'media mix'

At this stage our choice of media for each lesson objective should be relatively small. A final choice should now be made in the light of the following two factors:

(a) Certain groups of objectives, to be taught together, may well be taught by means of the same media, for convenience. Look for media common to several related objectives.

(b) The personal preferences of the teachers who will be involved in the course should be considered. If you are planning a course which you will teach, your personal preferences may already be partly mirrored by the weight you attach to various practical constraints and optional media characteristics. If however you are planning a course for other teachers (and you know who these will be) you would do well to investigate their instructional methods and preferences, and also the present level of their skills with respect to the media you are selecting.

6 and 7 Make or buy

These steps are self-evident from the flow chart of our procedure (Figure 2.3). Whether you decide to use existing materials (usually the more economical solution) or to produce tailor-made materials, the important point to remember is that the statements of objectives for the course, the detailed prescriptions of instructional events and the identified essential media characteristics (ie steps 1, 2 and 3 of the procedure) should be used as controls over the materials to check their suitability for the course being planned.

8 Design system of implementation and evaluation

This stage involves:

(a) Designing appropriate tests for the lesson's cognitive and psychomotor objectives. This is therefore very closely linked with stage 1. As soon as the lesson objectives are specified in behavioural terms, one can derive appropriate test situations directly from them. Indeed we suggest that tests for the cognitive or psychomotor objectives of a lesson should be developed at stage 1, so that the conditions and standard implied by the objective are mirrored in the test. Otherwise, there is a danger that tests may not reflect the objectives exactly.

(b)   Designing appropriate ways in which the long-term effects of the lesson, and in particular the affective objectives, may be assessed. Very often these cannot be directly measured, but can only be sensed from the general atmosphere of the class, or deduced indirectly from subsequent activities (eg increased popularity of certain library books). Long-term retention of cognitive objectives can of course be measured by re-testing at a later date. Alternatively, indicators such as sustained improved job performance may be used. Affective objectives may also sometimes be deduced from later performance. For example, a greater adherence to basic safety precautions in a factory is generally a sign of a change in attitude rather than knowledge. Similarly, attendance figures at a series of lectures are often a significant measure of whether the lecturer is achieving his affective objectives. A thorough and very entertaining discussion of how to measure the attainment of affective objectives has been written by Bob Mager[6]. In this he stresses the value of observing 'avoidance' and 'approach' behaviour on the part of students.

When planning the evaluation of a lesson, or a course, it is well worth considering carefully just which of the many characteristics of the lesson you really want to evaluate, and what indicators are available for these characteristics. All too often data is collected which cannot later be used for any purpose. Sometimes essential data necessary for course improvement is overlooked. Figure 2.11 gives a few examples of the sort of lesson characteristics which may be worth evaluating, (but not always). These are linked to some of the behavioural indicators you might use, and these in turn are linked to appropriate evaluation procedures. Stop to think how often inappropriate evaluation procedures are used for the course re-design activities envisaged.

Some further questions for consideration:

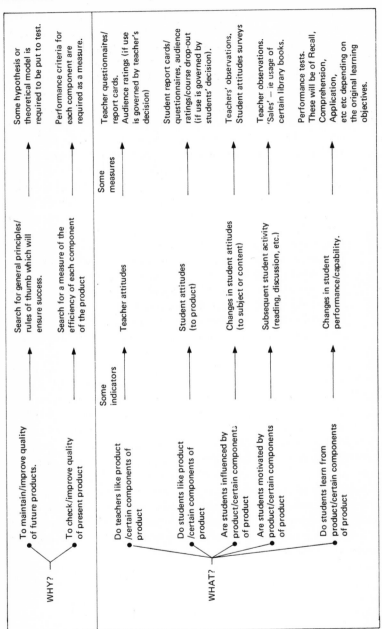

Figure 2.11 Some thoughts on evaluation

(a)   If we set a test of cognitive objectives (with a view to improving the course) do we wish to know which students make mistakes, or what mistakes are made (and why)? Surely for course evaluation we need lots of 'mini-questions' (at least one per objective) rather than 'global' questions which test whole areas of knowledge. Furthermore, we need to be able to diagnose a particular weakness in the lesson from a particular error pattern. Tests which do not allow us to do this are useless for course-evaluation purposes.

(b)   When do we want to compare students against each other? Certainly not when we are designing instruction. Nor when we are honestly engaged in instruction. In both these cases we really wish to compare students' performance against the desired learning objectives. Only if we are selecting students for some purpose do we need to compare their performances. Most educational systems are extremely selection-orientated in their final examinations, and unfortunately this tendency to 'grade' students percolates down into the daily routine in the classroom. Students are given 'marks' which relate to how they have performed in relation to their group (eg the 'ten best essays' are rewarded with an A grade). Whatever the overall essay-writing skills of the group are, the best ones get an A (unless the teacher is one of those who believes in never giving anything better than a B+ — he's presumably waiting to discover a budding Shakespeare).

This type of approach to lesson or course evaluation is quite useless. For our purpose we need to measure a student's performance against a performance criterion, not against the 'norm' of his group. Thus 'norm-referenced' tests should not be used for course evaluation purposes — neither should they be used for diagnosing individual student's problems. The category of norm-referenced tests includes any tests which are designed to spread results out in some approximation to a 'normal' distribution. It includes IQ tests, aptitude tests of various sorts and also the recently popularised 'objective' multiple-choice tests of attainment (eg those used now for many City & Guilds examinations).

What the teacher (as opposed to the social system) requires are 'criterion-referenced' tests, that is, tests which are rigidly bound to defined performance standards — tests based on and derived from behavioural objectives.

Conclusion

Thus we have come full circle to a re-emphasis of the critical importance that the precise statement of your course objectives (in behavioural terms) plays in the systematic design and evaluation of your course.

We have dealt in this chapter with a procedure for lesson design, concentrating particularly on the selection of presentation media. The procedure attempts to be systematic, and in the attempt, may be accused of being a trifle long-winded. Readers can however take heart in the knowledge that lengthier procedures have also been suggested. Briggs outlines a procedure, which together with exercises for practice, fills a book of over two hundred pages[7]. His handbook on instructional design is intended for study a few hours per week over a year or so by teachers in training. And who could argue that this is time mis-spent, on what is after all one of the basic skills of teaching.

Furthermore, although our procedure does appear lengthy, its use, with practice, does not take too much time. Many of the stages become intuitive. One 'telescopes' the procedure, performing several stages at one time. Certain types of objectives immediately trigger off certain approaches, because you have 'been here before'.

Briggs suggests that many of the procedures involved in media selection may be 'telescoped' into an 'If-Then' chart, rather like the one shown here in Figure 2.12. This chart illustrates very well the 'selection by rejection' motto that we have been applying in this chapter.

However, the problem with a chart of this kind, as with any procedure, is that it tends to be somewhat too rigid. The

Subjects were asked to prepare a lesson plan for given objectives, making full use of any media they thought fit. These lesson plans were judged by a team of educational technologists and experts in teaching method. The lesson plans were classed as ideal, acceptable and poor.

The given objectives were:

At the end of the lesson, students should be able to:

1 State when, how and why a new (decimal) currency system is to be adopted by the UK.
2 Identify the new coins.
3 State their equivalents in the old currency.
4 Carry out simple cash transactions in new and mixed old/new coinage.

The lesson plans were classified as follows:-

Experienced Teachers (N = 52)

Objective No.	Ideal Plan	Acceptable Plan	Poor Plan
1	19	23	5
2	19	31	2
3	17	20	11
4	15	15	10
total	70	89	28

Inexperienced Trainee Teachers With Job-Aids (N = 58)

Objective No	Ideal Plan	Acceptable Plan	Poor Plan
1	56	2	0
2	37	21	0
3	41	15	2
4	32	26	0
total	166	64	2

Figure 2.12 Summary of a study into the value of the algorithms and check lists presented in this chapter.

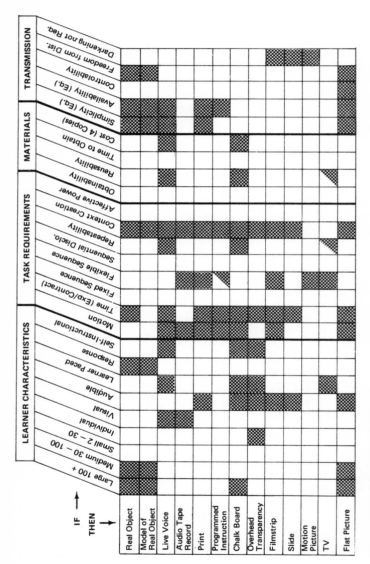

Figure 2.13 An 'If-Then' chart

Summarising characteristics which make certain media unsuitable or partly suitable for instruction. Produced by J G Wilshusen and R Stowe (from L J Briggs, *Handbook of Procedures for the Design of Structures*, 1970

more one 'telescopes' the procedure the more rigid it appears on paper. This is not necessarily true if the procedure is internalised. The experienced lesson designer may telescope the procedure in many ways, depending on the nature of the problem facing him.

We do not claim to have here a procedure which should be followed in every respect, every time. Rather it is offered as a framework, based on a particular view of the instruction process, which should enable the teacher to set about designing lesson plans which have a fair chance of being successful.

Does the procedure work? It certainly seems to. A small study using a prototype version of the job aids in this chapter was tested on groups of trainee teachers. Groups of experienced teachers were also asked to prepare lesson plans for the same instructional objectives. The results of the study were reported in full at an APLET conference in 1969[8]. Figure 2.13 summarising this report speaks for itself.

Of course, like any procedure, it works better for some than for others. Many past students at Enfield College have commented on or criticised certain aspects, and this has led to some modifications. No doubt further modifications will be made in the future.

References

1. A J Romiszowski, 'Classifications, Algorithms and Check Lists as Aids to the Selection of Instructional Methods and Media' in *Aspects of Educational Technology*, Vol 4, ed, Bajpai and J Leedham, Pitman, 1970.

2. Peggie L Campeau, *Selective Review of the Results of Research on the Use of Audiovisual Media to Teach Adults,* Council of Europe CCC/TE(72)5, 1972.

3. R M Gagné, *The Conditions of Learning,* Holt, Rinehart, Winston, 1965. (Second expanded edition 1970.)

4. L J Briggs, Peggie Campeau, R M Gagné, and May,

Instructional Media — a Procedure for the Design of Multi-Media Instruction, American Institute for Research, Monograph 2, 1967.

5. L J Briggs, *Handbook of Procedures for the Design of Instruction,* American Institute for Research, Monograph 4, 1970.

6. R F Mager, *Developing Attitude towards Instruction,* Fearon, 1969.

7. L J Briggs, op cit in n 5.

8. A J Romiszowski, op cit in n 1.

3   When To Use Still Visual Media

In this chapter we will discuss when and how to present still visual material. The approach will be a systematic evaluation of the role of each medium, based on user experience and research, together with indications of how the teacher may avoid pitfalls and obtain the greatest value from the materials used.

To begin with, why do we need to use visual aids at all? Why not the Real Thing?

Why not? Very often teachers bring samples of everyday objects into the classroom or take the class out to view real things in their natural surroundings. We soon come across objects which cannot be readily shown. They are too large, too small, too expensive, too dirty, too dangerous, too delicate, or they only come out at night! This is when the teacher turns to an alternative display — a model or a picture. Sometimes the object is available and could be shown, but the characteristics one wishes to demonstrate are not very obvious — (they are inside, for example) — so some other means of presentation becomes both more practical and more meaningful to the student.

Finally, the thing may not exist, or at least not in an observable form: you can only demonstrate its presence by its effects. Here again a model or chart may be helpful. Energy, for example, may be demonstrated directly — as when we take a swipe at Jones in the front row — but he will learn more about its nature and the way it is converted into other forms of energy by studying a chart or performing an experiment.

So the three main reasons why models or pictures are used

are:

1   It is inconvenient to use the real thing.

2   A model or chart can better explain the principle being taught.

3   The real thing cannot be seen anyway.
     If none of these objections applies, then by all means use the real thing, and you can put this book down till your next teaching problem arises.

Models or pictures?

It all depends which shows best the principle being taught. If the third dimension plays an important part in communicating your message, then you can expect better results from a model. If the shape, texture or inside structure is unimportant, or if it can be adequately represented in two dimensions, a diagram or picture will probably be just as good. Indeed, there is evidence that too much realism or detail may hinder the communication of your message. If a picture is sufficient, a model will not improve comprehension, and may indeed hinder it by introducing irrelevant and distracting detail.

Of course, both models and pictures can be made clearer by the omission of irrelevant detail, so focussing the student's attention on those points which are relevant to the problem in hand. For example, anatomy lessons are simplified by the production of separate charts showing bones, organs, the bloodstream, the nervous system, the musculature, and so on. To show all these details on one chart would be very messy and unclear. At a later stage, however, a model which can be dismantled is most helpful in showing how the various sub-systems fit and act together to give a real working human being. At a still later stage, when beginning to learn 'maintenance and repair' procedures, the real thing becomes necessary. This too can be messy, in a different way, and fatal for the patient, if perchance the early lessons using first charts, and then models, have not been learned well.

Occasionally, the transition from 2- and 3-dimensional representations to the real thing can be eased by the use of working models, or simulators. Our budding surgeons are at a disadvantage here, as no one has yet produced a complete simulator of a human being. In the main they have to rely on the traditional training technique of first 'sitting by Nellie', and then having a bash.

In many technical fields however — as in fighter pilot training — complex simulators are used to train operators in the use of dangerous or expensive machinery. Similarly, models and simulators are often designed specifically to guard human safety and comfort — as in the testing of safety harnesses. And of course, barbers have for centuries learnt to wield a cut-throat by laboriously shaving a wooden head, graduating progressively to softer and softer woods.

Such models and simulators are the subject of a later chapter. Here we are concerned with the visual presentation of objects, phenomena or ideas. The use of models is indicated when:

1   The shape of the object is complex and must be shown.

2   The inside detail must be observed and cannot be better shown by a cross-section diagram.

3   There is so much detail, all relevant, that pictures or diagrams are unclear or misleading (eg crystal or molecular structure; pipework installations in refineries; complex 3-D mechanisms).

In general, models should therefore be employed when the use of the third dimension aids communication. Only details relevant to the message being communicated should be included. Too much unnecessary realism may reduce effective communication.

If you can picture the object, concept or phenomenon

adequately in two dimensions, there is little to be gained in terms of learning efficiency by using a model. This does not rule out, however, the motivational value of the model, or the 'real thing'. Being able to play with objects is recognised by infant teachers as a valuable educational experience. This is no less true of adults. Many a motor mechanic enters his trade as a result of a love of 'mucking about' with cars. He would soon leave his apprenticeship if given no chance to play with a real engine. But his play will be all the more valuable if he understands, for example, the Otto cycle or the principle of the S U Carburettor. These can be learnt more efficiently from simplified diagrams or models which illustrate the processes.

Our man of the assembly line, however, may assemble the engine quite efficiently with very little knowledge of the principles on which it works. He will be trained on the real thing. However, his training may also be speeded by supplying visual aids, such as a series of photographs of stages in the assembly, or by means of a job aid: for example, a wall chart of instructions in chronological order.

So again we see the need for precise objectives. Only when we have specified the performance required of the learner and analysed the knowledge and skills required to perform, can we set about the systematic and intelligent design of visual display.

Two-dimensional visuals

There are three main types of visual display materials:

1   Pictures — including photographs, line drawings and paintings aiming at a true and lifelike representation of a real object.

2   Diagrams — including engineering drawings, cross-sections, schematic diagrams, flow diagrams — aiming at a clear representation of an object, or specific characteristics of an object, or a process, concept or phenomenon.

3   Graphic presentations — including graphs and charts — aiming to present a trend, or an inter-relation, or a set of figures.

These sub-divisions are more points on a continuous scale than watertight compartments. There is an increasing level of abstraction and increasing use of symbolic conventions as you proceed along this scale. Consequently, the further a visual lies along the scale, the more must a student learn 'how to read' the conventions before the visual will communicate the intended message. This is a point often overlooked by users of visual aids.

Reading of visual material

One learns to 'read' visual material partly by experience and partly by being taught. Even the understanding of quite simple pictures must be learnt. The appreciation of perspective, for example, is not inborn. Painters only mastered its use during the Renaissance. We now use it unthinkingly, by rule-of-thumb, to produce drawings. Children, however, have to learn to read such drawings by a process of experience — of comparing pictorial representations with the real things around them. Luckily for the users of visual aids, most of our students soon learn to comprehend perspective — at least this is true of Western Europe. Experiments in other cultures show that different experiences lead to different perception of visual material. A perspective drawing of a long room with several cut-out windows was shown to Europeans and Africans. An identical head was made to appear at each window. Europeans, used to perspective drawings and long rooms, judged the heads at the smaller (apparently farther) windows to be larger. Africans, not used to conventions and living in round houses, made no allowance for perspective and judged all the heads to be equal. Such aspects of a drawing as facial expression, attitude, or irrelevant detail content may be sufficient to alter or distort the message being communicated. Young children in particular tend to react emotionally to visual material, and the general atmosphere of the picture may register much more strongly than the factual content — 'I don't want to go to Heaven because God looks so strict'. We have also the recent example of a road safety campaign that went wrong. The sight of the badly mangled cars prominently displayed at accident black-spots was meant to communicate 'drive carefully'. What was in fact communicated was anxiety, and the accident rate went up. For similar reasons, one must control the content of a picture to ensure that the viewer's attention focuses on those aspects which are of significance for the lesson in progress. A photo of a nuclear reactor set in parkland with cows grazing may attempt to make the point that the locality is safe and free from pollution. A Hindu might only notice the cows.

Research on the comprehension of visuals

As one progresses to more abstract visual presentation, there is an increasing possibility that the target audience for our visual masterpiece will not be equipped with the skills necessary to read our meaning. We may be better off without the visual aid. Extensive research by Vernon[1] on the use of graphs to present numerical data and statistics showed that:

1 Intelligent and well-educated people could cope with graphical information, but less fortunate individuals needed written explanations and supporting textural material.

2 There was no difference in the effectiveness of line graphs and numerical charts for the communication of factual data, though graphs were a little better at communicating trends.

3 In no case was there evidence to suggest that graphs or charts would help to teach something that would 'otherwise be beyond the comprehension of the reader'.

Vernon also investigated the effect of pictorial illustrations on the comprehension of a text[2]. The same text was given to two matched groups of 16-18 year olds, but one group also had illustrations. There was no decisive evidence to suggest that the illustrated version was better understood. The points illustrated were better remembered, but at the cost of less understanding of the general theme of the text. Pictures were inefficient at presenting relations or explanations, but did arouse emotions and strong attitudes. Thus, the illustrated version resulted in a less thorough, less objective grasp of the argument presented in the text.

These, at first sight rather unfavourable, results require some qualification.

First, the choice of topic used for such research is likely to influence the results a great deal. The text referred to above dealt with social problems and presented data on divorces, mortality and so on. This is, no doubt by choice, a subject which can adequately be dealt with by a straightforward verbal presentation. The pictures and graphs used simply underlined or re-stated points which were already made in the text. It is not surprising that they added little to the overall comprehension. However, there are subjects which cannot be adequately expressed in words. In the early stages of learning to speak, the child relies heavily on making associations between the things he observes and the spoken sounds he hears. We cannot start using verbal explanations until he has built up a basic mastery of the language. Modern language teaching methods which involve a minimal use of the native tongue, could not be operated without the use of visual material. Much technical material in scientific or industrial training can best be presented visually. Imagine a motor car manual explaining engine dismantling procedures, or the wiring circuits, without the use of diagrams.

The *second* qualification one might make of Vernon's work relates to the choice of student for the research. We saw that the more intelligent, more educated, could cope more readily with graphs. It is all too easy to conclude that graphs are therefore more difficult to read and comprehend than equivalent written descriptions. Might the reason not be, however, that the more intelligent, more educated, simply had more previous experience in use of graphs, because they are encountered later in one's education? Is it not perhaps a question of the readiness of students to benefit from a particular presentation medium; a question of the amount of prior training they had received in the necessary graph-reading skills?

A *third* qualification might be made. We are all steeped in the traditions of a verbal, literate society. As he learns to read and write, a child becomes less receptive to other visual stimuli. He tends, through schooling, to be forced into a routine of expressing everything he sees or feels in terms of words. Communication through action is not encouraged. In fact it is often actively discouraged by our society. Two points arise:

1 Are the less intelligent, less educated students less successful with graphs because they have difficulty in 'translating' what they learn visually into a written answer to a question? Are they more successful with a written text because they simply learn to repeat what they read? Does this necessarily indicate greater comprehension?

2 Are we justified in assuming that everything a student learns from a picture is capable of being measured by verbal questioning. Vernon herself reported changes in emotion and attitude, as a result of illustrating the text. May this not be a valid educational objective in itself? Can it be effectively measured by a written test? There is evidence that information presented visually is better recalled in a visual rather than a verbal test[3].

There is a school of thought typified by the writings of Marshall McLuhan[4] which suggests that we are leaving the age of print — (the Gutenberg age). Due to electronic mass media, especially television, Western societies communicate more and more on a direct face-to-face level. Also, instantaneous two-way communication over any distance is possible. As a result, the role of gestures, visual displays and tone increases, and the importance of clear step-by-step logical presentation diminishes. Evidence for these views is mainly gathered from an examination of social and cultural changes in society, trends in the arts and so on. There is also, however, some evidence in educational research. This will be discussed in the chapter on television.

We should perhaps re-examine the present system in which children, reared from birth in an environment of electronic mass media, gaining more and more of their early education through instant, up-to-date visual presentation, are taught and tested in school predominantly by the written word. Do our children perhaps read the language of pictures better than their parents ever did?

Recent research by Hartley[5] tends to bear out some of these observations. He compared the way students reacted to lecture material supported by slides and by blackboard illustration. Although in general they preferred the slides, they learnt better from the blackboard. A detailed look at this experiment will illustrate once more that it is not so much the medium, as the way it is used and the purpose it is used for, that controls the efficiency of the message's transmission.

A lecture was delivered in a lecture theatre fitted with a projection room, where the experimenter sat out of sight of the lecturer and the student. The lecture was tape recorded through the theatre's amplification system. Points made in the lecture that were illustrated with slides were noted. Points made with the aid of the blackboard were noted and the time of their delivery recorded.

The lecturer tended to leave each slide showing until he was ready to show the next, so both the initial time of display and the display length were noted. Generally speaking, the lecturer continued to talk while directing the students' attention to the slides, but if he remained silent for a period this was also noted.

Ten days later the students were given a short test consisting of 12 questions, 6 of which tested material which had been taught in conjunction with slides, and 6 of which similarly tested material presented with the aid of the blackboard.

The students were asked to answer their questions with the aid of their notes, and to indicate whether they had, or had not, notes on the points in question. In addition, the students were given a questionnaire designed to test their opinion on the use of slides in lectures.

A comparison was made between the number of questions in each group of six to which students reported some reference in their notes. This showed no significant difference between the groups, but that there was a tendency for more notes to have been made from the board than from the slides.

A comparison was made between questions which were answered incorrectly, even when students reported referring to their notes. This showed (again not significantly) a tendency for more mistakes to have occurred from points made with slides. In addition, there were more omissions in the notes for material presented with slides than with the blackboard. The length of time slides were displayed did not seem to affect the results.

The questionnaire results indicated among other things that 90% of students thought that there were sufficient (or even not enough) slides used. Only 10% felt that fewer slides should have been used. However, 71% stated they would have liked to have had a pause in the lecture, to allow them to absorb the slide. So perhaps their relatively poor performance on the slide material was due at least in part to the way the slides were used — presented and 'talked-over' by the lecturer, as Hartley points out.

The criterion for the use of a slide by the lecturer often seems to be that it is a quick way of showing material that is too complicated to write or draw on the board. Such a criterion ignores the fact that if it is too complicated for the lecturer, then it will also be too complicated for the student.

Lecturers need to take more account of the objectives of their slides, and the difficulties of students when using them. For instance, one slide in this study, used to illustrate the size of a crater, did so without a scale. In answering a question on this point only four students gave the correct answer (¾ mile), whilst the rest gave answers of over 10, and one said 300 miles.

In conclusion, the results should not be taken as a condemnation of visual materials, but rather as another indication of the need for a systematic approach to visual aid design. A visual aid is not an aid unless it performs a specific function and performs it well. The points to consider are:

1 The objectives — is the student to remember, to comprehend, to form an attitude?

2 The target audience — are they ready for this method of communication; can they use the language?

3 Alternative methods — can the objective be achieved equally or better by a verbal description?

4 Evaluation — does the visual achieve the desired objectives? How can we validly measure this?

References

1. M D Vernon, 'The Use and Value of Graphical Methods of Presenting Quantitative Data', *Occupational Psychology,* Vol XXVI, 1952.

2. M D Vernon, 'The Value of Pictorial Illustration', *British Journal of Educational Psychology,* Vol XXIII, 1953.

3. C Duncan and J Hartley, 'The Effect of the Mode of Presentation and Result on a Simple Learning Task', *Programmed Learning and Educational Technology,* July 1969.

4. M McLuhan, *Understanding Media,* McGraw-Hill, 1964.

5. J. Hartley, 'Using Slides in Lectures', *Visual Education,* August/September 1971.

4   Still Media–Presentation Methods

There is a range of methods used to present still visual material — from the traditional chalkboard to flannelboards, magnetic boards, wall charts, opaque, slide and strip projectors, down to the modern versatile overhead projector. The various methods have particular advantages for certain types of visual material, so although modern equipment like the overhead projector can effectively present diagrams, photos, models and so on, it would not be fair to say that it has rendered other presentation methods obsolete. We will therefore consider the full range of methods at the teacher's disposal, identifying the advantages and limitations of each.

1 The chalkboard

This was called the *blackboard* until recently when someone noticed that modern blackboards are seldom black — they are blue, green, brown, and even yellow. Reasons for this are less glare and reflection, and less obvious 'ghosting' (the marks left when chalk is rubbed out). Unfortunately, they sometimes give less contrast to white chalk, and the user might experiment with other colours to get maximum readability.

The chalkboard has for long been the standard teaching aid. It is almost universally available, and nearly every teacher uses it. Paradoxically though, it is one of the more difficult teaching aids to use well. More training and skill is required to make good use of the chalkboard, than to screen a film, use a slide projector or a tape recorder.

First, one must learn to control the chalk. It takes practice to learn to write legibly and to form sufficiently large letters. It requires practice, together with a gift for drawing, to produce large, clear, freehand diagrams quickly. Standard manuals on the use of the chalkboard list a range of techniques to make its use easier[1]. The preparation of diagrams can be improved by the use of cut-outs or templates for any shapes which are often drawn. Complicated diagrams from books or slides can be projected onto the chalkboard and the essential details drawn by tracing over the image. Small pictures can be blown-up by use of a pantograph, or by dividing into a grid and copying each square separately. Any lines used regularly, such as coordinates for graph drawing, can be permanently printed on sections of the board.

Most of these techniques require the prior preparation of the diagrams. It seems a pity to spend great effort before a lesson preparing a clear diagram by, say, the 'project-on' method, only to rub it off within a short while. Would it not be better to make a more permanent visual which could be used over and over again? It would be economical to spend more time in preparing a better diagram, as re-drawing time would eventually be saved. There are now so many efficient ways of presenting pre-prepared visuals, that the use of a chalkboard for this purpose is obsolete. It's no use moaning that you have no other visual aids. A roll of wallpaper is sufficient to produce a whole range of clear re-usable visuals, for use as wall charts or flip-charts.

The real use for the chalkboard today is for impromptu material (words or diagrams which have become necessary due to an unexpected turn in the lesson) or for work which is developed through the lesson by contribution from the class (experimental results, ideas, theories, solutions to problems, summaries). Therefore, much of our chalkboard use is likely to be 'off-the-cuff' writing or sketching. Unless we have a pretty good idea what sort of contributions the class will make, we are unlikely to be equipped with appropriate templates or cut-outs. However, general purpose drawing aids such as rules, squares and mathematical instruments are invaluable, and their use should be mastered. In the long run, there is no substitute for practice in the use of the chalkboard, in order to achieve clear writing, fast sketching and tidy layout.

One should mention here a further development of recent

years — the white chalkboard, or white-board. Originally, these were used with soap or wax-based coloured chalks and crayons. Now, it is more common to use felt-tipped markers. There are obvious advantages in this equipment. First, there is no chalk-dust. Modern 'dustless' chalks have, it is true, improved the situation and silicosis is unlikely now to be an occupational disease of teachers. However, the term dustless is only relative. Dust is still produced, irritating the lungs of some and destroying the clothes of all. Secondly, the range and strength of colours that can be used on a white-board is much greater. Traditional chalk is available in a limited range of anaemic pastel shades. Wax-based crayons are obtainable in every standard colour — spirit markers in a range of pastel and strong colours. The white-board is therefore particularly valuable when sharp or true-to-life colours are an advantage (for example in art classes and design) as well as for improving the clarity and definition of almost any diagram.

There is one problem however: that of cleaning the board. Unless the surface is very smooth and hard, colours penetrate. The problem of 'ghosting' is much more acute. Certain wax-based crayons and spirit markers will not wipe off even with a damp cloth, but require special erasers or solutions. If you intend to use a white-board, it is well to get advice on cleaning methods, and the drawing materials permissible, from the manufacturers; or to first experiment with the available materials.

2 Felt-boards and magnetic boards

The felt-board is simply a board covered in felt or other suitable cloth. Shapes cut out of felt will stay put if pressed onto the board. Other materials such as paper cut-outs can be fixed by backing them with a piece of felt, or if they are heavy, with a special material incorporating thousands of minute nylon hooks. It is possible to use the felt-board to present a display of pre-prepared shapes or items. The main advantage is that these items can very quickly be added to, removed, or their relative positions altered.

The magnetic board is similar in function, but shapes and

objects are attached by means of small magnets fixed to their backs. Any sheet of steel would serve as the board itself. Commercially available magnetic boards are generally prepared for use as a chalkboard or a white-board as well, so that lines may be drawn on the surface as well as separate shapes fixed to it. This makes the magnetic board ideal for the presentation of a range of subjects such as work study, strategy or sport. Any problem which involves the movement of things from place to place, or changes in their relative positions, can be very effectively demonstrated, discussed and built up stage by stage.

Elementary school teachers use flannel boards to establish such concepts as 'above' and 'below', or to demonstrate sentence structure. They are used in secondary schools to illustrate Pythagoras' Theorem. Football coaches use them to discuss new tactics. Industry may demonstrate plant layout modifications, or the company structure.

You can equally well use a flannel or magnetic board as a lesson summary. Headings or major points can be slapped up as they are reached, removed for questioning and follow-up, then replaced, without the delay of writing them up and rubbing them off.

It is obvious that both flannel and magnetic boards require the pre-preparation of all materials used. They are therefore a supplement to the chalkboard. Material which is part of the lesson plan would be presented on, say, a magnetic board. Contributions from the students would be developed alongside, on the chalkboard. The chalkboard which is steel-backed, so that it can be used also as a magnetic board, is therefore particularly useful.

However, the special value of flannel and magnetic boards is restricted to display of fairly simple shapes or objects. Complicated pictures or diagrams can be better displayed by projection, or by the use of some form of chart.

3 Charts and posters

In this context, charts include all manner of non-projected materials — photographs, maps, diagrams, graphs and

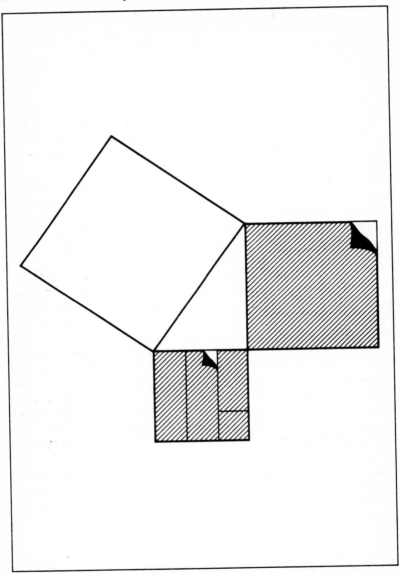

Figure 4.1 Effective use of a flannel or magnetic board
Pre-cut shapes are placed to cover the two small squares. They are then peeled off
and replaced on the larger square demonstrating that Pythagoras' theorem 'really
works'.

cartoons. The particular application of each type of chart or picture — when and how to make best use of its qualities — will be discussed later. From the user's point of view, these materials are all similar, in that they do not need any special equipment to project or display them, and they require preparation in advance. Whereas the chalkboard is used to develop the subject during the classroom session and magnetic and flannel boards to demonstrate a changing relationship between objects, charts and posters are a permanent, pre-prepared, static display.

It is of course possible to use a sheet of paper and chalk or pen to develop a chart in the classroom, thus using the paper as a substitute for a chalkboard. We will not consider this use here, but confine ourselves to discussing ways of using pre-prepared charts.

There are two main ways in which charts are used — as permanent displays (wall charts) or as displays which emphasise or summarise certain points in a lesson. The latter will only be shown for a short time, then taken away or replaced by another showing the next stage of development of the subject. The handiest way to store and use such charts is to mount them by the top edge to a horizontal bar, so that one can flip the charts over to reveal any one of them to the class. We will therefore refer to them as flip-charts. Of course, it does not matter in the least whether flip-charts are made to flip, or whether some other system is used, just as it does not matter whether wall charts are actually hung on walls. The essential difference is the amount of control exercised over their use by the teacher. Wall charts are a permanent or semi-permanent display which the student may use in many ways, flip-charts are designed to supply visual support to a specific lesson, and to be used in a specific way.

The use of flip-charts

Flip-charts, in use, perform the same function as slide or film strip projectors (to be discussed later). They present a visual display for a limited period of time. Each chart has a specific function, some specific message to communicate. A series of charts, may, like a film strip, develop a subject being discussed. Like a film strip, the effectiveness of the charts

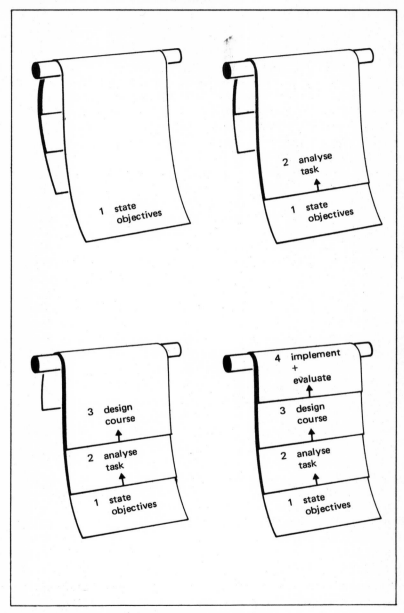

Figure 4.2 A set of flip-charts for lesson summary

will depend on how well the discussion and the visual is integrated. Flip-charts are seldom designed to stand on their own and communicate the whole message. The exception to this is when they are used as a summary of the main points. Generally, the visual on the chart supplements and illustrates the verbal commentary. To display a chart showing a verbal statement of the point under discussion, and then to read out the statement verbatim discloses either a total unawareness of the function of visuals, or else an awareness that the visual is so bad that the back of the class cannot read it. To re-read a visual presentation is valuable only in reading classes, or perhaps when making a very strong point in summary.

Flip-charts would therefore not normally be overloaded with words, as the reading of the chart interferes with listening to the commentary. Long paragraphs can best be given in hand-outs, but if they are presented as a chart, the teacher should remember to shut up for long enough to let the class read. This technique may be useful when training comprehension, or when introducing a case study.

Both these last examples involve the audience in active participation. Charts are an excellent method of obtaining student participation. The teacher has both the content and the time of presentation under his control. Furthermore, in many subjects the ability to respond to a visual stimulus is more appropriate. How many children do we know who recite their kerb drill faultlessly, yet are quite prepared to step out in front of a moving car. Much industrial training consists of learning appropriate responses to visual stimuli, rather than answers to verbal questions.

There is much experimental evidence that active participation by the class increases the effectiveness of visuals such as charts and film strips. In its simplest and most common form, this participation involves the copying of notes or diagrams from the visual display. This procedure is much favoured, on the grounds that it gives the student notes to refer to, and forces attention to details of diagrams. Others favour free note-making. Another school of thought favours hand-out notes as they are standard, correct and legible. Still another argues that students seldom, if ever, use notes, and the teacher should plan and carry out systematic revision instead of giving these. There is some truth in all views. It depends much on the level and motivation of the students. However, note copying is probably not very productive in relation to the time it takes, particularly when long paragraphs or complex diagrams are involved. More imaginative ways of obtaining student participation, by asking questions on the visual content, getting students to explain the function of the parts, or to suggest modifications, are liable to produce more effective learning. You should bear in mind the objectives of the lesson. Students should be active in ways which contribute to the behaviour patterns they are learning. Note copying is therefore relevant to lessons in spelling, writing or drawing.

Very often a chart is used to summarise the main stages or points in a lesson. It is often useful to present such a chart at the beginning as well as at the end. Sometimes you want to keep in mind the stages covered so far. When a series of charts is used, a stage-by-stage summary can be built up by so mounting the charts that each successive one is slightly shorter. The main point, or title of each stage is written at the bottom of the chart. When the next chart is flipped over, it covers the visual, but leaves the title at the bottom uncovered. As the lesson progresses, a stage-by-stage summary of the main points is built up. Thus at any time, students are reminded of the relevance of the present stage to the lesson as a whole.

The use of wall charts
Wall charts have many uses:

(a) They may stimulate interest, remind or motivate. These are the functions of posters. We have ample evidence from the world of advertising that well-designed posters can perform these functions. A study by Laner and Sell[2] investigated the use of safety posters in steel works. In this experiment, the display of posters increased the level of conformity with safety requirements by 20% or more.

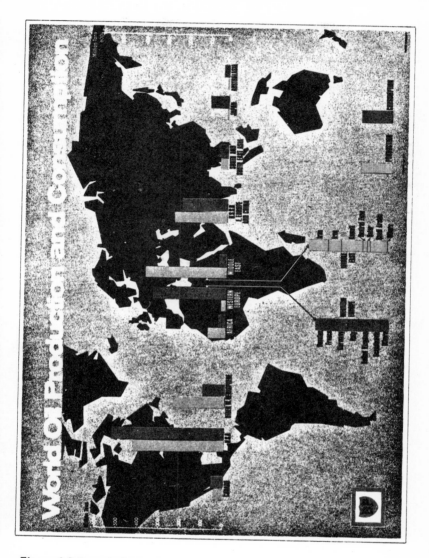

Figure 4.3 A typical wall chart
One of the series supplied to schools and colleges by British Petroleum. Designed
more for regular reference, or as a summary, than to make any one specific point.
A lot of information. A good teacher could put it to many uses.

Consider the points made in the previous chapter. What skills and knowledge
must students possess in order to fully understand this chart?

(b)   They may act as a source of ideas or discussion. Modern language teaching methods, which attempt to avoid the use of the native tongue, rely heavily on wall charts for visual presentation. The use of semi-permanent wall displays to stimulate the imagination is of special value in the earlier years of school life, and is widely used by primary school teachers. According to Bethers[3] young children react emotionally and imaginatively to the content of a picture. As they grow older they begin to look for factual content. The types of wall charts we would use would therefore be governed by the age of our students.

(c)   Provided the students are capable of reading their meaning, wall charts can be used to present factual data. This data may be:

Numerical: as the lists of drill sizes required for tapping holes of different diameters (usually displayed in engineering workshops)

Graphical: relation of height to weight for healthy children, steam pressures in boilers, etc

Pictorial: photographs of equipment, with the parts named

Schematic: this includes diagrams of equipment, processes, structures, engineering drawings, plant layout, flow of materials or cash through a system, the company organisation, procedures to be followed, etc

How a student uses charts

The student may use wall charts in several ways: (a) he may refer to them at random and gradually familiarise himself with their message — this is the action of posters; (b) his attention may be directed to them at certain points of a lesson by the teacher, and he may learn or gain inspiration from the content; (c) he may use the chart systematically as an information store; as a substitute for his memory. The chart becomes a job aid. This is most commonly the use made of charts loaded with factual details. Memorisation of the content would be difficult, if not impossible; the presence of the chart makes it unnecessary. The use of charts as job aids, thus reducing the need for extensive training procedures should not be overlooked. Unfortunately, at the school level, we are hog-tied by examinations which require the memorisation of vast quantities of data which can, in practice, be easily looked up. On the job, architects, engineers and chemists all realise that a reference book (or if we need to refer often, a wall chart) is a much more reliable information store than the human memory.

Recently, much work has been done in industry on task analysis, often for work-study purposes. It is a simple step from a task analysis to the production of a chart, listing, step-by-step, the operations a man must perform and the decisions he must take. Such charts, referred to variously as: process charts, decision trees or algorithms, can very often act as job aids, reducing the amount a learner must memorise, and the amount of practice he requires. Charts as job aids are being increasingly used in business and the professions, from operation on machinery and process plant, through complex office procedures such as tax assessment, to high-level diagnostic procedures such as nuclear reactor fault finding or the diagnosis of disease.

Use of charts as job aids

An example of the way charts (particularly those describing procedures or decisions) may simplify communication problems, is shown in Figure 4.4. This shows two pages from a self-instructional programme on the production of algorithms[4]. The reader is invited to compare the time he takes on the problem in the first page using the prose as a guide, with the time he takes on the second problem, using the algorithm as a guide. Clearly the chart is a more effective job aid. It saves time, as you read only those parts which are relevant to the job in hand. Also, it illustrates more clearly

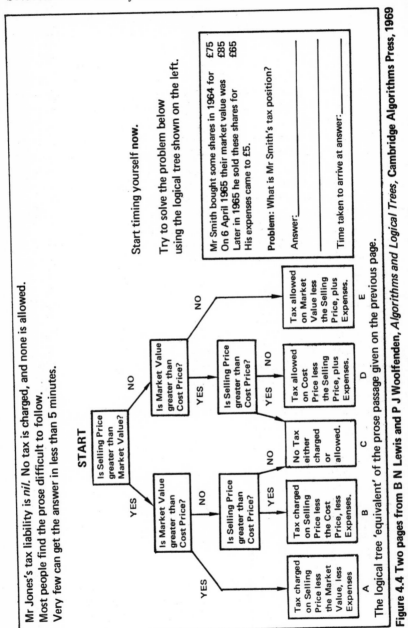

Mr Jones's tax liability is *nil*. No tax is charged, and none is allowed.
Most people find the prose difficult to follow.
Very few can get the answer in less than 5 minutes.

Start timing yourself now.

Try to solve the problem below using the logical tree shown on the left.

Mr Smith bought some shares in 1964 for   £75
On 6 April 1965 their market value was   £85
Later in 1965 he sold these shares for   £65
His expenses came to £5.

Problem: What is Mr Smith's tax position?

Answer: _____

Time taken to arrive at answer: _____

START

Is Selling Price greater than Market Value?

YES — Is Market Value greater than Cost Price?

NO — Is Market Value greater than Cost Price?

Is Selling Price greater than Cost Price?

Is Selling Price greater than Cost Price?

A. Tax charged on Selling Price less the Market Value, less Expenses

B. Tax charged on Selling Price less the Cost Price, less Expenses.

C. No Tax either charged or allowed.

D. Tax allowed on Cost Price less the Selling Price, plus Expenses.

E. Tax allowed on Market Value less the Selling Price, plus Expenses.

The logical tree 'equivalent' of the prose passage given on the previous page.

Figure 4.4 Two pages from B N Lewis and P J Woolfenden, *Algorithms and Logical Trees*, Cambridge Algorithms Press, 1969

During the first half of 1966, income tax forms were sent to about 20 million people in Great Britain. Accompanying each form was a small yellow leaflet, designed to provide 'general guidance' to the reader concerning the newly introduced Capital Gains Tax. Part of Section F, subsection (i) of the leaflet reads as follows:

(i) If the asset consists of stocks or shares which have values quoted on a stock exchange (see also paragraph G below), or unit trust units whose values are regularly quoted, the gain or loss (subject to expenses) accruing after 6 April 1965, is the difference between the amount you received on disposal and the market value on 6 April 1965, except that in the case of a gain where the actual cost of the asset was higher than the value at 6 April 1965, the chargeable gain is the excess of the amount you received on disposal over the original cost of acquisition price; and in the case of a loss, where the actual cost of the asset was lower than the value at 6 April 1965, the allowable loss is the excess of the original cost or acquisition price over the amount received on disposal.

If the substitution of original cost for the value at 6 April 1965, turns a gain into a loss, or a loss into a gain, there is, for the purposes of tax, no chargeable gain or allowable loss.

Mr Jones bought some shares in 1964 for   £2,000
On 6 April 1965 their market value was   £2,500
Later in 1965 he sold these shares for   £2,300
His expenses came to £50

Problem: What is Mr Jones's Tax Liability?

Answer: _____

_____

Time taken to arrive at answer: _____

what outcomes are possible and what decisions must be made to reach a particular outcome. Thus, although the main use of such charts is to 'avoid the need for teaching'[5] , they may also be useful as an aid to instruction.

However, one should not get 'carried away' by algorithms. Even if they are applicable, they are not always the best way of presenting a job aid. A long and complex procedure will lead to a very large, complex and unmanageable chart. It may be better to present the chart in prose form, in numbered paragraphs. Charts in Chapter 2 of this book, which deal with factors influencing the choice of media, can in fact also be laid out in prose form. An extreme example is presented in Figures 4.5 and 4.6. The algorithm shown is one developed to enable a student to place the correct verb-ending on any regular Latin verb[6] . Although it works, it is clumsy and may be frightening to a Latin scholar not accustomed to the notation. Figure 4.6 is a suggested equivalent job aid, laid out in a more familiar fashion, less frightening and probably easier to use.

Of course, not all algorithms can be reduced to a manageable, easily read chart. One can in the last case because of the total symmetry of the decision-making process. However if later decisions depend in various ways on earlier decisions, or if earlier decisions have to be re-considered in the light of later outcomes, then feedback loops appear in our algorithm and it becomes much more difficult to present it in any other way. Figure 4.7 represents another algorithm from the book by Lewis and Woolfenden[7] . This diagram, though fairly complicated, is probably as clear a way as any to lay out the procedures for not losing at noughts and crosses. As an exercise, the reader might like to try to improve on this chart and also on the one presented in Figure 4.4. The aim is to prepare a job aid (ie a set of complete instructions but not a learning aid). In the author's experience it is difficult to improve on Figure 4.7 but Figure 4.4 may be much simplified.

We are living through an information explosion. The amount of knowledge one must cover to reach the frontiers of one's subject, or even to perform effectively in one's job, is rapidly increasing. Automation tends to enlarge jobs rather

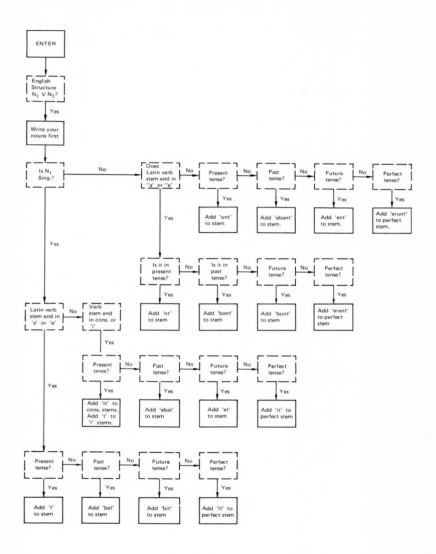

Figure 4.5 An algorithm for obtaining Latin regular verb endings

consider:
1 is first noun singular/plural
2 verb stem ending
3 required tense

Read off:
required verb ending
add it to the verb stem

		Present	Past	Future	Perfect
First noun is Singular	Verb stem ends in A or E	'nt'	'bant'	'bunt'	'erant'
	Other verb stem endings	'unt'	'ebant'	'ent'	'erunt'
First noun is Plural	Verb stem ends in A or E	't'	'bat'	'bit'	'it'
	Other verb stem endings ie consonant or 'i'	Stem ends with consonant: Add 'it' Stem ends with 'i' : Add 't'	'ebat'	'et'	'it'

Figure 4.6 Latin regular verb endings: an alternative chart to the algorithm

116

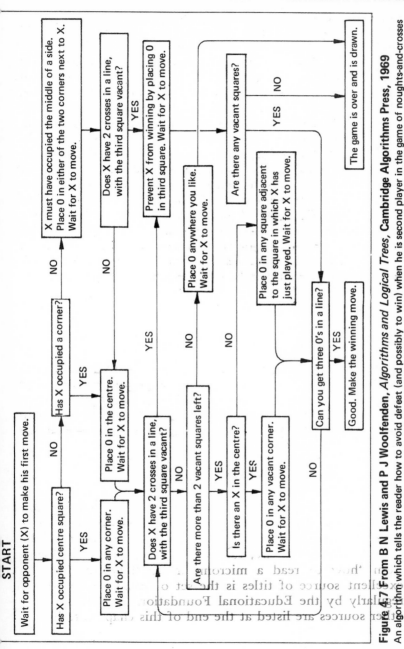

Figure 57 From B N Lewis and P J Woolfenden, *Algorithms and Logical Trees*, Cambridge Algorithms Press, 1969

An algorithm which tells the reader how to avoid defeat (and possibly to win) when he is second player in the game of noughts-and-crosses

than to fragment them, so even the operative is required to use vast amounts of information to do his job. Rapid obsolescence of jobs renders it impractical, if not impossible, to follow traditional educational methods of memorisation and recall. It is only a question of time before traditional school examinations must yield to the pressures of society. First principles are more important than ever before. The necessary factual information can be looked up. Open-book examinations are round the corner. The need is for books which yield their information quickly. Eventually, perhaps, the printed book will be replaced by microfilm, capable of instant recall on personal receivers through a computerised library system. Experience with computers however, indicates that specific banks of data, often used, and used for a limited range of purposes, can be more efficiently stored and recalled by simple files or charts at the place of work. Charts are by no means obsolescent. We can look forward to their increasing use, particularly in the form of job aids and data stores.

4 Projectors

Methods of projecting still pictures include the strip projector, slide projector, opaque projector and overhead projector. The last is a most versatile medium of presentation and warrants a section to itself. This section will deal with the first three more traditional and in many ways similar projection methods.

Film strips

These have been with us since the 1920's, but wartime development established their widespread use in education in the 1940's and 1950's. There are extensive libraries of film strips available for hire, for sale, or free, on topics ranging from 'how to read a micrometer' to 'bible stories'. An excellent source of titles is the set of catalogues produced regularly by the Educational Foundation for Visual Aids — other sources are listed at the end of this chapter. Industrial training film strips are produced by many visual aids companies, and also by companies in other fields, such as B P Petroleum. Catalogues can be obtained from these companies. Information on industrial training aids is available through the appropriate Industrial Training Board.

The quantity of material available unfortunately includes a fair proportion of film strips of rather doubtful quality. Many film strips fall short of the ideal in terms of visual content, arrangement and supporting commentary. Most of them include teacher's notes. Some are even supplied with a recorded commentary on tape or disc to support the visuals. We will discuss the use of such presentation again in the chapter on audio teaching aids. For the moment let us concentrate on the practical use made of film strips and strip projectors.

By far the most common film-strip projection equipment takes a 35 mm film. The film may have pictures taken on full-frame, as by any ordinary 35 mm camera, or on half-frame, which gives smaller pictures, but twice as many of them on the same length of film. Commercially produced film strips are most often half-frame, but most projectors can be modified, by means of a shutter arrangement, to screen either half or full-frame film strips. Thus a film taken by a standard 35 mm camera can be screened as a film strip. It is, however, much more common for the amateur to produce his material in the form of 2 in x 2 in slides.

Film slides

There are several reasons for the increasing use of slides by persons or organisations preparing their own teaching materials:

(a)   *Ease of filming* One bad photo on one film would require re-shooting the whole film, or else splicing in an alternative shot. If multiple copies of the finished product are to be prepared, this is no problem. The final strip will be in one piece. If only one copy is required, only the slide which is below standard needs re-shooting and mounting. The same applies to later damage. Only the one damaged slide need be replaced.

(b) *Flexibility in use* As the slides are individually mounted, the teacher has much more control over which visuals he shows, and the order in which he shows them. He may show only part of a sequence to some group. Any changes in the subject matter which affect some of the slides can be accommodated without re-making the whole sequence. Film strips tend to become obsolescent, particularly when they deal with industrial processes or human problems.

(c) *Durability* Slides stand up to wear and tear better than film strips. The film surface is protected by glass, or the mount, so that it does not come into physical contact with parts of the projector mechanism.

There is less standardisation among slides and slide projectors in the sizes catered for. The most common slide is cardboard-mounted standard 35 mm film frame. This is the format used by the home-use slide projectors, and the standard mounting supplied by photographic companies. With modern high-class projectors this size of slide gives adequate definition for most educational purposes, except perhaps the largest auditoria. But larger slide sizes are still used. Glass-mounted 2 in x 2 in or 3 in x 3 in slides are used and occasionally even larger ones are found. Before producing or ordering sets of slides, it is best to make sure that the projection equipment available is capable of screening them. Some projectors, though not all, will take either the 2 in x 2 in or the smaller cardboard mounts. The larger sizes generally require special projectors.

In terms of impact, or the qualities which make them effective, there is no difference between film strips and slides. The main difference in use is the degree of flexibility, already mentioned. Film strips are supported by carefully prepared teacher notes, even scripts. This task is performed by the teacher when using slide presentations. There is no less need for a well-designed commentary with slides, but the teacher has more scope to use his own ideas. Because of cheap mass production, film strips will continue to be made. For reasons of individual teaching style, teachers will continue to buy them, chop them up, edit them and mount them as slides.

Projectors

Projectors are chosen either for versatility or for special qualities useful to the task in hand. As with most equipment the versatile machine gives adequate service in many applications, but is perfect in none. The small school or training establishment, possessing only one or two projectors, would settle for a versatile model taking several sizes of slide mounts, and possibly film strips as well. Such projectors are available, and the better ones have a selection of lens units available, to give adequate projection in various sizes of rooms. Modern projectors are quite small and robust, so are easily transportable.

If a projector is to be used solely for slides, you should consider a magazine-loading machine. The advantages are:

1 Easy loading of slides.

2 Fixed order of presentation (unless you drop the magazine).

3 Easy storage in correct order.

Of course, deliberate re-arrangement of the order of presentation is simplicity itself. Some projectors take a straight magazine, others a circular drum. These have the advantage of automatically showing the first slide after the last one — very useful for continuous presentation at exhibitions. Most magazine-loading projectors have the further advantages of remote-control slide progression. This increases the flexibility enormously. Being able to sit back with the class and watch is the least advantage. A series of slides of stages in an assembly task can be presented at a fixed rate, which can be increased as learning progresses. Slides may be processed by other equipment, such as a tape recorder, by a simple process of synchronisation. Synchronised slide and tape presentations, to be discussed later, are a popular and valuable communication method in industry — in training and in sales. Such versatility can be purchased quite cheaply. The Kodak Carousel, for example, is an inexpensive machine with all the extras, and gives excellent results although designed primarily for the holiday slide enthusiast. Educational and industrial models are more robust, but carry the penalty of a higher price-tag. You can also buy zoom-lens models which enable you to 'fill your screen' every time.

If expense is no object, one can purchase random-access facilities, to pick out any slide at will, or even a battery of two such projectors, mounted as one, with fade-in, fade-out facilities, ·capable of presenting the equivalent of a Hollywood epic in still pictures.

Automatic strip projectors are also available, and there are various gadgets on the market that sychronise film strip to recorded discs or tapes. You can have random access, and fantastic storage capacity at the price of several hundred pounds. The E S L 2004 teaching machine has the technical facilities to select any one of 2004 frames on a film strip at any instant. Who would ever want to do that in a classroom presentation? Teaching Programmes on the machine only use a fraction of its capability. It is not surprising that the machine has proved to have greater application in the fields of information retrieval and storage.

Screening

There are two possibilities — direct projection and back-projection. Back-projection requires special equipment in the form of a projection box, or a room with a translucent screen in the wall. Its advantage is a better picture in daylight conditions. Back-projection was all the rage a few years ago. Recent advances in projector design now give excellent results in daylight when projected directly on to a screen. The advantages of daylight projection are very worthwhile (eg class control, note taking), but back-projection is no

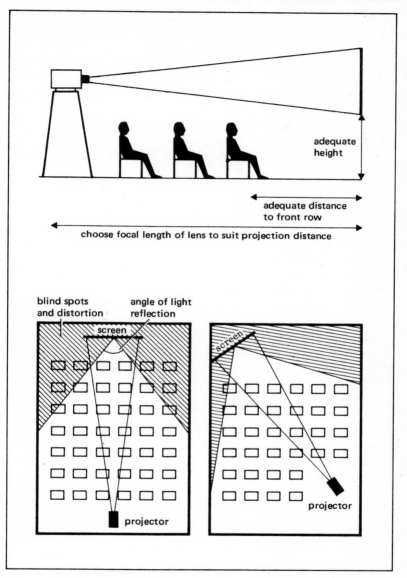

Figure 4.8 Optimum positioning of projector and screen

Positioning screen across a corner removes blind spots. A beaded screen could thus be used in a square room.

longer the only way to achieve this. Most portable back-projection set-ups are limited to a small picture size. Thus the attractions of back-projection for occasional use in a general-purpose classroom are lost — extra equipment to set up with no special advantages. The method is still of value in a permanent auditorium, as all equipment is out of sight and out of harm's way.

Whether front- or back-projection is used, the screen should be positioned for easy viewing — high enough for the back rows to see the bottom edge, not so high that the front rows get a crick in the neck.

The material of the screen should also be chosen with the room in mind. If the room is wide, a matt white screen will reflect the light in all directions, so that those in the corners can see. This of course carries the penalty of a less bright picture. A beaded, or silver screen will reflect light more directly, giving a brighter image within a smaller viewing angle, (eg long narrow rooms).

Permanently fixed screens are preferable to the portable, wobbly tripod type.

Design of slides and film strips

We have already discussed factors which may render subject matter suitable for visual display. Once you have made the decision to use slides or a film strip, there are a few commonsense design considerations.

First, *clarity*. This is affected by the quality of photography, choice of colours or contrast and size of detail, as well as by the quantity of information presented on one slide. Intelligent use of colour may add clarity, but the use of too many colours may add only confusion. Similarly, too much information on one slide will not be taken in during the limited time of display normally allowed. The observations made earlier in the chapter contrasting the use of the flip-charts and wall charts apply here. If your subject cannot be broken down into simple visuals, use a hand-out diagram in preference to a projected image.

Secondly *legibility*. This will again be influenced by how

much you cram into your slide, as the more verbal material you present, the smaller the print size. Again, overloading the slide with verbal content is using the medium for something which can better be achieved by a hand-out. A useful guide to the production of verbal content for slides is to work to an absolute limit of 8 lines of print if a slide is used with its larger dimension vertical, or only 6 lines of print if the slide is to be screened horizontally. A good way of planning content is to use a standard typewriter, with cards (or pencil-drawn rectangles) of 2 by 3 inches. If you type your message into this space, laid out as well as possible, you will get a model for a legible transparency. Note that with normal line spacing you could get over twice the recommended maximum number of lines in the space.

Incidentally, provided you have a 35mm camera with the facility for close-up work, so that the 2 in x 3 in card can be photographed to fill the slide, this is an excellent way of preparing artwork. The use of a carbon ribbon on the typewriter gives results every bit as good as the use of Letraset on larger cards, with considerable time and cost savings. A further dodge: If you don't have a carbon ribbon typewriter, try interleaving a thin polythene sheet (such as thin overhead projector transparency material) between the master and carbon copy (ie paper I, polythene, carbon paper, paper II). The polythene tends to even out the pressure of the typeface, giving a much-improved carbon copy. You may need to experiment with different grades of plastic to achieve the best results. The eventual clarity and legibility will of course depend on the distance of the screen from the viewer and on the size of image on the screen.

In the typical classroom (Figure 4.8) the front row may be about 8 or 10 ft from the screen and the back row about 30 ft. A typical screen size for such a room would be 5 or 6 ft square. If we project a 35mm transparency made by the above method, to 'fill' a 5 ft square screen, we will get a letter height of about 3 or 4 in depending on the typeface on our typewriter. This is quite large enough to be read with comfort from the back row — more than adequate as research shows that letters half this size should be legible under these conditions. However, the aim of our rule is to limit the content as well as to ensure legibility.

Opaque Projectors

Opaque projectors are not high on the popularity poll of visual aids. They have suffered in the past from the disadvantages of bulk, noise from the fans needed to cool the powerful lamps, and the need for total blackout in the classroom.

Every school or training institution nevertheless seems to have one. No doubt an excellent case for purchase can be put up on the grounds that any visual material already available can be utilised. No preparations of slides is required, illustrations in books, postage stamps, or even small objects can be instantly projected for all the class to see. Nevertheless, opaque projectors, or as they are traditionally called, episcopes, do not get much classroom use. Recently there have been vast technical improvements. Episcopes have become lighter and some can be used in semi-blackout conditions. They have become more versatile. As epidiascopes, an extra lens system enables them to project slides and even film strips. It would seem that the opaque projector should make a comeback — and so it no doubt would, if it was not for the development of the overhead projector, and its related facilities for cheap, rapid copying of original visuals onto transparencies. Meantime, one major use of opaque projectors is to transfer diagrams from books onto chalkboards or charts by the 'project on' method.

5 The overhead projector

Historically, this is the most recent addition to the range of still projection equipment. It is also the most versatile. It can perform nearly all the functions listed earlier for other still media. Some authors would claim that the overhead projector will replace all other still media in time. This is unlikely, and undesirable. Some materials can still be better projected on slides, some on charts, and in any case, variety is the spice of life. Over-use of one medium may kill some of

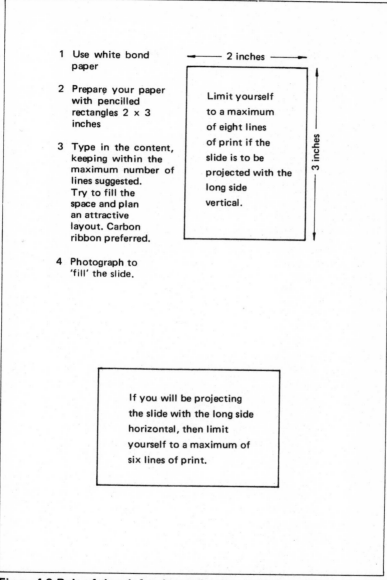

1 Use white bond paper

2 Prepare your paper with pencilled rectangles 2 x 3 inches

3 Type in the content, keeping within the maximum number of lines suggested. Try to fill the space and plan an attractive layout. Carbon ribbon preferred.

4 Photograph to 'fill' the slide.

2 inches

Limit yourself to a maximum of eight lines of print if the slide is to be projected with the long side vertical.

3 inches

If you will be projecting the slide with the long side horizontal, then limit yourself to a maximum of six lines of print.

Figure 4.9 Rule-of-thumb for the production of slides of verbal material
To ensure legibility and avoid overloading with information

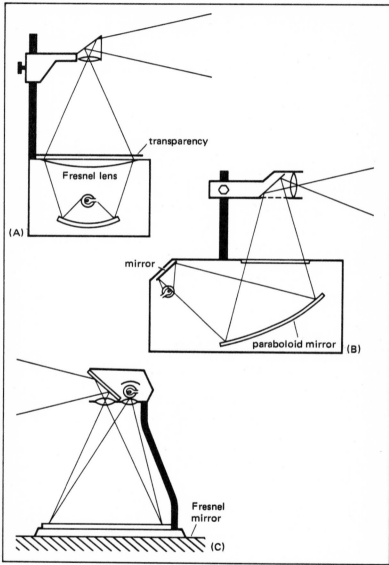

Figure 4.10 Systems of overhead projection

(A) Fresnel lens system. This type is small, often portable. (B) Condensing mirror system. Large lecture-hall machines. (C) Fresnel mirror system. Table top mounting or collapsible for portability.

the impact of visual presentation. However, if you are limited to only one presentation method, the overhead projector would certainly be the best choice.

Basically, the overhead projector consists of a horizontal table, 10 in x 10 in, on which you place the material to be projected. Light from the bulb below the table is condensed by a concave mirror or by a Fresnel lens, passes through the transparency and is focused and turned through 90 degrees by a lens system mounted on a stalk or bracket above the table (see diagram). One recent model uses reflected light, from a bulb above the table. This gives a more compact, table (see figure 4.10). One recent model uses reflected light, from a bulb above the table. This gives a more compact, table-top or portable model, at slight cost to the brilliance of the image.

1   Daylight projection. There is no need for any form of blackout unless there is strong direct sunlight on the screen.

2   In use, the teacher faces the class from his normal position at his desk. There is no need to turn your back, no need to·stand at the back of the room.

The advantages in use can best be summarised by contrasting with each of the media so far discussed:

(a)   *As a chalkboard or scribbling pad* Most overhead projectors (except some portable models) can be equipped with a 10 in wide roll of acetate sheet, on rollers, enabling it to be wound over the projection table. The 10 yards or more of acetate on the roll, gives a writing surface equivalent to several of the biggest chalkboards imaginable. The instructor may write on the roll with 'chinagraph' wax pencils, felt-tip pens, or Indian inks. It would seem that we are sounding the death-knell of the venerable chalkboard. There are, however, some disadvantages to the overhead projector. Some materials, especially the wax pencils, tend to be difficult to use in the heat of the projector lamp. Most users find it more difficult to write clearly on the acetate sheet than on a chalkboard. The large lettering necessary on the chalkboard forces the user to form his letters carefully. On the overhead projector one writes small, under difficult conditions, with unfamiliar materials — and any faults are magnified tenfold.

Orthographic problems can be overcome, however. The main argument in the 'save the chalkboard' campaign is that the overhead projector really comes into its own when used to display pre-prepared materials. Using both acetate roll for scribbling and prepared drop-on transparencies is both inconvenient and bad presentation. Use of a chalkboard or similar medium for spontaneous work, leaves the table of the overhead projector clear for the main-stream visual presentation — switch on, show transparency, make point, switch off. Impact!

(b) *As a magnetic board* The stage or table of the overhead projector is horizontal. You can project the silhouette of any object placed on the table. If objects are made of transparent material, such as perspex, you may have colour, or may draw details on the object in Indian ink. Models of inter-connected parts thus may be made up of different coloured perspex, and the relative position of the parts projected, even when the parts overlap.

A further advantage is that to give a reasonably projected image, the shapes or objects to be used can be quite small. Not only are they cheap to make and easy to store, but it becomes a feasible proposition to market them commercially. Sets of plastic letters, working models, geometrical theorems kits etc, are now available for use with overhead projectors. If you have one, you don't need flannel or magnetic boards.

(c) *As a flip-chart* Any original of the right size can be used as a master to produce a near-instant, cheap transparency for the overhead projector. Larger or smaller diagrams can be copied photographically. Transparencies are easily handled and stored and are less bulky than charts.

As mentioned earlier, an excellent technique for using the overhead projector is to switch on only when a visual is being viewed, and then to switch off. This gives the same control over presentation as do flip-charts, with much more dramatic impact. Furthermore, with the overhead projector there are techniques possible which are far beyond the capabilities of charts:

1　The 'cover-up' technique. As the visual lies horizontally, it is simplicity itself to cover up parts of it until required, by a sheet of paper, or by cardboard 'windows' fixed to the transparency by sticky tape.

2　The 'overlay' technique. Successive details of a diagram may be superimposed, one on top of the other, by the addition of more transparencies. In our earlier example of an anatomy lesson, our teacher, with only one set of transparencies, could superimpose the musculature, bloodstream, respiratory system etc, on the outline of a human body one at a time, all at once, or in any required combination.

Whenever diagrams or charts are used, they may be built up, or broken down for analysis, by means of the overlay technique. Obviously the overhead projector can perform all the functions of flip-charts at an equally low cost of materials, with less trouble in preparation and with great impact and imagination.

Wall charts are of course another matter. As we defined them, their function is to provide a permanent or semi-permanent source of information or inspiration. It would not be practical to use any projector for this job, unless special visual impact was required, as for example, at exhibitions or fairs.

(d) *As a projector of pictures* Some of the points under this heading have already been mentioned. To begin, the overhead projector, due to the ease of transparency preparation from originals in books etc, is taking over the role of opaque projectors. No one seems to worry too much about matters of copyright. Secondly, any materials available in the original, or easily drawn, can be made into transparencies and presented with a degree of control even greater than is possible with charts, film strips or slides.

However, most methods of transparency preparation do not cope very well with half-tone pictures or colour photos. Photographic methods can produce positive transparencies of adequate size, but the processes are long and expensive, particularly if colour is involved.

It is, therefore, far better to use film strips or slides for photographs and detailed pictures. Also, it is uneconomical to use the material in a film strip or an original for a set of transparencies. The cost of blowing-up the picture is excessive unless, of course, one projects a small image onto paper or acetate and traces the diagram. There is so much material available in strip or slide form, that there is a good economic argument for being equipped with strip/slide projectors as well as overhead projectors. They are complementary to each other in their function.

In conclusion, it must be mentioned that overhead projector manufacturers produce gadgets which clip to the column, and which can be used to project slides or film strips. The method is quite effective. However, it does involve much setting up and dismantling. It is a way of using slides when a slide projector is not available, but for ease of presentation of different materials, the teacher would do well to have both types available.

Screening

The overhead projector will, even in daylight, give a large clear image — much larger than could normally be obtainable from a 'daylight' slide projector. Provided there is room in the classroom to give sufficient 'throw', a screen up to 8 ft square can be used. It is probable that for most classrooms, to get this size of image and yet have the projector near the teacher's desk, a wide-angle lens head should be used. However, a screen of 5 — 6 ft square is adequate for classrooms up to 40 ft long.

If the screen is mounted high enough for a clear view, it will probably be necessary to tilt the head to throw the image upwards. This will cause the familiar 'keystoning' of the image, unless the screen is mounted to compensate. As shown in Figure 4.11 the top edge of the screen should be tilted forward, so as to give a true, rectangular, undistorted image. The seat positions from which the image will be clearly visible, will depend on the choice of screen/material, as outlined earlier.

Figure 4.11 also shows one advantage of putting the overhead projector screen in a corner rather than directly in front of a group. There is less obstruction from the lens head of the projector and the teacher's body. The 'straight ahead' position is also left available for projection of films or slides onto another screen, or for a chalkboard, flannel board etc. Other factors such as classroom width-to-length ratio, seating arrangements or the position of windows and direct sunlight will of course influence the possible screen positions for a given room.

Figure 4.12 shows the relationship between ideal screen size and room size, for clarity in the back row. Also, some idea of the distance of projector from screen and comfortable distance from screen for the front row of viewers. The projector distance may be reduced by use of a wide-angle lens system.

Methods of transparency preparation

Many transparencies are, of course, prepared by hand. The materials used have been mentioned. In addition to coloured wax pencils and transparent inks, one can use transparent stick-on sheet for cut-outs, perspex, or any other material

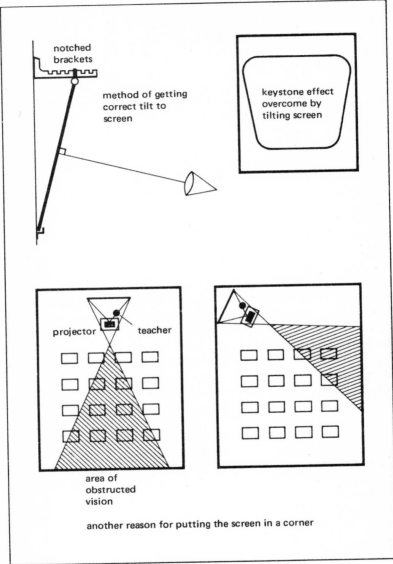

Figure 4.11 Positioning of screen for overhead projection
Keystone effect may also be a problem with slide projector fitted with a wide angle lens.

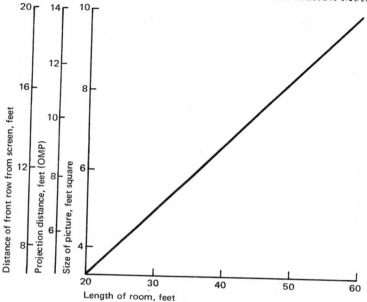

Figure 4.12 Relation of room and screen size for effective projection
(And distance of overhead projector with standard lens.)

that the ingenuity of the teacher suggests. Suggestions for transparencies in particular subject areas abound in the literature listed at the end of the chapter. We will confine ourselves to a very brief look at the relative advantages of the more common automatic transparency production methods.

(a) *Photographic methods.* Transparencies can be produced by normal photographic methods eg from negatives, using an enlarger. The processes are slow, materials expensive, and a darkroom and equipment necessary — in other words, it's a specialist job. One way to cut corners is to use a polaroid camera, with a special positive transparency film. This will take colour, but gives only a small transparency — 3½ in x 2½ in.

(b) *Diffusion transfer processes* (eg A B Dick). These are similar in principle to photographic processes, employing a developer. Transparencies of quarto

135

(10 x 8) or foolscap (11 x 8) size can be produced. Production time is not too long, but transparencies must be left to dry. It produces excellent results from black and white and will tackle half-tone. Can be messy and equipment needs periodic cleaning.

(c) *Heat processes* (eg Thermo-Fax). Suitable for most single-colour originals. It does not cope too well with vegetable inks (eg Biro) as they do not absorb heat sufficiently to register on the heat-sensitive copy paper. Extremely fast — the transparency is ready for use in seconds. A clean, dry process.

(d) *Dyeline process*. If you have a map-copying machine, all you need is some Diazo colour foil. The original must be drawn on translucent material (eg tracing paper). It takes longer than heat process and more preparation is necessary.

(e) *Verifax*. Uses liquid developer. It is similar to diffusion transfer in time and work.

(f) *Xerography*. Rank Xerox will take transparency material. It is quick and clean, and will copy any original.

(g) *Spirit duplicator* (eg Banda). Masters will give reasonable impression on acetate sheet.

Without going into details of how to produce transparencies by any system, it is clear that the processes are not complicated. Almost every training establishment will have at least one method already at its disposal. Extensive use of the overhead projector, however, demands a really efficient transparency-making machine, so that every teacher may produce a transparency at a moment's notice, from a newspaper, book, or the notes of a student.

New models are hitting the market every few months. When making your choice, try to combine as many as possible of the following features, giving priority to those of

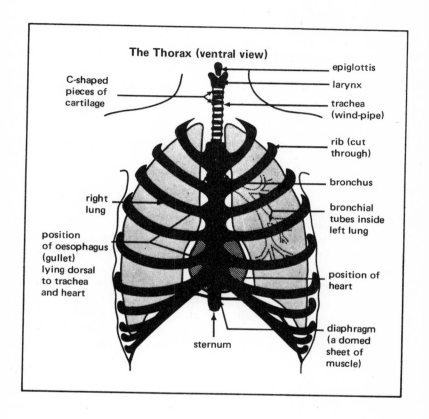

The Thorax (ventral view)

C-shaped pieces of cartilage

epiglottis

larynx

trachea (wind-pipe)

rib (cut through)

bronchus

right lung

bronchial tubes inside left lung

position of oesophagus (gullet) lying dorsal to trachea and heart

position of heart

sternum

diaphragm (a domed sheet of muscle)

Figure 4.13 Overhead projector transparency

This is a pre-prepared transparency, one of a series on Human Anatomy and Physiology by Wheeler and Carr, marketed by ESA.

Such a subject is ideal for use of the overlay technique. The rib cage, lungs and the organs may be printed onto separate acetate sheets, and then viewed separately or superimposed.

137

particular value to your own situation:

Fast copies — matter of seconds.

Dry copies.

Copies from any ink or colour.

Copies in negative as well as positive (white or black background).

Copies in coloured film.

Copies from bound books as well as loose sheets.

There is no doubt a machine available that fits your ideal combination of qualities.

Clarity of transparencies

As the majority of transparencies for overhead projectors are prepared by hand, it is important to have some rules for letter size etc. The general rules specified for slides may be taken as a guide, although, due to the greater versatility in use of overhead projector material (eg by overlay or cover-up techniques) it is common for transparencies to carry more material than a single slide should. This is not necessarily bad, though the limits for legibility and good instructional practice would outlaw a fair proportion of the materials we often see at conferences and meetings, even occasionally at conferences on educational technology.

Guidelines do exist however. Useful sources of information are listed at the end of this chapter, including an article by J M Adams[8] listing some of the visual parameters involved.

Line width — The main visual parameter controlling the design of a transparency is the resolving power of the eye. This varies with the illumination and the contrast of the subject, but under good illumination and with moderate contrast may be taken as two minutes of arc. This corresponds to a line thickness of 0.036 in at 10 ft and 0.108 in at 30 ft viewing distance. The thinnest line on the transparency visible at 30 ft, assuming a magnification of six, is 0.018 in.

Type height — At a normal reading distance 3 point type is just readable to people with good vision, 6 point type can be read by most people, type for easy continuous reading should ideally be about 12 point. Letters on the screen will have to be 30 times these sizes if they are to be read from the back row. As the magnification of the original transparency is six, we may specify letter sizes on the film as: just readable — 0.1 in letter height; preferred minimum — 0.2 in letter height; preferred for continuous text — 0.4 in letter height.

Another field in which research has been done into readable letter sizes is road signs. The design recommendation here is 1 in letter height for every 50 ft viewing distance. This would lead to a letter height of 0.6 in on the screen under our viewing conditions, or 0.1 in on the film. It is stated that 99% of drivers can read signs drawn to this specification.

These recommendations are in approximate agreement, and it would seem reasonable to take 0.1 in as an absolute minimum for letter height on the film. One might note that 0.1 in is about the size of a normal typewriter typeface, and we all know what results that gives as a transparency. The preferred limit of 0.2 — 0.4 in is recommended.

Tints and shading — If hatching is used to give a solid or tinted effect (some printing processes use this method) then to appear uniform to all members of the audience, the screen ruling must be finer than 85 per inch. On the other hand if hatching lines or dots in dotted lines are to be visible to all members of the audience, the ruling must be coarser than 28 lines per inch.

Polaroid techniques

In conclusion, we must mention a recent development — the use of the overhead projector to simulate movement. A sheet of polarised material is spun in the light beam above the stage. The transparency of, say, a pipework layout, is treated with stick-on pieces of plastic sheet, polarised in specific directions. As the 'spinner' rotates, the impression of moving liquid is created along the pipes. This technique of 'technanimation' is becoming popular. It has been applied to mechanical diagrams, flow charts, and recently to kinetic art and the light shows of the younger generation. Excellent sets of transparencies have been produced commercially. The techniques are now also being applied to 35 mm slides.

References

1. W A Wittich and C F Schuller, *Audiovisual Materials: Their Nature and Use* (Chapter 3 on the use of the chalk board), Harper and Brothers, 1962.

2. S Laner and R E Sell, *Pictorial Methods — Occupational Psychology*, Vol XXIV, 1960.

3. R Bethers, 'What I Know about Making Drawings for Children', *Visual Education*, October 1956.

4. B N Lewis and P J Woolfenden, *Algorithms and Logical Trees — a Self-Instructional Course*, Cambridge Algorithms Press, 1969.

5. C P Gane, I S Horabin and B N Lewis, 'The Simplification and Avoidance of Instruction', *Industrial Training International*, July 1966.

6. J L Evans, 'A Potpurri of Programming Technology' in Ofeish and Meierhenry (eds), *Trends in Programmed Instruction*, Department of Audiovisual Instruction, National Education Association, USA, 1964.

7. Op cit in n 4.

8. J M Adams, 'Design Recommendations for Overhead Projector Transparencies', *Visual Education*, June 1971.

Further Reading

Chalkboard etc
CEDO, *Flannelgraph, Magnetic Board and Plastigraph as Aids to Teaching and Training,* 1967.

B Pringle, *Chalk Illustration: a Manual for Technical Teachers,* Pergamon, 1966.

H G Ramshaw, *Blackboard Work,* O U P.

J Stewart Crichton, *Blackboard Drawing,* Nelson, 1954.

Preparing Visuals
CEDO, *Aids to Drawing and Enlarging,* 1969.

CEDO, *Information on Material for Making and Projecting Wallcharts and Handouts,*

Helen Coppen, *Wallsheets; Choosing, Using and Making,* NCAVAE, 1971.

Marjorie East, *Display for Learning: Making and Using Visual Materials,* Holt, Rinehart, Winston.

R Leggatt, *'Showing-off' or Display Techniques,* NCAVAE, 1970.

G C Weaver and E W Bollinger, *Visual Aids, Their Construction and Use,* Van Nostrand Reinhold, 1949.

Slides and Filmstrips
R Stephen Judd, *Teaching by Projection,* Focal Press, 1963.

M K Kidd and C W Long, *Projecting Slides,* Focal Press, 1963.

Brydon Lamb, *Use of Slides and Film Projection in Teaching and Training,* NCAVAE.

Overhead Projection

(a)   *Books Specifically on the Overhead Projector*

A H Crocker, *A Survey of Overhead Projectors (Experimental Development Unit Report No 6) 1969.* Also *Supplement* published in 1970. National Committee for Audio-Visual Aids in Education, 1969. (Note- Reports of later models appear in some of the EDU's *Technical Reports* which are published three times per year.)

A King and W Shelley, *Learning with the Overhead Projector,* Chandler Publications, 42 Gray's Inn Road, London WC1.

L S Powell, *A Guide to the Overhead Projector,* British Association for Commercial and Industrial Education.

M J Schultz, *The Teacher and Overhead Projection,* Prentice Hall, 1965.

Ronald Uhl, *How to Prepare Your Own Transparencies,* Visual Arts Press, 1963.

A Vincent, *The Overhead Projector, (Experimental Development Unit Report No. 8),* National Committee for Audio-Visual Aids in Education, Revised 1970.

(b)   *Photography, Photocopying and Colour Lift for the Overhead Projector*

J H Burnard, 'The Preparation of Illustrative Material for the Overhead Projector', *British Journal of Photography,* 13 June 1969.

J G Fennell, 'A Method for Making Transparencies from Pictures in Glossy Magazines and Books',Vol 50, No 172, *The School Science Review,* March 1969, pp 630-631.

H S Griffiths, 'A Modified Process for Picture Lifting for Transparencies', *Visual Education,* August/September 1970, pp 17-19.

Peter Wicks, 'A Simple Photographic Method for Two-colour Overhead Projector Transparencies', *Visual Education,* June 1965, p8.

J B Young, 'Hardware for O H P Software . . . Five Years Development by a New Technical College', *Visual Education,* May 1971, pp 22-23.

J B Young, *Reprographic Principles Made Easy,* National Committee for Audio-Visual Aids in Education, 1970.

(c) *Specialised Aspects and Techniques*

J M Adams, 'Design Recommendations for Overhead Projector Transparencies', *Visual Education,* June 1971, pp 19-23.

S Adams, R Rosemier, P Sleeman, 'Readable Letter Size and Visibility for Overhead Projection Transparencies', *Audio-Visual Communication Review,* Vol 13, No 4, pp 412-417, Winter 1965.

D B Thomas, 'Simple Animation Techniques for Overhead Projectors', *R A F Education Bulletin,* No 4, pp 64-67.

S J Willis, 'Introducing the "Mini-roll" ', *Visual Education,* February 1971, pp 22-25.

(d) *Applications in Subject Teaching*

N H Alyer (comp), *Tops in General Chemistry (Tested Overhead Projection Series).* Reprint from *Journal of Chemical Education,* Wood & Son, 23 Leman Street, London E1.

T D Best, *Geography via the Overhead Projector,* National Council for Geographic Education, Illinois State University, Normal, Illinois 61761.

H N Cleeve, 'Out of Focus — a Novel Way of Using a Visual Aid (OH Projector)', *School Science Review,* No 179, December 1970, pp 377-378.

Walter Eppenstein, *The Overhead Projector in the Physics Lecture (ED 015 650),* Rensselaer Polytechnic Institute, Troy, New York, 1961. Reprinted by ERIC Document Reproduction Service, 4936 Fairmount Avenue, Bethesda, Maryland 20014.

Dennis Johnson, 'The Overhead Projector and the Use of Scientific Demonstrations and Models', *Visual Education,* February 1971.

Stephen Krulik and Irwin Kaufman, *How to Use the Overhead Projector in Mathematics Education,* National Council of Teachers of Mathematics, 1201 Sixteenth Street, NW, Washington DC 20036, 1966.

D J Lucas, 'The Overhead Projector in the Physics Laboratory'. *Physics Education,* Vol 2, No 6, November 1967, pp 324-326.

H Lucas, 'Demonstrating Probability on an Overhead Projector', *Visual Education,* June 1965.

R McRae, 'Working Anatomical Models for the Overhead Projector', *Medical and Biological Illustration,* Vol XVIII, No 4, October 1968, pp 249-252

D H Revill, 'The Use of Audio-Visual Aids in Education for Librarianship with Special Emphasis on the Overhead Projector', *Visual Education,* December 1966, pp 13-17.

D W Thomas, 'Overhead Projector Transparencies for Geography Teaching, A Review', *Geography,* No 241, Vol 53, Part 4, November 1968, pp 400-403.

J E Wrathall, 'The Overhead Projector — A New Aid for the Geographer', *Geography,* Vol 51, Part 1, January 1966, pp 38-41.

The Software — Major Producers of Film strips

E J Arnold and Sons Ltd, Coal Road, Seacroft, Leeds LS14 28W.

BBC Publications, Marylebone High Street, London W1A 1AR.

British Transport Films, Melbury House, Melbury Terrace, London NW1.

Camera Talks Ltd, 31 North Row, London W1R 2EN.

Carwall Audio-Visual Aids, P O Box 55, Wallington, Surrey.

Common Ground Filmstrips, Longman Group, Pinnacles, Harlow, Essex.

Concordia Films, Concordia House, 117-123 Golden Lane, EC1Y OTL.

Educational Productions Ltd, East Ardsley, Wakefield, Yorks.

EAV. Educational Audio-Visual Ltd, Coal Road, Seacroft, Leeds LS14 28W.

EFVA, The National Audio-Visual Aids Library, Paxton Place, Gipsy Road, London SE27 9SR.

Encyclopaedia Brittannica International Ltd, 18-20 Regent Street, London SW1.

Gateway Educational Films Ltd, St Lawrence House, 29-31 Broad Street, Bristol BS1 2HF.

Guild Sound & Vision Ltd, Kingston Road, Merton Park, London SW19.

Hulton Educational Publications Ltd, Raans Road, Amersham, Bucks.

McGraw-Hill Publishing Co Ltd, Audio-Visual Dept, Shoppenhangers Road, Maidenhead, Berks.

Rank Audio-Visual Ltd, P O Box 70, Great West Road, Brentford, Middlesex.

The Slide Centre, 17 Brodrick Road, London SW17.

SPCK. Audio-Visual Aids Dept, 69 Great Peter Street, London SW1.

Sunday Times, Thomson House, 200 Gray's Inn Road, London WC1.

Visual Information Service Ltd, 12 Bridge Street, Hungerford, Berks.

Visual Publications, 197 Kensington High Street, London W8.

Weston Goods Studios Ltd, P O Box 2, Henley-on-Thames, Oxon.

Wills and Hepworth Ltd, Loughborough, Leics.

Diana Wyllie Ltd, 3 Park Road, Baker Street, London NW1.

Major Producers of slide sets
E J Arnold and Sons Ltd, Coal Road, Seacroft, Leeds LS14 28W.

Educational Films of Scotland, 16-17 Woodside Terrace, Charing Cross, Glasgow C3.

Miniature Gallery, 60 Rushett Close, Long Ditton, Surrey.

Slide Centre Ltd, 17 Brodrick Road, London SW17.

Woodmansterne Ltd, Hollywell Industrial Estate, Watford WD1 8RD.

Diana Wyllie Ltd, 3 Park Road, Baker Street, London NW1.

Publishers and Suppliers of Pre-Prepared Overhead Projector Transparencies

E J Arnold & Son Ltd, Butterley Street, London LS10 1AX.
Map outline, ruled isometric grids, ruled music staves, etc.

Common Ground Ltd, 44 Fulham Road, London SW3.
Biology, Geography.

Educational Productions Ltd, East Ardsley, Wakefield, Yorks.
Biology, Geography, Geometry, History, Physics and Chemistry. Technical graphics, etc. Most of these are from the American Keuffel & Esser Co and can be supplied either as transparencies or as translucencies for diazo reproduction.

Educational Suppliers Association Ltd, Pinnacles, Harlow, Essex.
Biology.

Encyclopaedia Brittannica International Ltd, Dorland House, 18-20 Regent Street, London SW1.
Biology, English, Geography, History.

G A F (Great Britain) Ltd, Stourton House, Dacre Street, London SW1.
Wide range of transparencies of American origin.

Rupert Hart-Davis, Educational Publications, 3, Upper James Street, London W1.
Transparencies accompanying the book *Biological Science, An Enquiry into Life — The BSCS Yellow Version.* Also sell Transart's Flipatran books.

Irwin Technical Ltd, 109-123 Clifton Street, London EC2.
Chemistry.

International Computers & Tabulators Ltd, 112-124 Upper Richmond Road, Putney, London SW15.
Computer Technology. Sets of transparencies loaned to educational establishments.

International Tutor Machines Ltd, Ashford Road, Ashford, Middlesex.
Anatomy, Astronomy, Atomic Science, Biology, Botany, Chemistry, Electricity, Engineering, Geography, Mathematics, Meteorology, Solid Geometry, Space Science.

Longmans Ltd, Pinnacles, Harlow, Essex.
Chemistry.

MacDonald Educational, Sales Department, 49 Great Marlborough Street, London W1.
Importing Hammond transparencies from U S A. Astronomy, Geography, Meteorology, Oceanography. May also publish Biology transparencies.

MacMillan & Co Ltd, 10 St Martins Street, London WC2.
Geography. Also be importing Biology and Mathematics transparencies from the extensive list published by The International Visual Aids Centre, Brussels.

McGraw-Hill, Shoppenhangers Road, Maidenhead, Berks.
Geography, Physics.

Methuen Ltd, 11 New Fetter Lane, London EC4.
Atlas of transparencies in Flipatran binder.

Minnesota Mining & Manufacturing Co Ltd, 3M House, Wigmore Street, London W1.
Paper masters from which transparencies can be produced by photocopying. Very large range of subjects including some of British origin on Geography, Decimal Currency, Biology, Chemistry, Technical Drawing, etc.

Pergamon Press Ltd, Headington Hill Hall, Oxford OX3 OBW.
Flipatran books on Chemistry, Geography, History and Technical Drawing.

George Phillip & Son Ltd, Education Department, Victoria Road, London NW10
Geography.

Pitman Publishing, 39 Parker Street, London WC2.
Motor Engineering, Electricity, Anatomy and Physiology.

Scientific Teaching Apparatus Ltd, Colquhoun House, 27-37 Broadwick House, London W1.
Importing Hubbard Scientific Co transparencies from U S A. Astronomy, Engineering, Geology, Human Body, Light, Machinery, Magnetism and Electricity, Map Reading, Meteorology, Oceanography, Plants, Sound, Space Exploration.

Scott, Foresman & Co, 22 South Audley Street, London W1.
American transparencies on Reading, Psychology and Sociology.

Transart Visual Education Division, Cambridge Street, Godmanchester, Huntingdon.
Flipatran Book System, Biology, British Standards, Geography, Mathematics, Science. All sheets with graph rulings.

The Hardware — Manufacturers of Slide and Filmstrip Projectors

Agfa-Gevaert Ltd, 27 Great West Road, Brentford, Middlesex. 01-560 2131

Campkins of Cambridge, 15 Kings Parade, Cambridge. 0223-51791

CZ Scientific Instruments Ltd, P O Box 2AR, Zeiss England House, 93-97 New Cavendish Street, London W1. 01-580 0571

Dixons Photographic Ltd, 18-24 High Street, Edgware, Middlesex. 952-7011

George Elliott & Sons Ltd, Worcester House, Vintners Place, EC4 V3HH. 01-236 2248

Gnome Photographic Products Ltd, Gnome Corner, Caerphilly Road, Cardiff CF4 4XJ. 0222 63201

Hanimex (UK) Ltd, Hanimex House, 15-24 Great Dover Street, London SE1. 01-407 8161

R F Hunter, 51-53 Gray's Inn Road, London WC1. 01-405 7311

Johnsons of Hendon Ltd, 335 Hendon Way, London NW4. 01-202 8200

Kodak Ltd, P O Box 33, Swallowdale Lane, Hemel Hempstead, Herts. 0442 58621

E Leitz Instruments Ltd, 30 Mortimer Street, London W1. 01-636 3774

Paul Plus Ltd, 29 King Street, Newcastle, Staffordshire. 0782 65131

Rank Audio-Visual Ltd, P O Box 70, Great West Road, Brentford, Middlesex. 01-568 9222

J J Silber Ltd, 11 Northburgh Street, London EC1. 01-253 8031

Manufacturers of Overhead Projectors
Bell and Howell A V Ltd, Alperton House, Bridgewater, Wembley, Middlesex. 01-902 8812

Block and Anderson Ltd, Cambridge Grove, London W6.

Clarke & Smith Manufacturing Co Ltd, Melbourne Road, Wallington, Surrey. 01-467 46696

Elite Optics Ltd, 354 Caerphilly Road, Cardiff CF4 4XJ.

ESL Bristol Ltd, St Lawrence House, 29-31 Broad Street, Bristol BS1 2HF. 0272 25351

Fenn Import Ltd, 35 Hartshill Road, Stoke-on-Trent, Staffordshire. 0782 45141

International Tutor Machines Ltd, Ashford Road, Ashford, Middlesex. Ashford 56222

Minnesota Mining and Manufacturing Co Ltd, 3M House, Wigmore Street, London W1A 1ET. 01-486 5522

Ofrex Ltd, Ofrex House, Stephen Street, London W1. 01-636 3686

Omal Group Ltd, Omal House, North Circular Road, London NW10. 01-387 8282

5 When To Use Sound Media

The need for sound media

In earlier chapters we discussed how both still and moving visual media can seldom stand on their own. We saw the need for spoken or written captions or commentaries in order to focus the student's attention on the important aspects of the visual. We know that pictures or graphs do not necessarily teach better than verbal descriptions, or even clarify the message that the verbal caption communicates — it depends on the type of learner we have and on the type of subject matter we are communicating.

Our theme has been that visual aids should have a precisely defined function, they should be designed to fulfil that function, and they should be evaluated to measure their effectiveness.

This chapter and the next deal in the main with sound media — in particular the radio, gramophone and tape recorder, but audio-visual methods employing any of the above, together with supporting diagrams or pictures, are also covered. Such methods, using a recorded commentary and related visual material, are very similar in function to the cine film. The only difference is that the pictures do not move. The audio-visual presentation tells the whole story. For a time, the medium takes over from the teacher. We would therefore expect that audio-visual presentations of this type would be of value in similar teaching situations as films, with the further provision that the actual movements of objects on the screen are of no importance to the learning process.

Let us first consider pure audio presentations — radio programmes, records, recorded tapes. These may be used in two ways, First, they may be used by a teacher to bring into the classroom sounds which are of significance to the learning process, for example music, language pronunciation, bird-calls or the noise of a rattling big-end bearing. The sound material is only part of the teacher's presentation. He introduces it for a specific purpose, and demands specific reactions from the class. Students may be required to comment on the sound presentation (as in a music appreciation class), to recognise the sound and discriminate it from others (as in learning musical scales or bird-call recognition) or to discriminate and repeat the sound (as in the language laboratory). The teacher decides to use a sound presentation on the basis of analysing his subject matter. This analysis pin-points areas of the subject which rely on sound. The teacher then decides whether to use a teaching aid. He may prefer a native Frenchman's presentation to his own (perhaps imperfect) accent. It may be impractical or impossible to demonstrate the sound other than by a recording. We do not have the time to track down birds in the field, or the space in our classrooms for a symphony orchestra.

The Royal Navy have a training course which aims to teach submarine personnel to recognise ships passing overhead by the noises they make. This high-level discrimination skill, when well mastered, enables the seaman to distinguish not only between a ship and a school of whales, but between different types of ships and their countries of origin. As the opportunity to use the skill only occurs in wartime, and then it's usually too late to learn, one naturally turns to recorded sound media for training. The set-up involves a battery of tape recorders capable of supplying the student with any of 20 characteristic ship noises in any combination. The student must identify each noise as it occurs. If he is wrong, the original noise and his own choice are played together to illustrate the difference. In time he learns to discriminate between more and more similar noises. The structure of the course is based on programmed instruction principles. The choice of presentation medium was dictated from the start by the subject matter. Nothing but sound recording would do.

Sound media may be used as an integral part of a teacher's presentation. Alternatively, they may be used to take over the verbal presentation altogether. The teacher may record his lesson, or he may play a broadcast or recording prepared by someone else. Such a recorded commentary differs little from the classic lecture situation. The message source — lecturer or recording — emits information which is (we hope) received at the message destination — the audience. This is essentially a one-way traffic. No feedback to the message source on the effects being produced at the destination is provided for. Similarly, the slide-tape audio-visual presentations which we will be discussing later are analogous to the lecturer who uses visual aids. This use of a recording to replace the classroom teacher is often quite justified. The broadcast speaker may be a better lecturer, or be better informed. Even if the teacher records his own voice, advantages may result. He has greater opportunity to revise, edit and re-organise what he says. His presentation should be more professional as a result. Furthermore, if a teacher can record his presentation, this may free him for other work which the recording cannot do — individual help, checking progress etc. Indeed all the old arguments as to why teachers should benefit from the use of programmed instruction may be applied in this case, provided of course that broadcast talks are as effective as a live presentation. Experimental research comparing recorded and live lessons has generally yielded inconclusive results.

Research on sound media

Scupham[1] summarised Danish research which assessed the comparative effectiveness of matched communications through print, radio, television lecture and a more elaborate televised presentation using film, animation and other visual devices. Of the 500 subjects participating in the study, 120 were soldiers and the rest were students at agricultural colleges. No significant differences were found in the test scores of groups in the various treatment conditions, but there was a significant difference between the average score of the soldiers, whatever the presentation medium, and that of the students.

Stuck and Manatt[2] conducted an investigation into the

relative effectiveness of audio-tutorial and lecture methods of teaching concepts of school law to preservice teachers in the senior class at a state university in Iowa. The entire class of 219 students was divided arbitrarily into two groups. Pre-post-test gain scores indicated that the audio-tutorial group was significantly superior to the traditionally taught group.

Audio programmes may in some cases have positive advantages over the equivalent written texts. For one thing, they do not require that the student can read. Where students are used to learning from books, or the subject matter is of an academic nature, there seems to be no clear advantage for either method.[3] Where the students are not trained scholars, and the subject matter is mainly composed of simple instructions to be followed, rather than concepts to be understood, a taped presentation often promotes a much better performance. We have found[4] that with apprentices learning to name and operate machine tools, a taped programme may promote better learning and take up to 50% less learning time than the equivalent written programme. This may be explained partly by the type of student, partly by the task, (which already employs his hands and eyes — using the ears for instructions seems more efficient), and partly by the environment: the learner wears earphones which shut out other noises and distractions.

Another experiment attempted to compare the effectiveness of the same lesson when presented by radio, television and a live teacher. Students of media would expect the radio presentation to be at a disadvantage in this experiment from the start, as vision is excluded. When tested immediately after the lesson, the 'live' groups were slightly better, but re-testing two months later showed, rather suprisingly, that the television groups remembered most, and there was no difference in the long-term effects of the teacher and the radio programme. As is so often the case with such controlled experiments, however, the differences between the groups were small, and did not point conclusively to the superiority of any one medium. Much greater differences can be expected between the success of different teachers, than on the same teacher using different media.

It is here that we have the real value of the recorded lesson and radio broadcasts. You can spend more time in preparing the presentation, use the best subject experts and employ the best available teacher. Most important (though seldom done systematically) you can evaluate the presentation before release and eradicate any weaknesses. Such a presentation is sure to communicate more effectively than many a 'live' lecturer, mumbling into his sketchy, jumbled, obsolete notes.

Of course, the good teacher does much more than simply read his notes. He acts not only as a message source, but also as a monitor of the effect of the message. Is it understood? Is further explanation necessary? He then uses this information to plan subsequent messages. Teaching is a dynamic two-way communication process. Normal broadcasts, such as films or large group lectures are capable only of one-way communication. Like all such methods, they rely for long-term effectiveness on well-designed exercises which involve the student actively. Normally, these take the form of a follow-up session or seminar immediately after the presentation. Occasionally, an element of programming is built in by breaking the sound presentation into short units, with questions or appropriate student activity interspersed.

Whichever method is used, sound recordings share with films a permanence and an inflexibility of presentation. In some subjects this is a disadvantage, as opportunities for spontaneous off-the-point but nevertheless useful discussions may be lost. In other subjects, however, this may be a positive advantage, in ensuring an accurate, standard presentation every time, resulting in reliably predictable course results and uniformity of practice on the job.

A design project may have as many solutions as there are designers. There may be much value in studying all the designs, even the unsuccessful ones. But before the designers can get together and discuss intelligently, they must

(a) all understand the terms of reference (in the same way),

(b) all have a mastery of relevant data and information, and

(c) all speak the same language (technical jargon, symbols, convention).

Every subject has such areas where uniform understanding and practice is essential. It is these areas which may benefit from a fixed, standard presentation. If the information can be effectively communicated without visual aids, then here is an area where one might consider using sound media.

Thus, all decisions on whether to use sound media spring from the task analysis. There are three possible types of application which may be identified by asking the following questions:

1 Do my students need to have their interest aroused in the subject? If so, are there any broadcasts or recordings which may help to do this?

2 Are there any topics which involve sounds the student should hear that I cannot produce?

3 Are there any topics which must be understood by all in exactly the same way, and which I cover fairly frequently?

A positive answer to any question indicates a possible application of recorded sound media. Which media to use, and how to obtain or produce recordings is discussed in the following chapter.

References

1. J Scupham, 'Broadcasting and the Open University', *British Journal of Educational Technology,* Vol I, No 1, 1970.

2. D L Stuck and R P Manatt, 'A Comparison of Audio-Tutorial and Lecture Methods of Teaching', *Journal of Educational Research,* No 63, 1970.

3. M C Davison, J A G Davison and M J Apter, 'A Comparison of the Effectiveness of Book and Audio-Visual Presentation of Two Linear Programmes', *Aspects of Educational Technology*, Vol 1, Methuen, 1967.

4. R J Amswych, 'An Investigation into the Use of Tape-Recorded Programmes for Craft Training', *Programmed Learning and Educational Technology,* July 1967.

6 Simple Audio and Audio-Visual Media

Radio

The use that a teacher can make of radio broadcasts is limited in very much the same way as his use of national television broadcasts. He has no control and sometimes little prior notification of the content and treatment of an impending programme. If the programme is designed specifically for school use, or for further education, then there might be a booklet describing the content and supplying follow-up and preparatory work for the students. In such a case, we can apply our normal criteria of selection. What are the objectives of the course? Do these objectives agree closely enough with our own? If they do, we might wish to use the course. This is where we meet problems of time-tabling and of evaluation. Generally, the course is broadcast at one time only, and this may not be very convenient. Schools broadcasts are put out during normal school hours, but of course it's just sheer luck if the timetabled Physics period coincides with the programme on Heat. Programmes designed for further education or for industrial training are generally put on at the most inconvenient hours — late evening or early Sunday morning are favourite times. Obviously the designers of the programmes really intend them for private study at home or is it simply pressure on peak listening times by the mass audience?

Even supposing that by some chance we can incorporate a series of programmes into our course, we have the second problem, of evaluation. Having established the course objectives, we structure an appropriate test situation. If, after listening to a radio programme, students do badly on the test, what do we do? If we have time, we may re-teach. We would certainly decide not to use the programme again, as we have no powers to modify it. If, on the other hand, students do well on the test, we would like to use the programme with subsequent groups, but of course it is not going to be repeated.

Here we see one valuable use of a tape recorder. Successful programmes may be stored for subsequent use at convenient times. Partly successful programmes may be edited or modified by the teacher in the light of his students' performance.

Having said this, we are immediately up against problems of copyright. Recently, copyright laws have been relaxed in the case of certain educational programmes, such as the schools broadcasts, enabling teachers to record the programmes and use them at will for the length of the school year. Unfortunately, this does not necessarily apply to other broadcasts. While this situation lasts, the use which can be made of radio for instructional purposes will remain limited. For one thing, the amount of learning which takes place during the broadcast itself is not very large. Research carried out by the BBC on the amount learnt from a short 5 minute discussion revealed some startling figures.[1] The average listener took in only about 28% of the material. Even university graduates — (the top 1% in terms of prior training in learning from lectures) — only managed to take in 48%. Early school leavers learnt as little as 21%.

Now, these figures are for a 5 minute programme, using volunteers as experimental subjects. How much lower are the figures for a 20 minute programme broadcast to a captive, unmotivated audience? The efficiency of the learning depends largely on the effectiveness of the follow-up and preparatory materials.

There are two ways in which one could achieve efficient learning from radio programmes. First, the programme authorities could set up their own evaluation studies prior to broadcasting. These would aim at refining the content of the programme, and at designing the most efficient preparatory and follow-up materials. We end up with a sound presentation, prescribed preparatory exercises, prescribed follow-up exercises and standard method of testing the student — a sort of instructional package or kit. Now the way to get the best out of an instructional package is to ensure that it is used according to its design. Some measure of control over the teacher is required. BBC schools broadcasts suggest that the use of their booklets is beneficial, but they cannot insist on their use. Some developing countries use radio as a backbone of their educational system, in order to reach scattered communities with few teachers. They have found that the effective use of the mass media for this purpose does involve the establishing of control over teaching methods, and the standardisation of curricula.

In an educational system such as in Great Britain, relatively well supplied with teachers, and with a history of local autonomy as regards syllabus and teaching methods, the controlled systematic use of the mass media in education is unlikely to succeed. In industry and commerce the training needs of different industries (and different firms within the same industry) are so diverse that systematic use of the mass media is again out of the question.

The second way of utilising radio for efficient learning is of more value. This is to use it as a source of material. It is left to the individual teacher or instructor, or to a group with similar teaching objectives, to produce an instructional course, or package, based perhaps on a radio programme. The production of such a package involves preparation of student exercises, testing and evaluation — in one phrase, a lot of work. Such a package, if successful, will teach successive groups to the same high standard.

The gramophone

It would seem that gramophone recordings should overcome many of the limitations of 'live' radio broadcasts.

As with radio, a gramophone recording may bring into the classroom the voices of well-known people, music by virtuoso performers and discussions by experts. The resources of the record company, as those of radio, generally ensure high standards of subject-matter expertise, background research and presentation. Unlike radio however, the gramophone record may be played over and over to successive groups at any convenient time.

One snag, however, is that gramophone records are expensive, and it is this factor which has limited their use in education.

Nevertheless, very extensive use is made of records in the teaching of music, the cost being shared over many schools and institutions — central record libraries charge a moderate hiring fee, or if they are subsidised, no fee at all. Similarly, much material such as historical speeches, animal noises and indeed lectures on certain topics are available on records.

In recent years, as the need for following-up and integrating student activity has been realised, there has been a tendency to produce multi-media presentations and planned instructional kits. Some of the earliest of these took the form of gramophone records linked to a film strip. As the commentary progressed, a recorded bleep would indicate to the instructor, or to a member of the group, to move to the next visual. The advantages of such a presentation are less need for skilled instructional staff, and a standardised unchanging presentation. One of the first applications of linked record and film strip presentations was in the training of personnel during the last war. Such tasks as the assembly of a Bren-gun could be treated adequately by a recorded commentary related to a set of visuals. Once the trainees mastered the names of the parts and the general principles involved, practice could be supervised by a sergeant who need not be a highly skilled teacher. The gramophone disc performs well in this sort of situation, as there is a constant supply of new trainees. The rigidity of the teaching is a positive advantage and the large number of copies required makes the recording process economical.

Here we have the reasons for the relatively limited use of the gramophone record in education. First, the presentation is rigid, so is suitable only for subjects where uniformity of procedure is an advantage or a necessity. Language learning, and much industrial training at the operative level, fall into this category. Secondly the subject must be sufficiently studied to make the production of records in quantity economical. We have noted that schools in particular seldom buy records outright. As soon as the cost of individual records drives groups of schools or training establishments to set up libraries, the potential market for a record is reduced drastically, and the whole project becomes uneconomical from the producer's viewpoint.

The advent of the magnetic tape recorder has put new life into the movement for pre-recorded lessons.

The telelecture

Before we discuss the tape recorder and its applications, we should mention briefly a technique which is used in the United States, particularly in the fields of university education and management education. As we noted earlier, one advantage of radio or television, is that it can bring the well-known personality or the acknowledged expert into the classroom. This not only guarantees an authoritative presentation, but also students pay greater attention and learn more when they listen to someone known to them, either personally or by repute. What if there is no suitable radio programme? What if the authority on the subject does not appear on TV? The traditional method of getting information 'straight from the horse's mouth' is to invite the authority to speak. The bulk of management training courses are largely staffed by a 'circus' of visiting lecturers. These are able speakers, well-informed in their subject, who have the time to devote to such activities. People who combine these three qualities are scarce, and so demand fairly hefty lecturing fees. As one proceeds higher up the academic ladder, closer to the frontiers of knowledge, they become scarcer and yet more in demand. A course staffed by visiting speakers is usually one of two things. Either it will be a social occasion (such as most conferences) which brings together various interested parties at various levels of expertise. The speakers will find that some sections of the audience are at least as well informed as they are, while others do not have the necessary background to benefit from their presentation. They do their best, trying neither to preach to the converted nor to aim way above the audience's head. The presentation is really an interlude in the real work of the conference which takes place between individuals over meals or in the evenings.

Otherwise, visiting speakers are called in because the organisers of a course cannot perform the teaching themselves — through lack of time or knowledge. In the latter case, no systematic control over course content can usually be exercised by the organising teacher. Even in the former case, it is a bit difficult to invite a speaker and then tell him how to treat his subject. One selects a visiting speaker by repute. At worst, he is someone with a reputation in a particular area. At best, one has heard him before, and his treatment of the subject agrees with one's own views and objectives.

However, to return to the telelecture. Basically this is a lecture delivered over the telephone. A telephone line between your classroom and the lecturer's place of work or private house is hired for an appropriate time. Amplification equipment is installed at each end, so that the lecturer simply speaks while sitting in a chair, or in bed, in a normal voice, and the distant class listens to a loudspeaker installed in the classroom.

In the summer of 1967 the author attended a telelecture in California. The lecturer was in New York. The presentation dealt with the uses of the computer in education and the audience were mainly head teachers of local schools, some already using computer-assisted instruction, some not. The speaker was able to illustrate his presentation with slides which had been sent by post and were screened at his direction by one of the class. The class could interrupt or ask questions by means of a roving microphone. Thus there was a two-way communication facility over some three thousand miles between a class of fifteen and an acknowledged expert on the subject, at about ten per cent of the cost in fees, travel and hotel expenses which would have been incurred by fetching the lecturer to the class. Compared with face-to-face confrontation as in the normal lecture, the telelecture did seem a trifle mechanical. One missed the lecturer's gestures and the lecturer no doubt lost a lot of audience feedback by being unable to observe them. However, these are the disadvantages of any sound broadcast. Against these must be weighed the advantages of two-way communication and the greater accessibility of our rare subject experts.

In America, the telelecture system uses standard telephone lines. The exclusive or temporary hire of telephone lines is becoming more and more common, for a range of purposes, such as news reporting or the installation of remote computer terminals. We may look forward to the increasing use of telephones for teaching. Pundits who delight in forecasting the future predict vast information libraries, computer controlled, available for reference to every citizen by dialling in from his home telephone. Prototypes of such systems, capable of limited information retrieval, already exist. The all-embracing public information system may still be some way off, however. The telelecture method is here and now.

The tape recorder

Just as the overhead projector has revolutionised the presentation of still visuals, and the cheap, easy-to-use 8 mm cine camera has made every teacher a potential film director; so the magnetic tape recorder has created a whole range of new teaching methods. Its impact has been most felt in language teaching and related subjects but it is now being applied most effectively to other school subjects and to commercial and industrial training. What makes the tape recorder of especial interest is the control which can be exercised over the recorded content by the teacher or instructor, and the flexibility with which it can be used by the student. Teachers may record their own materials, geared towards their own teaching objectives, and can follow-up, evaluate and revise their recordings. Students may stop a recording in order to make notes or solve a problem, record their own comments, and can re-play or re-record as often as they need.

These qualities of flexibility and control make the tape recorder a much more versatile and much more useful teaching aid than radio or the gramophone. Whereas you can only select suitable materials from radio programmes or records; you can, with tape, produce recorded materials specifically designed to meet your training objectives.

The tape recorder places a number of technical facilities at the teacher's disposal:

(a) *Instant playback* As soon as a recording is made, it is ready for listening. No developing or transcription delays. This is the facility which has made the tape recorder such a powerful medium of language teaching. The student can listen to a phrase, imitate it, then immediately compare his own efforts with the master recording.

(b) *Instant erasure* No complicated procedures are required to erase unwanted material from the tape. If a section is badly recorded, you simply re-record a second attempt over the top. The original recording is automatically wiped off. This makes for very simple production of tapes and correction of faults — even by novices.

(c) *Four-track recorders* These are recorders which can record on four parallel bands of the tape. Two recording heads are fitted. By switching between heads, one can record either on track 1 or track 3 as the tape passes through. By reversing the spools and replaying the tape through the other way, tracks 2 and 4 are available. Four-track recorders get twice as much material onto the same tape. However, they also enable more sophisticated techniques of recording to be used. For example: the language-learning situation described above generally uses a 4-track recorder. The master phrase is on track 1. The student uses track 3. He can play back both tracks simultaneously, to compare his efforts, but can only erase and re-record on track 3. This enables the student to practise a particular phrase as often as he likes, using the same master recording.

(d) *Mixing or dubbing* The 4-track recorder also allows one to dub, or to add commentaries to existing recordings. The commentary goes onto track 3 while track 1 plays back. They are then played back together and recorded onto another tape.

Another technique may be used which produces a mixed recording in one stage. Some recorders have a number of input jacks. These may be used for several microphones, or one may be used for a microphone, while another records directly from a gramophone, radio or another tape recorder. Both the original message and the teacher's comments appear on one track of the final tape. This technique requires more rehearsal than the former to get good results, as you cannot alter the two inputs separately after recording.

(e) *Automatic stop* Many tape recorders are equipped with a device which will stop the tape automatically. It is activated by sticking a piece of metallic tape to the recording tape, at the point you want the machine to stop. It is standard practice to have a metallic section near each end of a tape to prevent it running right through the machine and off the spool. The user can, however, arrange for the tape to stop at any point he desires, simply by sticking on some aluminium tape. This enables you to leave recorders unattended, or to present a recording section by section. You can by this means present an 'audio-programme' which stops automatically after each 'frame' of information to allow the student to respond. The student can re-start the tape by pressing the start button which over-rides the metal strip.

(f) *Automatic slide progression* The automatic slide projectors discussed earlier, operate by an electrical impulse from the remote control. This impulse may be generated by an audio signal of a particular frequency. Some tape recorders are modified to be used in conjunction with an automatic slide projector, to give an automated audio-visual presentation. Recorders which do not have this facility can be modified by an item of equipment designed to supply the impulse. This is simply placed beside the recorder, and the tape is re-threaded to pass through this extra gadget.

(g) *Speed variations and recording facilities* Generally, the faster the tape speed, the higher the quality of reproduction. The most common tape speeds are 7½, 3¾ and 1⅞ inches per second. 15 ips and ¹⁵⁄₁₆ ips are occasionally found. Other things being equal, the faster the recording speed the better the recording. 3¾ ips has, however, virtually become the standard speed for sound tape recorders. There is very little pre-recorded material that is not available at that speed, and there is much that is available at no other. The next most useful speed to have is probably 7½ ips. Most tape recorders accept 7 in diameter tape reels, corresponding to 1200ft of standard play tape, 1800ft of long play, 2400ft of double play or 3600ft of triple play. Recording times are, respectively, more than one, one and half, two or three hours on one track at 3¾ ips.

Many of the more expensive tape recorders are not supplied with microphones, to enable the purchaser to buy what is best for his purpose. If you say what you want to do, the manufacturers will usually recommend suitable microphones.

It is useful to have a device to enable you to 'index' a recording, so that you can find your way back to any particular section. Recorders fitted with digital counters for this purpose are marked. However, it is worth checking that the counter fitted to the recorder that interests you really does work consistently. For all but the most straightforward recording work it is desirable to be able to mix at least two sound sources — say, a spoken commentary and background music or sound effects. It is possible to obtain separate mixing units, and these are more versatile than anything normally built into a recorder. It is also very useful to be able to monitor a recording while it is being made. With a lot of recorders it is only possible to listen to the sound as it is being recorded. It is much better to be able to listen to the sound re-played a fraction of a second after it has been recorded so that you can judge the quality of what you are doing. Many other facilities are offered on some tape recorders. Some of them, such as automatic volume control, are useful in some situations. It will pay you to try out a recorder to satisfy yourself that you are paying for something you will find useful.

(h) *Cassette tape recorders* Over the last few years these have become especially popular in education and training, being cheap, reliable, robust, extremely portable and easy to handle.

Some cassette recorders now have built-in synchronisation facilities for the operation of automatic slide projectors (Phillips and Hanimex notably). Cassette recorders have also been used as the basis for inexpensive, portable language laboratories, often intended as a supplement to the larger installation.

Language laboratories

This specialist application of the tape recorder is now well established as a language teaching method. It is also being increasingly used as a testing device or to present audio-programmes in many other subjects, so is of more general interest to teachers. Indeed, the Americans are beginning to refer to the equipment by the more general title of 'electronic learning laboratory'.

Essentially, a language laboratory provides facilities for a student to listen to a master recording, and to record his own responses. This is generally achieved by the use of a 4-track tape recorder. When side 1 is being played, track 1 contains the master recording and the student may record, erase and re-record on track 3. This procedure is possible on some sophisticated or modified tape recorders, but the system does not really become a 'laboratory' until a number of such recorders are connected to a central console operated by the teacher. Generally, the teacher may listen in to any one student and can communicate directly to any one or a group of students.

Thus, the student may act as his own judge of his responses, but the teacher may monitor and if necessary supply individual help and guidance. For instance, in learning a language the student may use the language laboratory to listen to words or phrases and then repeat them. He will then compare his pronunciation with the master recording and try again. However, at this stage he is by no means an expert judge of pronunciation. What appears a reasonable attempt to him may jar on the more skilled ear of the teacher. The teacher may then take over, point out the error and eradicate it without disturbing the class. The effective use of a language laboratory for pronunciation training relies heavily on the skill and efforts of the individual teacher.

A later use of the laboratory may involve the practice of sentence construction. The master tape may ask a question, and the student phrases an answer, or the master makes a statement in English and the student translates it. The master then gives the correct response. Here the judgement to be made is much more within the student's capabilities. His effort either agrees with the master or it does not. There is little scope for fine degrees of error as in pronunciation. When used for such a purpose, the teacher's role is much more limited. We have in effect a self-presenting lesson.

It is this technique which is now being applied to 'programme' other subjects. Whether such programmes are effective depends as always on whether the subject is appropriate for such treatment, and on how the programmes themselves are structured. The subject must be one where verbal responses are appropriate, and where the responses are standard and unchanging — subjects which require drill and practice. The rate of progress to more difficult material must be such that at each stage the learner is capable of judging the correctness of his responses, and if necessary identifying his error. In addition to language learning, this .technique has been successfully employed in teaching backward readers, giving practice in mental arithmetic and training in sound identification. The one advantage over the use of individual tape recorders is that the teacher may listen in unnoticed to monitor the individual's progress and to pick out those who need remedial work or who lack motivation.

Equipment

Language laboratory equipment is both expensive and varied. Many systems exist giving progressively greater facilities for student/tape/teacher communication at progressively higher prices. Some have simple tape recorders at the student booths, the master being played from the teacher's console. These have the disadvantage of a lock-step presentation. Others require a 4-track recorder in each booth with an individual tape complete with master recording on track 1. Still others get by with one master tape which can be recorded from the teacher's console onto the student's track for as long as it is required and then replaced with another lesson. This last system is most versatile as it generally allows the use of individual pre-recorded tapes as well.

There are two systems in common use — the audio active comparative (AAC for short) and the audio active (AA). The audio active comparative system, sometimes called listen-respond-compare, requires recording facilities for each student. In the audio active, or listen-respond, system the student hears his voice, as he 'speaks, by way of his headphones but it is not recorded. Less equipment is needed, so the system is cheaper than an audio active comparative one. There is much debate about the benefits of the AAC system, and many manufacturers supply both types of laboratory. Some of them offer a 'mixed economy' system, providing a teacher's console with up to half the positions in a class being AAC, the rest being AA.

Generally speaking, AAC systems have to be wired in to a classroom and cannot be moved about. There are a couple of so called transportable systems, but moving them involves moving 20 to 30 lb of equipment for each student, so they are of interest only where a small number of positions are required. There are also individual units, requiring only a power supply, that can be used, say, in a library or other quiet rooms. Because the student requires little more than a headset, a number of transportable AA systems are marketed which do not require fixed wiring though, after a while, this is often installed.

The teacher's console is usually equipped to transcribe tapes, records or the teacher's voice, onto the student's tapes as shown in Figure 6.1.

Using programme tapes, there are two ways in which the material may be made available to the student. One is to maintain a library containing sets of duplicate recordings. Where a laboratory has to be used by different groups at the same time, this is often a convenient — though expensive — system. The other method is to 'broadcast' a master recording, using the students' recorders to make duplicate copies which will be erased at the end of the lesson. It is not always easy to do this without the students' presence, and it does take time at the beginning of a lesson.

Language laboratories vary considerably in the facilities they provide. It is not always easy, from the sales literature or from a demonstration, to decide whether the presence or absence of some facility will significantly affect the operation of the system. Ask the manufacturer to give you the addresses of some installations that have been in use for at least a year. Visit them, and find out what snags have occurred.

The versatility of the equipment is but one of the potential buyer's considerations. There are further considerations of reliability, student comfort, earphone hygiene, sound-proofing of booths and laboratories, and so on. In a new and fast developing market, where a new system appears almost every month, you would be wise to seek up-to-date professional advice at the time of purchase. The Educational Foundation for Visual Aids is most helpful in advising on equipment available. *Language Laboratory Facilities,* by A S Hayes, is an excellent guide for those contemplating the purchase of language laboratory equipment. First published in 1963 by the US Government Printing Office, it was re-issued in 1968 by Oxford University Press, with some additional material. Early in 1968 the Ministry of Technology, on behalf of the Department of Education and

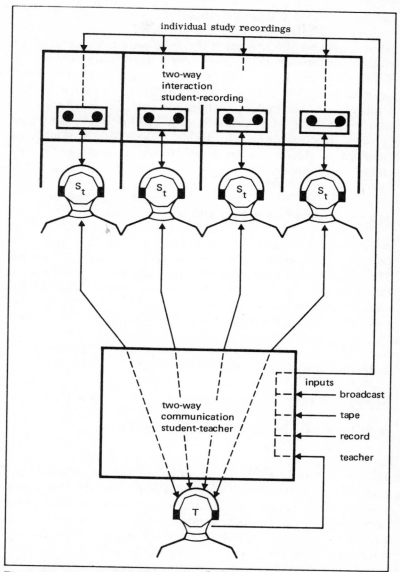

Figure 6.1 The communication facilities provided by a language laboratory

Obviously such a communication system may have many other applications: review, drill and practice testing.

Science, carried out an examination of a number of audio active comparative laboratories. For some reason, not all the laboratories on the market at the time were tested, and other equipment now on the market was not in production at the time. Some of the laboratories tested have been superseded or modified. The Ministry's report was published by the Ministry of Technology (HMSO). The Experimental Development Unit of NAVAC is now continuing to test new systems. Reports appear in *Visual Education*. A number of standard works on the language laboratory are listed at the end of this chapter.

The use of slide-tape presentations

Synchronised slide-tape presentations have become very popular, particularly in industrial and commercial training. The Ford Motor Company, for example, uses the technique in just about every foremanship, supervisory or management course they run.

The practical advantages of such courses are:

1 Instant availability — day or night shifts.

2 Standard presentation — leading to uniform practices.

3 Self-presentation — saving an instructor's time.

However, Ford's have found in practice that although the courses are professionally prepared and although the visuals are designed to communicate and are produced to the highest technical standards, the greatest value of the slide-tape presentation is to stimulate interest, motivate for further study, and give the general outline of the subject. Long-term retention of detail information was low, a result very much in agreement with studies discussed earlier. In order to ensure retention and enable the foreman to pass a qualifying examination, supplementary texts were required which gave the man practice in applying the information he received from the tape.

Such results do not cast doubt on the value of the slide-tape presentations. Rather they pin-point the functions each media can perform. The retention figures obtained are every bit as good as one gets from a well-prepared, well-delivered lecture. Like the lecture, slide-tape presentations (and traditional training films) give very little opportunity for the learner to participate actively and practise his mastery of the information. They are one-way or open-ended, communication channels. They can be made two-way, or closed loop channels, by supplying material for student practice, checking student performance, and if necessary, using this feedback to modify the lesson. This can be done by the methods of programmed instruction, by eliciting appropriate responses at every stage of the presentation.

The techniques are not limited to written programmes. There are now many audio and audio-visual programmes in use, not only in language teaching but in many other subjects ranging from liberal studies to machine operations.

A recent article in *Visual Education*[2] summarised some research comparing conventional teaching with slide-tape and other audio-visual methods, for topics from school science such as laboratory safety precautions and how to use a bunsen burner, a microscope and a thermometer. This study found a marked superiority of the audio-visual methods over the conventional (although many possibly relevant factors, such as teacher quality or novelty effects do not appear to have been controlled). Students using the audio-visual materials generally scored 10% better and took between 30% and 60% less learning time.

This study used carefully developed visual materials and taped commentaries. The students were expected to perform relevant procedures during study. The conventional instruction was administered by a teacher who had not been involved in the preparation of these materials, although he no doubt used his own visuals to supplement his own spoken commentary. One wonders to what extent the much improved learning reported above was the result of the 'automation' applied to the audio-visual lesson, or to the extra analysis and care that went into its preparation. How would the author of the packaged course, using the same visuals, compare to the package?

Certainly other controlled experiments in this field show less startling differences between media. However, the above results are a strong argument for the careful preparation of well-tested audio-visual programmes, to be used by many teachers who do not themselves have the time to devote to such detailed preparation.

There are also many machines and devices specially adapted for presenting such programmes. In machines such as the RITT equipment[3] the teacher no longer has to use metallic tape. Stop, start, and rewind can be achieved by recording impulses onto a separate track of the tape.

In many subjects however, equivalent results can be achieved by following a short unit of 'straight' audio, or audio-visual presentation, by an exercise (written or spoken or manual) which gives the learner practice in using his new knowledge, and the teacher an opportunity to observe and correct mis-conceptions. The principles on which such follow-up materials are designed are again the principles of programmed instruction. Whether one refers to the complete course 'package' (eg part film, part tape, part text, part teacher) as a programme or not, is purely academic. What matters is that it has been systematically designed, evaluated and found to work.

Radiovision

In recent years, the BBC has been using a technique they call 'radiovision' for some of their schools broadcasts.

Still film strips, produced to accompany radio broadcasts, are provided in advance of transmission dates by the BBC for schools wishing to use them. During transmission, teachers may listen to the sound broadcasts with their classes or they may record them for later use. The resultant recording is then replayed accompanied by the filmstrip at whatever time is convenient for the class.

The advantages of radiovision are low cost of production,

flexibility in use and the advantages gained by the use of a large, high-quality projected colour picture. Additionally, radiovision uses equipment already available in schools. Tape and film strip may be used by the teacher whenever and wherever needed, as the medium is not limited by broadcast transmission times and the equipment is simple and portable. Repetition and revision are easy. Tape and film strip can be stopped for discussion, or reversed to replay sections which have caused difficulty. Single frames can be shown. The teacher can use film strip or tape separately, and can 'edit out' or add material as he wishes. Against this, radiovision lacks animation, which makes it unsuitable for some sequences.

To investigate the two media, a controlled experiment was set up by Anna Foxall[4]. 847 children from South Wales participated, from fourth year primary and first year secondary groups.

The control group watched programmes 1 to 5 of *Maths Today*, while the radiovision group used a radiovision version of those programmes, produced by the investigator and resembling the television programmes as much as possible.

Graphics were designed by adapting photographs taken from the screen while videotape recordings of the television programmes were in progress. The resulting pictures were adapted slightly, where animation demanded this, and colour was used, not only to add interest, but also to convey information where animation had been used by television. The sound tracks needed slight adaptations from the television programme scripts.

A questionnaire and interview techniques were used to obtain reactions of teachers and pupils on the media in use, and on the suitability of programmes; and to assess pupils' achievements. Two tests were given, to both experimental and control groups, before and at the end of the experiment.

Test results showed no significant difference between the learning achieved from the two media compared. However, there were surprisingly strong preferences for the radiovision series among both pupils and teachers, and considerable cost and flexibility benefits as well. Some of the general conclusions were as follows:

1   Children's reactions, which were obtained collectively, showed that primary children liked both media, and generally enjoyed programmes whichever medium they used. In secondary schools taking both media, two teachers reported better reactions from children when using television, and two others found their classes responded better when radiovision was used.

2   Primary teachers varied very little, between radiovision and television groups, in opinions on programme suitability, though there was a very slight bias in favour of radiovision. In the secondary schools, teachers' ratings as to the 'level of difficulty' of programmes, favoured radiovision a little, perhaps because programmes can be 'held' while difficult subject matter is absorbed.

3   Reactions obtained on the media in classroom use showed that primary teachers very strongly favoured radiovision and would have preferred it to television.

4   Primary and secondary teachers, without exception, favoured radiovision, rather than television, for follow-up activities, since radiovision is not subject to restrictions of pace and can be shown in whole or in part as often as necessary.

Thus, decisions to use an expensive medium if a cheap one is as effective should be more carefully considered. The areas in which television offers unique advantages should be re-examined, and its use more carefully considered.

Radiovision involves savings in costs, but no loss of quality. It should not be considered a poor relation of television but as a medium in its own right.

There are two further ways in which its use could be extended:

(a)   Radiovision can be used as an alternative to television, especially in areas where television is not available.

(b)   It is also possible to use radiovision, in conjunction with television, as a cheap means of revising and backing up television programmes.

Special training by tape recorder

Like cine film, the tape recorder presents information at a fixed pace. One might argue that this is a disadvantage to the learner, as he cannot proceed at his own learning rate. This may be sometimes true, though recent research[5] indicates that the importance of student-paced learning may have been over-emphasised. However, there are many teaching situations where the speed or pace of the task is of vital importance. Here the paced-presentation of the tape recorder, far from being a potential disadvantage, makes it an ideal choice for a presentation medium. Pacing by taped instructions has been used in training of machine operations, assembly tasks, typewriting and shorthand skill, mental arithmetic and so on. The basic procedure in all cases is to produce a tape which presents instructions or problems to the learner at a comfortable rate. When performance reaches a satisfactory standard, the rate of presentation is stepped up. The decision to step up the rate may be taken by an instructor, on the basis of the percentage accuracy of a set of problems or a sheet of typing; or by the learner himself, based on whether he feels he is keeping up with the instructions. Two practical examples of pacing by tape may illustrate the method.

1 Paced typewriting

Variations of this method are used by many commercial schools and secretarial colleges. The method described here is operated by Sight and Sound Ltd, who have a number of installations throughout the country. Novice students are first trained by means of a simulator. This takes the form of a visual display of the typewriter keyboard on the wall of the class. A tape recorder is synchronised to the display. The voice on the tape slowly reads out a succession of letters. As each letter is spoken, the appropriate key on the visual display lights up. The colour of the light indicates the finger to be used. Students type the letters as they are called out. In successive lessons the rate of presentation increases somewhat, but the main purpose of the first stage of training, with the simulator, is to establish the basic skill of touch-typing without looking at the keys.

Once students have mastered the motor-elements of the skill, and can type accurately (but very slowly) without the aid of the simulator lights, they are transferred to speed training. They now perform standard copy-typing exercises, reading from printed sheets. However, their pace of typing is controlled by tape which reads the exercise, letter by letter, into individual earphones. Students progress to a faster tape once their typing error rate drops below a pre-determined level.

The method produces good results, in terms of reasonable touch-typing speeds after 12 or 18 hours of training. What is most interesting is that experienced typists may in a few hours increase their typing speeds by an appreciable factor in these paced-practice conditions.

Similar courses now exist for home study, such as the American one illustrated in Figure 6.2.

A well-documented study of typing training[6] which compared conventional methods of instruction with individual automated audio-visual instruction, found that students using the audio-visual methods consistently outperformed the others to a significant degree. Only a proportion of the audio-visual course was paced instruction on tape, other media such as loop films or books being also used when appropriate.

2 Paced operative training in industry

The techniques of paced practice on machine or assembly operations are now well established in British Industry. Much of the early work was carried out in Sweden by the L M Ericsson Corporation, who now produce and market the RITT system of tape-teaching equipment[7]. In its simplest form, this is a robust tape playback unit with remote foot controls for stop, start and re-wind. The instructions from the tape are fed to earphones worn by the learner. To give

Figure 6.2 The tape recorder as a training tool

Top: A schematic representation of an induction loop system used for operative training (RITT).

Above: A trainee using a tape to guide and pace touch-typing (Mind Inc).

the learner greater mobility in the workshop, and to eliminate the danger of trailing wires, an 'induction loop' system is used. The signal from the tape unit is fed into a loop of wire draped round that part of the workshop where training is progressing. The earphones are equipped with miniature radio receivers to pick up the signal. The loop gives a uni-directional signal, so that the earphones will pick up the taped instructions only while the operative remains within the loop of wire. By this method a number of different training operations can be carried out in different parts of the workshop, without long wires to earphones and without radio interference.

The training procedure is as follows: the first part of the tape gives detailed instructions on the job, together with all the background information necessary. The novice and a skilled operator both put on earphones, and the novice watches the skilled operator follow the instructions for one or two cycles of the operation. They then swap position, the skilled man supervising the new man's attempts to follow the instructions, and where necessary, re-winding the tape, demonstrating again, or guiding the novice's hand. When the skilled man is satisfied that the novice has mastered the basic principles, he puts him onto the second stage of the tape, and leaves him to it.

This is the pacing stage. The instructions for performing the operation are repeated cycle by cycle, but progressively explanations and redundant words are omitted, and the pace of instruction increases. All the learner has to do is to follow the instructions. If he finds that he cannot cope with the increase in pace, he is free to re-wind to an earlier, slower section and try again. So although the tape is pacing the operation, the rate of progression is under the learner's control. Such tape-pacing installations have now been installed in many industrial training workshops. Often they have proved most effective, paying for the cost of the installation by improved productivity after only one or two operatives have been trained. Some typical results and advantages of this method, as reported by researchers, are listed below[8].

(a)   Uniform, high-quality instructions.

(b)   Less embarrassment for learners (particularly the older worker).

(c)   The best method is learnt by all.

(d)   Training times reduced by 50% or more.

(e)   Poor readers can learn quickly.

(f)   Foreign workers can be trained by translation of the tape.

(g)   Better labour relations, less turnover.

Many other electronic firms are now producing similar equipment, and the facilities available to the course programmer are increasing. He can now arrange for automatic slide or cine film presentation synchronised to his tape, group instruction, wind-back or forward to pre-determined points on the tape (allowing a modicum of 'branching'). Whether he can, or would wish to use all these facilities is another matter. It does seem however, that tape-teaching has come to stay. One big attraction is the ease with which the relative amateur can record and synchronise his course materials.

The two examples of tape-teaching discussed above are in many respects similar. They each involve two stages — prior training in the principles and skills involved, followed by paced speed training. In both cases tape was used in the first stage to replace the human instructor, but in both cases tape was not enough. Simulators, guidance, practice on the equipment was also required. The exact requirements can be isolated by performing a task analysis. Of course, tape need not have been used at all in the first stage, it was merely convenient, and just as effective as the instructor (there may even be the advantages of uniformity and language mentioned above).

In the second stage of training however, the tape is essential. It provides the criterion of speed by which the learner can judge his progress. The tape (together with the machine being used) is also sufficient. The student can judge for himself when he is ready to progress. He gains all the feedback he requires from the tape and the quality of his work. We have a teaching process which is adaptive to the student's learning rate.

The speed at which a task is performed is often an important criterion. When the task is complex, very long, or varies much from attempt to attempt, then tape-teaching may not be the answer. When, however, the task is simple and repetitive, this method has much to recommend it and should be seriously considered.

References

1. W A Belson, *An Enquiry into the Comprehensibility of 'Topic for Tonight'*, BBC Audience Research Dept, 1952.

2. I Townsend, 'Tape, Film and Slide Teaching Manipulative Skills in Science', *Visual Education*, March 1973.

3. C H Lundin, M M Grant and A Ehnborg, *RITT Audio Instruction Programming Manual*, Ericsson, Instruktion-steknik AB, Stockholm Sweden, 1968.

4. Anna Foxall, 'Television and Radiovision in the Teaching of Modern Mathematics: A Comparative Study', *British Journal of Educational Technology*, Vol 3, No 3, October 1972.

5. H Kay, B Dodd and M Sime, 'Clock-Paced System', pp 132-134, in *Teaching Machines and Programmed Instruction*, Pelican, 1968.

6. R K Edwards, M L Williams and W W Roderick, *An Experimental Pilot Study to Explore the Use of an Audio-Visual Tutorial Laboratory in the Secretarial Offerings at the*

Community College Level in Michigan, Lansing Community College, 1968.

7. See op cit 12 n 3.

8. Agar, 'Instruction of Industrial Workers by Tape Recorder', *Affarsekonomi,* No 10, 1962 (Swedish). Also, 'Swedish Training System Breaks the Language Barrier', *Industrial Training International,* September, 1966.

Further Reading

J D Halloran, *The Effects of Mass Communication,* Leicester University Press, 1964.

R Milton, *Radio Programming: a Basic Manual,* Bles, 1969.

J Scupham, *Broadcasting and the Community,* Watts, 1967.

School Broadcasting Council, *Research and School Broadcasting; School Broadcasting and the Newsome Report; Science Teaching and School Broadcasting.*

Tape recorders have a literature of their own, as regards their technicalities. The use of particular models for educational purposes however is reported on in technical reports appearing in *Visual Education.*
  Some books on the educational use of tape recorders and tape recordings are:

Andrew Phelan, *The Law and Your Tape Recorder,* Print and Press Services Ltd.

Sound Effects on Tape. A Tape Recording Handbook, Print and Press Services Ltd.

J Aldred, *Tape and Cine. A Tape Recording Handbook,* Print and Press Services Ltd.

R Hack, *The Tape Editing Guide,* Focal Press, 1961.

J Weston, *The Tape Recorder in the Classroom,* NCAVAE, 1973.

C N G Matthews, *Tape Recordings,* Museum Press, 1968.

P Spring, *Tape Recorders,* Focal Press, 1967.

J Graham Jones, *Teaching with Tape,* Focal Press, 1971.

The Software — Sources of Tapes

Except for specialist applications, such as music or language teaching (which is discussed in the language laboratory section of this source guide), there has not, till recently, been a great variety of pre-recorded tapes available. Now the situation is changing, due to the growing popularity of 'packaged' slide-tape lectures, the availability of BBC and Open University broadcast materials, and the cheapness and ease of use of the latest cassette tape recorders.

Much pre-recorded sound material is listed in the EFVA range of catalogues of Audio Visual Aids. In addition, in 1972 a new updated edition of the EFVA catalogue *Records and Tapes for Education* was published. The references on language tapes (given in the language laboratory section) also include courses for self-study on standard tape recorders. Music is catered for by the established record companies — the 'Musicassette' range of pre-recorded music (using the Philips cassette) is continually growing.

Some producers of pre-recorded tapes on other subjects are:

BBC Radio Enterprises (REB, REC, REGL and REM series records), Villiers House, Haven Green, London W5.

Discourses Ltd, 34 High Street, Royal Tunbridge Wells, Kent.

The Linguaphone Institute, 207 Regent Street, London W1.

Students Recordings Ltd, 15 Devon Square, Newton Abbot, Devon.

Sussex Tapes, 62 Queens Grove, London NW8 6ER.

Tutor-Tape Co Ltd, 2 Replingham Road, London SW18.

The Software — Sources of Language Tapes, etc

The Centre for information on Language Teaching, State House, High Holborn, London WC1, maintains a substantial reference library, including an audio-visual section, and publishes bibliographies on individual languages. The Audio-Visual Language Association, 7 Shelly Close, Langley, Buckinghamshire, publishes occasional bibliographies of laboratory and course materials.

Another useful publication is *Recorded Material for Teaching English* published jointly by the British Council and NCAVAE. This includes materials other than tapes and covers the teaching of English as a first language and as a second language.

NCAVAE also publish, in co-operation with EFVA and the Audio-Visual Language Association (AVLA) a catalogue *Audio Visual Materials for Modern Languages* as part of the VENISS service.

Books on the Use of Language Laboratories

P J Vernon (ed), *Audio-Visual Approach to Modern Language Teaching — A Symposium*, NCAVAE, 1973.

Audio-Visual Materials for Modern Languages, NCAVAE, 1965.

Audio-Visual Materials for English Language, A Teaching Catalogue, published for the British Council by Longmans, 1973.

Professor John D Turner, *Introduction of the Language Laboratory*, University of London Press, 1965.

Language Laboratories, Educational Surveys, HMSO,

The Language Laboratory in Higher Education — an Experiment, Harrap, 1967.

E M Stack, *The Language Laboratory and Modern Language Teaching*, Oxford University Press, second edition, 1971.

J B Hilton, *The Language Laboratory in School*, Methuen, 1964.

F M Hodgson, *Language Learning Material*, Educational Explorers.

Robert Lado, *Language Teaching — A Scientific Approach*, McGraw-Hill, 1965.

J D Turner (ed), *Programming for the Language Laboratory*, University of London Press, 1968.

F Gennys (ed), *Programming Languages*, Academic Press.

The Hardware

Manufacturers' Addresses — Tape Recorders
AEG (Great Britain) Ltd, AEG House, Chichester Rents, Chancery Lane, London WC2. 01-242 9944

Bang and Olufsen, Eastbrook Road, Gloucester. 0452 21591

Bell and Howell A-V Ltd, Alperton House, Bridgewater Road, Wembley, Middlesex. 01-902 8812

Bosch Ltd, Rhodes Way, Radlett Road, Watford, Hertfordshire. Watford 44233

Brenell Engineering Co Ltd, 321-5 Liverpool Road, London N1. 01-607 8271

British Radio Corporation Ltd, 284 Southbury Road,

Enfield, Middlesex. 01-804 2477

Ferrograph Co Ltd, The Hyde, Edgware Road, London NW9. 01-205 2241

Grundig (Great Britain) Ltd, 42 Newlands Park, London SE26. 01-778 2211

Hanimex (UK) Ltd, Hanimex House, 15-24 Great Dover Street, London SE1. 01-407 3161

Magnetic Tapes Ltd, Chilton Works, Garden Road, Richmond, Surrey. 01-876 7957

Philips Electrical Ltd, Century House, Shaftesbury Avenue, London WC2. 01-437 7777

Sharp Electronics, 48 Derby Street, Manchester M8 8HN. 061-832 6115

Sony UK Ltd, 11 Ascot Road, Clockhouse Lane, Bedfont, Middlesex. Ashford 50021

Farnell Tandberg Ltd, 81 Kirkstall Road, Leeds LS31HR. 0532 35111

Van Der Molen Ltd, 1 Mildmay Road, Romford, Essex. Romford 41904

Manufacturers' Addresses — Language Laboratories
Aveley Laboratories Ltd, Arisdale Avenue, South Ockendon, Essex. South Ockendon 3444

W J & M Baylis Ltd, 611 Gortom Road, Reddish, Stockport. 061-223 0583

Bosch Ltd, Rhodes Way, Radlett Road, Watford, Herts. Watford 44233

Connevans Ltd, 1 Norbury Road, Reigate, Surrey. Reigate 47571

Cybernetic Developments Ltd, 111 Chertsey Road, Byfleet, Surrey. Byfleet 41131

ESL Bristol Ltd, St Lawrence House, 29-31 Broad Street, Bristol BS1 2HF. 0272 54159

Farnell Tandberg Ltd, 81 Kirkstall Road, Leeds LS31HR. 0532 35111

Hird-Brown-Laycock Ltd, 32 Wilkinson Street, Sheffield S10 2GB. 0742 24281

Sign Electronics Ltd, Lakedale Road, London SE18. 01-854 4321

7   Film

Cine film is now well established as a teaching medium. Nearly every school or training centre possesses at least one cine-projector, and it is difficult to choose from the large selection of off-the-shelf training films now available.

However, the path to acceptance has been long and not without setbacks. Indeed, it seems that the path has led us in a rather unexpected direction. As long ago as 1920, popular writers, as well as serious educators, were predicting a revolution in education, based on the widespread use of films. This revolution has not yet materialised. Although films are plentiful, the proportion of time spent watching them by the average student is very low. The predictions of higher student motivation and interest, as shown by the 1923 cartoon shown in figure 7.1, have not materialised either. Opponents of the present trend towards educational technology might perhaps take heart from this example. They might also note that the same has happened, or is happening, to the latest educational 'gimmick' — programmed instruction. But as we pointed out earlier, the essential elements of programmed instruction do not form a communication medium, but a communication technology. Teaching machines are a medium. As such, they will fail if applied inappropriately. Educational films have probably as many failures as successes to their credit. Many of the failures were due to the inappropriate use of film and the *Chicago Tribune* cartoon illustrates this. Study carefully the second pair of pictures. As an educational technologist, why would you doubt the likelihood of such a transformation in the attitude of the children?

The timetable, *To-day's pictures,* indicates that the cartoonist expected the filmed lesson to do exactly the same job as the teacher — automated chalk-and-talk. But is this not exactly what many educational films do? Think back over the films

Figure 7.1 'The Changing World' (Mr Edison predicts motion pictures will take the place of books in the schools). 1923 cartoon from the *Chicago Tribune.*

you have seen. How often did they include lengthy shots of a commentator or teacher talking at the audience or even writing on a chalkboard. True, the film has certain advantages: we can guarantee an accurate, clear exposition, supported by well-produced visual material, which can be reproduced, without change, to successive audiences. But there are disadvantages: the exposition may not be as clear as we hope to all members of the audience; opportunity for questioning and discussion of the visual material may be lost. Such an opportunity can of course be provided by the teacher, during the introduction or follow-up of the film. There is much evidence to suggest that the educational value of a film is dependent on the way it is used.

A quick look at some research in this field will help us to build some principles for the selection of educational films.

Research on cine film

1 Are films generally of educational value?

The short answer is yes, based on many large studies carried out throughout Europe and America. These measured the attitudes of teachers and students who had used films. However, these studies tell us little about any precise changes in attitude, knowledge or skill produced by the films. More detailed studies are needed to examine these points. Many of the results are inconclusive.

2 Can films change attitudes or emotions?

Most certainly. For example the U S Army has used a film entitled 'Why We Fight' in a controlled experimental situation. The film presented the facts behind the case without any emotional treatment. However, the group who had seen the film contained twice as many who were prepared to go to war, as equivalent groups who had not seen the film.[1]

When a film deliberately sets out to change attitudes and emotions, and employs all the actor's and ad-man's tricks, it can indeed be a powerful tool. The teacher should be aware of this power, and be on his guard in case it is abused. For example, films shown to groups of schoolchildren by

Furhammar[2] produced strong anti-German attitudes. Furthermore, the teacher should watch for unexpected or irrelevant attitudes that a given film may produce. We might mention here Belson's study.[3] A series of French language films, aimed at the potential tourist, had the odd effect of teaching efficiently a range of useful words and phrases, but at the same time increasing the general level of apprehension in the group about the difficulties of foreign travel and communication!

3 Can films increase interest and motivation?

Generally yes. There are innumerable reports on individual films. A wide survey, by Brooker, of instructional films produced by the U S Office of Education, showed that the vast majority of users considered that the films 'made the class work more interesting and resulted in less absenteeism'.[4] It should be noted, however, that the interest or motivation produced by a film stems from its content and the treatment the content is given, not from the film medium itself. Gone are the days when seeing a movie was an experience in itself. Today's younger generation accept films as commonplace, and expect surprisingly high standards of production. They 'learn the language' of film almost from birth.

4 Do students learn more effectively from film?

There is no one answer: the research has often been inconclusive. There is no doubt that you learn from a film, as from any experience. A film may present material which could not otherwise be demonstrated: documentaries from overseas, the interior of furnaces, animated sequences, slow-motion sequences. In such cases, one is using the medium to expand the teacher's normally available resources. It is doubtful, though, whether films per se have any advantage over other presentations. Laner compared two methods of teaching the assembly of a sash-cord window — a sound film, and a set of slides linked to a recording of the same commentary as the film used. No difference in the amount learnt was found.[5] Experiments on tasks which involved the mastery of skilled movements (such as in athletics) do however point to the superiority of moving film. Mackintosh[6] compared a sound-film presentation on *Water Power,* with a silent presentation of the film supported by a commentary prepared and given by the normal class teacher. He found that, provided the teacher's commentary was well prepared, he could achieve better results than the standard soundtrack, due no doubt to his greater familiarity with the students and their backgrounds. Experiments in London medical schools[7] compared an 8 minute silent film on *How To Inoculate a Plate* with live practical demonstrations. The carefully prepared film proved no more effective than the run-of-the mill demonstration. However, the film had greater practical advantages — more people could view at one time, they could view at any time, and as often as they liked.

In case we are accused of quoting only old research, it may be worth stating at this point that there is precious little recent research on the instructional effectiveness of film, or at any rate, precious little worth quoting. Most of the worthwhile research in this field was done before the war. Since then we have had a few experiments repeating and confirming earlier findings and a host of comparative studies so loosely controlled that one cannot in any way generalise from them.

Back in 1924 Freeman[8] reported on the experiments conducted at the University of Chicago in the early 1920's. This consisted of 13 individual experiments, representing the first systematic, experimental investigation of relevant instructional media variables and making the first use of experimentally designed media for this purpose. A few of the major conclusions were:

(a) The relative effectiveness of verbal instruction as contrasted with the various forms of concrete or realistic material in visual media depends on the nature of the instruction to be given and the character of the learner's previous experience with objective materials.

(b) The comparison of film with other visual media

(slides, still pictures) as a means of instruction when the medium variable is motion (eg a film showing the motion of a steamboat was compared with a still picture of the same object) indicates that the film is superior within a restricted range and type of content, but that outside this range the other media are as effective or more effective.

(c) The value of a film lies not in its generally stimulating effect, but in its ability to furnish a particular type of experience.

(d) It is inefficient to put into films actions which can be demonstrated readily by the teacher.

(e) In teaching science and how to do or make something, demonstration is superior to the film.

(f) Films should be so designed as to furnish to the teacher otherwise inaccessible raw material for instruction, but should leave the organisation of the complete teaching unit largely to the teacher.

(g) The teacher has been found superior to all visual media in gaining and sustaining attention.

(h) Each of the so-called conventional forms of instruction which employ visual media has some advantage and some disadvantage, and there are circumstances in which each is the best form to use.

Since then, little has been added to this list of findings. The results are consolidated by the extensive research during the 1950's sponsored by the U S Air Force, and reported later in this chapter. A review by Saettler[9] in 1968 found no new trends in research to that date and a recent review by Peggie Campeau[10] prepared for the Council of Europe, and covering all media research during the years 1966 to 1971, reported not one study in this field which satisfied her research criteria: carried out recently (1966-1971); completeness and availability (fully reported); sample at least 25 subjects per group; study at least one hour in duration; measures of effectiveness taken; statistical analysis carried out. A surprising finding, don't you think, when we consider the number of specialist magazines and journals filled every month with articles about film and its use.

Campeau argues strongly that, in any case, most research into film and indeed most media (with the possible exception of programmed instruction) is on the wrong track. Investigators are obsessed with comparisons of one medium against another for total courses, when they should be matching media to specific types of educational objectives. This is the argument laid out in Chapter 1 of this book — the argument supported by theoretical models such as those of Bloom, Gagné and others. However, even this is not all that new. Back in 1930, Weber[11] was arguing that we already knew all we ever would from comparative studies, and that future research should be conducted to determine optimum length content and treatment of the subject matter of films.

So the general picture emerges that cine film might enhance the acceptability of almost any presentation, but it only enhances the instructional value significantly if the material to be learnt involves the recognition or mastery of movements which cannot, for various reasons, be otherwise demonstrated. This is not by any means an argument for a reduction in the use of film in education. Most films are used as a general introduction to or summary of a topic. As such, their prime objective is to stimulate interest, motivate, paint the broad picture and establish certain attitudes — objectives easily achieved by the use of interesting photogrpahy and strong personalities.

We might add here that there are limitations to the research described above. Most studies, of necessity, measure the learning that has taken place by some sort of verbal or written test. Perhaps sometimes the apparent lack of learning is really a lack of ability to express verbally what has been learnt. Furthermore, many would argue (and there is evidence to support their argument) that the 'total involvement' produced by a good film might result in learning which is not capable of being tested verbally.

If the film objectives are of a specific training nature however, (eg to learn the names of parts or how to operate them) we should first carefully consider whether cine film is the ideal medium for presentation, and secondly show how the film should be structured to ensure efficient learning.

The systematic design of a training film

1 The objective

If we limit ourselves to training film we are back in the sphere of behavioural objectives — we should be able to define precisely the behaviour changes we wish to produce in the audience. In the light of research findings, film is most appropriate if these objectives involve the mastery or the recognition of movements. The correct motions to be used when filing may be learnt by watching a film and imitating. The principle of the Otto cycle can best be learnt from a demonstrated presentation showing the four strokes in sequence and then together. The fishing habits of the otter can best be learnt by observation — for practical reasons — on film. The objective of a film sequence will normally be one of the sub-objectives which are isolated during a task analysis.

2 The target audience

As with any presentation, one should ensure that the treatment used in a film is appropriate for the proposed audience — is the vocabulary used by the commentator appropriate; are examples or analogies referred to within the normal experience of the audience? For example, as discussed earlier, the use of graphs and tabular displays is not suitable for all age groups and intelligence levels.

In addition, specific photographic techniques may cause difficulty. Symbolic presentations and simplified diagrams do not always mean anything to young children. The treatment of time also causes problems. Brandy[1][2] found, for example, that the flashback technique was seldom understood by children under 12 years of age, and often caused problems with older children. He also found that all age groups gained much more from sequences involving action or imagery. Film sequences on abstract facts only worked well if heavily supported by introductory work. We see again that films cannot always stand on their own.

3 The method of use

Brandy's findings are supported by numerous other researchers, all indicating that a film is more effective if it is well followed-up by class work, even more effective if well introduced, and most effective if both introduction and follow-up are well planned and carried out. The basis for such systematic planning should be the task analysis of the subject being taught. From this we decide how the film should be used — whether, for example, the audience should simply watch the sequence of operations, or should imitate the movements — and also how it should be introduced and reinforced. Notes for the teacher, and perhaps supplementary written exercises, should therefore be planned at the same time as the planning of the film.

4 Photographic techniques

We have already mentioned some of the difficulties caused by symbolic, abstract or flashback techniques. In general, the treatment should be as simple and straightforward as possible.

In particular, one should consider the point of view of the camera shots. If an action is to be studied or observed, several points of view may be required. These should be selected because they are the views which yield most information, or which are normally encountered. For example, when explaining the action of a large machine such as a power press to a trainee, the most appropriate shots would be taken from the positions where the operator usually stands, as the film presentation then is closest to the 'real-life' situation that the trainee will eventually face. Unusual shots, such as a close-up of the hydraulic system or a bird's-eye view are only justified if they help to explain a vital theoretical point. The point of view is most important in film sequences used to demonstrate motor skills. If a man is expected to carry out the actions illustrated, it is a great help if they are shot from the point of view of the operator, rather than — as is often the case — from in front. Studies have demonstrated much more effective learning of manual operations when the film is shot from the operator's point of view. Indeed, shooting from in front often causes learning difficulties in the reversal of the process — right and left hands get muddled and so on. Incidentally, here we have one big advantage of the film medium, as in practice it is seldom possible to arrange a demonstration which can be observed from the correct point of view by more than one or two people at a time.

We might, at this point, mention some special photographic techniques which make the film medium particularly useful and versatile. The most important of these is slowing-down or speeding-up the action. Slow-motion photography enables the detailed study of movements and, by giving more time to the learner, is useful in the early stages of learning a motor skill. Single-frame photography enables long processes to be telescoped and presented in a short space of time. The technique has been used with great success in the fields of biology and chemistry, to illustrate such processes as plant or crystal growth.

One other technique which has proved effective over and over again in training films is animation. By this we mean in particular the animation of diagrams as, for example, the illustration of the flow of fluids or electricity in circuits. Such animated diagrams can be used to present visually processes which are not normally observable, or to simplify the visual presentation of observable processes by omitting irrelevant details.

5 The commentary

We have already discussed the need to use language appropriate to the target audience. Any new technical terms or names of parts will have to be defined before they are used. The function of the commentary should also be considered — if indeed, a commentary is necessary at all.

If the film sequence is attempting to teach a theoretical concept with the aid of pictures or animated diagrams, some commentary is almost always essential. As with still pictures and graphs, some explanation and some focussing of attention on the relevant points in the visual display is required to ensure efficient learning. These explanations can be on the sound track or as captions on the film. Excessive use of captions should be avoided — one cannot read them and attend to the visual display at the same time. They are very effective, however, in summarising key points or introducing new words. It is more efficient in general to supply a sound commentary. Research suggests that this might best be left to the teacher. However, this involves the teacher in studying the film and the supporting notes, and preparing a commentary carefully geared to the needs and abilities of his students. Human nature and the pressures on the teacher's time being what they are, it is perhaps optimistic to rely too heavily on live commentaries, so most films aiming to communciate knowledge have a recorded commentary.

Films which aim to demonstrate skills sometimes have no need for a commentary. The motions involved are often self-explanatory. Such films are usually short (though they may be watched over and over again in a loop projector), and have an introduction explaining the job, the components and tools used and their functions. The final training sequence merely demonstrates the actions to be learnt, and words of explanation are superfluous.

It should be noted that some training situations may require a sound track because of relevant noises associated with the subject being taught. For example, a dangerously overloaded electric motor or machine tool is often first recognised by the sounds it produces. By the time you see that something is wrong it's generally too late anyway (how sensible to demonstrate such danger symptoms on a film, rather than by a real-life demonstration, though of course other symptoms such as smells of burning will be lost).

6 Evaluation

Training films can be evaluated against their objectives in exactly the same way as other media. The evaluation of interest, stimulation or motivational effects is more difficult, as some valid measure of motivation (hours of private study per week?) must be found.

Evaluation against learning objectives can be more easily carried out. The existence of a precise behavioural objective implies that a valid test can be drawn up. If the audience performs well on this test after using the film, we celebrate — if they do not, we get the sack! To avoid this possibility, developmental testing of each film sequence can be carried out. As the draft script of each sequence is completed, it is 'acted out' in front of one native member of the target audience. He is then asked relevant questions or invited to perform relevant actions. If he is not successful, he is invited to ask questions. The script-writer uses the questions to identify where and why the sequence failed and modifies it accordingly. By using a series of three or four such guinea pigs, major bloomers are eradicated before filming. We make sure that we've got all the information in and kept most of the 'noise' out of the communication channel.

If the film uses animated diagrams, location shots, or other material which cannot be demonstrated 'in the flesh', then the developmental testing technique outlined can still help with the editing and of course the production of the commentary. With any luck, the final product should produce reasonable performance levels from the target population, without the need for extensive revision of the film.

The selection of off-the-shelf films

In many ways, the problems of selecting an appropriate training film off-the-shelf are similar to those of evaluation. One selects a film with the same objectives, aimed at the same type of student, and tests its effectiveness. However, off-the-shelf films are rarely explicit about their target population, and still more rarely have any statement of objectives, let alone one phrased in terms of student behaviour. There is no alternative but to sit down and watch it. Teachers have always done this, but all too often with a view solely to checking the factual accuracy of the material presented. While this is of vital importance, the factors of film structure we have discussed above are equally important in deciding whether a film is worth screening to your students. For example, if the objectives differ widely from your own, or if the commentary assumes vast amounts of pre-knowledge which your students do not have, then it is a waste of time to even attempt to use the film. Greenhill[13] produced, as part of an extensive study into instructional films, a set of questions the potential film user should attempt to answer when deciding the merits of a film.

The final version of his 'Film Analysis Form' contains 17 questions on the structure of the film, and 10 on the subject matter content. Each question can be answered as a matter of degree, and is rated on a 6-point scale. High scores indicate a strong yes, low scores — a strong no. The questions dealing with structure are:

*1   Are the objectives clear?

*2   Will the *target audience* find the film interesting?

3   Does the film build on previous knowledge, skills or experience of the target audience?

*4   Is the subject matter appropriate for the course of training?

5   Does the content relate directly to the main objectives?

6   Is the content presented in a well-organised, systematic pattern?

7   Are the important ideas or procedures clearly emphasised?

8   Does the film attempt to present too much material for the audience?

9   Are new facts, ideas, terminology or procedures introduced at a rate which will permit efficient learning (not too fast or too slow)?

10 Does the film provide for adequate repetition of the important content (eg revision, summaries, outlines)?

11 Is the method of presentation suitable to the subject matter?

12 Is the difficulty of the *pictorial presentation* appropriate for the target audience?

13 Are the details of the information or demonstration clearly presented pictorially (camera angle, lighting, close-up etc)?

14 Is the verbal difficulty of the commentary appropriate?

15 Does the commentator contribute to the effectiveness of the film (appearance, tone, manner, speed)?

*16 Is the sound track clearly audible?

17 Is the information presented in the commentary well integrated with that presented in the pictures?

Further questions on subject matter content are:

*1 Is the information *technically* accurate?

2 What is the relative importance of any inaccuracies?

3 Is the content up-to-date?

*4 Is the content specific (precise factual material rather than broad abstract generalisations)?

*5 Is it highly probable that the information or procedures presented will be confirmed by subsequent experience?

*6 Is it highly probable that the target population will be

able to *use* or *apply* the information or procedures presented?

*7 Is the subject treated more effectively than it would be through some other medium? (Lecture, demonstration slide film, textbook.)

8 Is it the most feasible or economic way of teaching the subject?

9 Does the kind of film used (colour or black and white) effectively show the essential details of the subject matter?

10 Does the film show common errors (in the performance of a skill), or common misconceptions (in understanding of theory), and how to correct them?

The answers to most of these questions are of course subjective. Individuals will differ in the exact rating given to a specific question. However, Greenhill found that if training was given in the use of the film analysis form, by practising on standard films, a surprisingly consistent and reliable level of rating was achieved. It is suggested that when rating a film, a low score (1 or 2) on any of the questions marked with an asterisk is sufficient to disqualify the film. Those without an asterisk are deemed less important and one or two low scores can be tolerated. The analysis form was originally developed for pinpointing weaknesses in film during production. It has, however, been extensively used for the systematic selection of off-the-shelf films. Finally, we should not ignore the possibility of using only part of a commercially available film. More and more film users are employing the technique of analysing a range of available films, and using only those parts which pass the test.

Film equipment

Most teachers and instructors are probably aware of the types of equipment available for film presentation. The large 35 mm format is seldom used. Most training films are available in 16 mm stock, but there is an increasing tendency towards 8 mm.

16 mm films

Films have been made in this format for entertainment and for training purposes since the 1930's. Initially the smaller size of the film limited the maximum size of image, and therefore the audience. Improvements in optics have overcome this limitation, and 16 mm film gives an adequate picture in all but the very largest auditorium. Silent and sound films are available. The sound tracks may be magnetic or optical. In practice this does not matter, as long as the projector you have can handle the type of sound track on your film. It's just as well to check beforehand. Many projectors will handle both types of sound track and these are obviously the ones to go for. In addition, it is best to obtain a projector with speeds for silent and sound film. The old silent films run at a slower speed. If run at the speed of the modern sound film, life seems to progress at a Chaplinesque pace and it's all over far too soon. High entertainment value, but doubtful educational merit. It is just as well to invest straight away in a multi-speed projector which will allow one to slow down or speed up certain sequences, or indeed to stop the film at any desired frame. A further facility which increases versatility and the control that the teacher can exercise over the presentation, is a socket for a microphone, enabling the standard commentary to be replaced by the teacher's own.

With these facilities the teacher may use standard films (or parts of them) in the most appropriate way for his teaching objectives. To regard the film medium as a 'canned' unvariable presentation totally out of the teacher's control, is to lose much of its teaching value.

8 mm and Super 8

Unlike the 16 mm format, 8 mm films do have a practical limit on the size of image which can be clearly screened. They are not therefore suitable for very large conference and lecture rooms. However, modern projectors have so improved that 8 mm films can now be effectively shown in quite large rooms, and are more than adequate in the typical classroom. Gone are the days when the image was limited to a 30 inch square. We can now project bigger images in full daylight conditions.

The 8 mm format is not yet all that popular in education and training. This is because there is such a lot of material already available in 16 mm, and most establishments are equipped for this film. However, the impetus behind the 8 mm movement is mainly from the home-movie market — potentially much bigger than the education market. The home-movie enthusiast is primarily interested in making his own films. The trend has therefore been towards the simplification of the cine camera. Today, a good 8 mm cine camera is simplicity itself to use. Every adjustment is automatic. Like Matt Dillon, you just point and shoot. It is through the production of special purpose training films, that 8 mm film has gained a foothold in education. Its use is liable to extend to off-the-shelf films as well, as the relative costs make it economical to buy a personal 8 mm copy of an often-used film rather than hire a 16 mm version. A further application of 8 mm which is boosting its popularity, as the concept loop film discussed later. The well-established 'Technicolor' range of concept loop projectors utilises a pre-loaded cassette giving a maximum film length of 4 minutes. An extensive library of cassettes is being built up in this format. Recently introduced projectors take a larger cassette enabling a longer film to be screened, and also incorporate a sound track.

The drive for sound and for better picture definition has led to the introduction of a 'Super 8' film format. There is a greater difference from the standard 8 mm film than the name implies. The image size on the film is larger — special cameras and special projectors are required. This apparent confusion in the 8 mm world will no doubt resolve itself in time.

Super 8 was introduced in 1965. The major difference is that Super 8 allows about 50% more room for each individual picture, mainly by reducing the size of the sprocket holes which, on Standard 8, are the same size as those used on 16 mm film. The normal speed for Super 8 film is 18 frames per second as against 16 frames per second with Standard 8. Both these differences help to give a rather better picture with Super 8. You may sometimes see a reference to Single 8. This is the name given by a Japanese manufacturer to his version of Super 8. The only difference from the projectionist's point of view is that Single 8 is on a thinner base, so that you can get more of it on a reel. But Super 8 is now coming available on the thinner base also.

Although there were many protests about the introduction of Super 8, there is now very little equipment made for showing only Standard 8. There is even less equipment available, other than second hand, for making Standard 8 films. Indeed, it may well be that within a few years Standard 8 will be in the same position as 9.5 mm now, supported only by a relatively small number of enthusiasts. However, a large number of dual format projectors are now available, for those who wish to change to Super 8 but have Standard 8 film they still wish to use. As long as one is using self-produced films, no equipment problem will arise, but as libraries of Standard 8 and Super 8 films grow in size, problems of compatability between film and projector will arise.

Sound systems

16 mm silent films are projected at 16 frames per second, sound films at 24 frames per second. The sound system used on professionally made 16 mm films is an optical one. The sound appears down the side of the film as a pattern of lines. As the film passes through the projector, this pattern is scanned by a photo electric system and turned back into sound. You have to use studio facilities to record optical sound. A number of 16 mm projectors also have a magnetic sound system. Here the sound is recorded on a magnetic stripe along one edge of the film, in the same way as on a tape recorder. Some projectors enable the user to record and

replay his own magnetic sound track. Others are designed only to replay a recording made on another machine. At present almost all 8 mm sound projectors use only the magnetic system.

The picture on a film is projected one frame at a time, so that the film is, in effect, jerked through the optical part of the projector. To replay the sound track, on the other hand, the film has to run continuously. This means that the sound associated with a particular picture is some distance away from it. In 16 mm the 'picture-sound separation' distance has been standardised. There are standards in 8 mm (different ones for Standard 8 and Super 8) but these have not been so long established and some projectors, identified in our list, do not conform to them.

Speeds and film capacity

As we have said, the 'standard' speeds for 16 mm are 16 and 24 frames per second. The standard speeds for Standard 8 were 16 and 24 frames per second, but a number of manufacturers have substituted 18 for 16 frames per second, particularly in dual format projectors. There are even one or two 16 mm projectors on which this has been done. Some projectors provide a variable speed control, so that films can be speeded up or slowed down. The ability to slow down a film, or to project still pictures, is useful in such things as skills analysis. When the film is stopped for the projection of a single frame, a loss of light is experienced because an additional heat filter is brought into use to prevent the frame being burned. Some projectors also allow for reverse projection, useful if one wishes to re-examine a section of film. On sound projectors it is often arranged that the sound track is automatically switched off during reverse projection.

Most 8 mm projectors take reels that hold 400 ft of film. This gives a little more than half an hour running time at 16 frames per second, 25 minutes with Super 8 at 18 frames per second. Most 16 mm projectors take 2000 ft reels, giving about an hour's show at sound speed, or an hour and a half at silent speed. Some, particularly 16 mm projectors, are designed to accept larger reels. This information is included in our list.

Many cine projectors now feature auto or self-threading facilities. In some cases this is a reel to reel section, in others the film is threaded automatically over the most tiresome parts of the threading course and attachment to the take-up reel has to be done manually. There are so many variations that it is wise to ask to use the equipment to see if it suits you. If a partially used film which has become damaged can be removed with ease from a self-threading projector so much the better.

Single concept loop films

Very often, a task analysis will pin-point certain concepts or skills which can best be mastered by watching a moving display or demonstration. In the case of skills, the learner may be required to imitate the demonstrator. In either case it is often necessary for the learner to watch the demonstration more than once. A film has advantages over other methods in that it can be readily repeated, and the details of a job can be seen equally well by all the audience. For example, it can give the whole audience the operator's viewpoint.

A technique which is increasing in popularity is the *concept loop film*. This is now generally in 8 mm form, and projected by a special loop projector. The method is not new, and 16 mm loop films have been used since well before the last war.

A loop film is so mounted that it automatically repeats itself. The two ends of the film are spliced together, and the film is so wound that it automatically re-winds. The 8 mm versions are wound in special cassettes. The earlier 16 mm loop films require special, often grotesque, attachments to the projector.

Concept loops may, as the name implies, present one phenomenon, or concept (eg the behaviour of a bi-metallic strip on cooling and heating). They are very effective when demonstrating some cyclic process, as they give the impression of a continuous film. Thus, the internal combustion cycle may be filmed once, and screened as a continuous process.

Loop film may also be used as a visual aid in the training of skills. The film repeats a set of actions, perhaps at slow motion, which may be studied by the learner. One of the

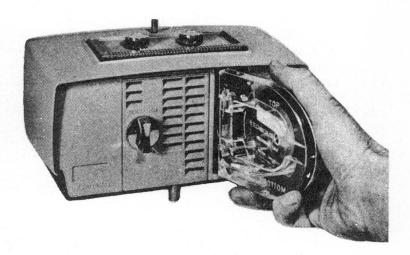

Figure 7.2 Technicolor 8 mm concept loop projector

Simple cassette loading, daylight projection, stop facilities make this a versatile training tool. Film length limited to just over 4 minutes. Both standard and Super 8 models available, supported by growing libraries of films.

earliest applications of such films was to athletic training, enabling one to watch at leisure (and as often as required) the finer points of the expert's technique. Now such films are increasingly being used to train industrial or craft skills. Often the learner imitates the film while watching. Loop films are available for training such diverse tasks as the use of a potter's wheel, the cutting of a mortice joint or the production of a screw thread on a lathe.

More likely than not, however, there will not be a loop film available for your requirements. In that case one source to consider is, as outlined earlier, a section of an existing long film. It used to be cheaper to obtain permission to use a section of an existing film, than to produce one from scratch. Now, with cheap 8 mm filming equipment, this is not necessarily the case. The short, single concept loop film is one of the easiest for the amateur to produce. The task is generally one which can be easily demonstrated and no complicated filming techniques are required. Often just one position of the camera is sufficient.

More important to success is the choice of suitable material for concept loops. At present these are generally silent films. The ideal topic is therefore one in which movement plays an important part, but where sound is unimportant. Furthermore, it should be one which we know by experience requires to be shown over and over to students to ensure understanding and mastery. Such topics abound, particularly in the training of motor skills. When used appropriately the concept loop is an effective training device which can save the teacher much repetitive instruction.

Film loop projectors

There were magazine loading cine projectors before the first single concept loop projector appeared in 1962, and there are still quite a number available, as will be seen from the previous section. But only the Technicolor system has aroused much interest in education and training. Certainly the support given to it by film makers in the past ten years is impressive. At first only Technicolor's own projectors were available, but now two British firms, ECEM and THD, have produced equipment that accepts the Technicolor cassette.

Because the loop projector represents education's major interest in 8 mm film, the introduction of Super 8 caused quite a stir, and British film makers attempted to make a stand against the new format. However, a growing number of loops are being made in Super 8, and Super 8 versions are being made of existing Standard 8 loops. For some extraordinary reason, while the normal speed for ordinary Super 8 projectors is 18 frames per second, Super 8 loop projectors run at 16 frames per second.

Recently, Bell and Howell, Eumig and other projector manufacturers have produced *cassette* loaded, automatic, Super 8 projectors, with a rapid-rewind facility. These may show long films in the normal manner, or may be used like a loop projector, at will, re-winding rapidly and re-playing a desired section of the film, of any length. Synchronised sound is also a feature. These projectors combine all the features of a high-quality projector for normal film, with all the qualities of a loop projector, save one — childishly simple, foolproof loading and operation. Where 8 mm film is used by the teacher or the mature student, these projectors are well worth considering though they are a bit too delicate and complicated for use by young children.

The screening of films

It is not the purpose of this book to teach the loading or operation of particular film projectors. There are, however, some general points. First, do we need blackout? The days of total blackout are over for good. It is generally an advantage to have partial blackout, or at least to avoid direct sunlight onto the screen. However, for many teaching purposes it is an advantage to use the minimum of blackout as it enables the teacher to exercise better class control, and the students to take notes. Some recent films require the audience to write down responses at certain points. Work rating films have used this technique for some time. More recently, 'programmed' films, requiring audience participation, have appeared on a variety of subjects.

Modern high-quality projectors, both 16 mm and 8 mm,

will give adequate images under daylight conditions, provided the size of the required image is reasonable. The use of a back-projection set-up gives excellent daylight viewing results. As mentioned earlier when discussing slide projection, the quality of the optical systems used has so improved recently, that the previous advantages of back-projection have been much reduced. Now, in a country like England where direct sunlight is a problem seldom encountered and easily overcome, back-projection does little to improve the image. It may of course hide the works and keep the projector noise down. These are both worthwhile advantages in the typical classroom where the projector is set up only occasionally. There is nothing so distracting as a lump of chattering machinery slap in the middle of the audience. Though back-projection helps, a separate projection room is better. The position of the speaker is also important. Ideally, it should be behind or below the screen. An alternative idea is to have two speakers, one to each side of the screen. Thus, the source of sound coincides with the image. If back-projection is used, this position also helps drown the projector noise.

The choice of screen was discussed in the chapter on slide projection. A matt white screen reflects the light in a wide angle. A beaded or silver screen reflects light more directly. It can therefore be viewed from a narrower angle, but gives a brighter image. For most cinema installations, where the front row is at a reasonable distance from the screen, and the room shape tends to be long and narrow, a beaded screen would be the right choice. For occasional use in a squarish classroom, a matt white screen will give better overall results at the cost of some brilliance.

Finally, one should not ignore the comfort of the viewer, particularly if a permanent cinema installation is planned or long films are to be used. The screen should not be too high for comfort, or so low that the front row obscures it. Seats should be comfortable, ventilation adequate. One is reminded of the famous research into subliminal advertising. Was the increase in ice cream sales due to the advertising flashes, or to the failure of the air conditioning plant?

References

1. J R Miles and C R Spain, *Audio-Visual Aids in the Armed Services,* American Council for Education, 1947.

2. L Furhammer, *Film Influence on Attitudes,* University of Illinois, 1963.

3. W A Belson, 'Learning and Attitude Changing Resulting from Viewing a Television Series "Bon Voyage" ', *British Journal of Educational Psychology,* Vol XXVI, 1956.

4. F E Brooker, *Training Films in Industry,* US Office of Education Bulletin No 13, 1946.

5. S Laner, 'The Impact of Visual Aid Displays Showing a Manipulative Task', *Quarterly Journal of Experimental Psychology,* Vol IV, Part 3, 1954.

6. D M MacKintosh, *A Comparison of the Efficiency of Sound and Silent Films as Teaching Aids,* Scottish Educational Film Association, Publication 3, 1947.

7. W H Hughes, P Collard and P N Cardew, 'The "How To Do It" Teaching Film, an Experiment in its Use', *The Lancet,* 1953.

8. F N Freeman (ed), *Visual Education,* University of Chicago Press, 1924.

9. P Saettler, *Design of Selection Factors in Instructional Materials: Educational Media and Technology* — Special issue of *Review of Educational Research,* April 1968.

10. Peggie L Campeau, *Selective Review of the Results of Research on the Use of Audio-Visual Media to Teach Adults,* Council of Europe, Strasbourg, Publication No CCC/TE (72) 5, 1972.

11. J J Weber, *Visual Aids in Education,* Valparaiso University Press, USA, 1930. Reported in reference (9).

12. W Brandy, *The Child Between the Feature Film and the Classroom Film* (in German), University of Munich, 1954.

13. L P Greenhill, 'The Evaluation of Instructional Films by a Trained Panel Using a Film Analysis Form', *Instructional Film Research Reports,* Vol II, US Instructional Device Center, 1956.

Further Reading

Use of Film
H C Butler, *8 mm in Education. Experimental Development Unit — Report No 5,* National Committee for Audio-Visual Aids in Education, 1966.

Gerald Fleming,'Language Teaching with Cartoons', *Film User,* June 1964, pp 284-287.

Louis Forsdale (ed), *8 mm Sound Film Education,* New York Teachers College, Columbia University, Bureau of Publications, 1962.

J A Harrison, '8 mm Sound in Education', *Visual Education,* July 1968, pp 54-55.

J A Harrison et al, 'Round Table Discussion on 8 mm', *Visual Education,* August/September 1968, pp 35-41.

8 mm Film Techniques
N Bau, *How to Make 8 mm Films as an Amateur,* Focal Press, 8th ed 1966.

J A Beveridge, *Script Writing for Short Films,* Reports and Papers on Mass Communication No 57, UNESCO, 1969.

Experimental Development Unit, *Practical Aspects of Sound*

Recording on 8 mm Magnetic Strips (Occasional Paper 8), National Committee for Audio-Visual Aids in Education, 1966.

D M Neale, revised by R A Hole, *How to Do Sound Films,* Focal Press, 4th ed 1969.

In addition, a series of further practical guides to the art and craft of film making is published by Focal Press.

Other Sources of Information

The most comprehensive source of information about films is the *British National Film Catalogue,* published by the British Industrial and Scientific Film Association, 193-197 Regent Street, London W1R 7WA. The subscriber receives quarterly details of newly released films in all gauges. At the end of the year this information is collected together in a bound volume. BISFA also produce, from time to time, subject catalogues. Less comprehensive, but also less expensive, is the list of new releases that appear monthly in *Audio-Visual* (formerly *Film User*). Indeed, the *Audio-Visual* synopses are so much more informative that some subscribers to the *Catalogue* also take *Audio-Visual. Visual Education* also publishes a monthly list of films of interest to educational users. If they don't already know it, even those with experience of using films will find much of value in Margaret Simpson's *Film Projecting — Without Tears or Technicalities,* published in 1966 by EFVA.

In 1967 the Educational Foundation for Visual Aids published a *Catalogue of 8 mm Cassette Loop Films.* Details of new releases appear monthly in *Audio-Visual* and *Visual Education.* The most comprehensive catalogue is the *Silent Film Loop Source Directory,* now in its sixth edition, published by the Technicolor Corporation and available free of charge from Technicolor Ltd, 20 Jermyn Street, London SW1. Loops produced in Britain, Canada, America and some other countries are listed under subject headings with an indication of the educational level intended.

Books on the making and use of 8 mm concept loop films are:

G H Powell and L S Powell, *A Guide to the 8 mm Loop Film,* British Association for Commercial and Industrial Education, 1967.

Commission on College Physics, *Production and Use of Single Concept Loop Films in Physics Teaching,* Commission on College Physics, University of Maryland, 1967.

Software—Sources of Commercially Prepared Film Loops

Camera Talks Ltd, 31 North Row, London W1R 2EN.

Ealing Scientific Ltd, Greycaine Road, Watford WD2 4PW.

EFVA, the National Audio-Visual Aids Library, Paxton Place, Gipsy Hill, London SE27 9SR.

Eothen Films (International) Ltd, 70 Furzehill Road, Boreham Wood, Herts.

Gateway Educational Films Ltd, St Lawrence House, 29-31 Broad Street, Bristol BS1 2HF.

Guild Sound & Vision Ltd, Kingston Road, Merton Park, London SW19.

Longman Group Ltd, Pinnacles, Harlow, Essex.

Macmillan and Co Ltd, Brunel Road, Basingstoke, Hants.

Rank Audio-Visual Ltd, PO Box 70, Great West Road, Brentford, Middlesex.

The Software—Catalogues of Films

We give below some of the major producers and suppliers of educational and training films. They all produce individual catalogues, although the *British National Film Catalogue* is the most comprehensive. The series of catalogues on Audio Visual Aids, produced by EFVA, are a useful source of information, classified under subject headings, allowing available films to be compared with other media on the topic.

Finally, EFVA also produce a *Classified Guide to Sources of Educational Film Material.*

BBC TV Enterprises Film Hire, 25 The Burroughs, Hendon, London NW4.

British Film Institute, 81 Dean Street, London W1.

British Transport Films, Melbury House, Melbury Terrace, London NW1.

CFL, Central Film Library, Government Building, Bromyard Avenue, Acton, London W3.

Concord Films Council, Nacton, Ipswich, Suffolk.

Connoisseur Films Ltd, 167 Oxford Street, London W1.

Contemporary Films Ltd, 55 Greek Street, London W1V 6DB.

Educational and Television Films Ltd, 2 Doughty Street, London WC1.

Encyclopaedia Brittannica International Ltd, 18-20 Regent Street, London SW1.

Gateway Educational Films Ltd, St Lawrence House, 29-31 Broad Street, Bristol BS1 2HF.

Guild Sound and Vision Ltd, Kingston Road, Merton Park, London SW19.

McGraw-Hill Publishing Co Ltd, Audio-Visual Department, Shoppenhangers Road, Maidenhead, Berks.

The National Audio-Visual Aids Library, Paxton Place, Gipsy Road, London SE27 9SR.

Petroleum Films Bureau, 4 Brook Street, London W1Y 2AY.

Unilever Film Library, Unilever House, Blackfriars, London EC4.

Manufacturers' Addresses — Film Projectors

Ambrico, 27th Street, Airport Industrial Estate, Stansted, Essex. 0279-4591

Bell and Howell A-V Ltd, Alperton House, Bridgewater Road, Wembley, Middlesex. 01-902 8812

British Films Ltd, 260 Balham High Road, London SW17 7AN. 01-672 6677

CZ Scientific Instruments Ltd, PO Box 2AR, Zeiss England House, 93-97 New Cavendish Street, London W1. 01-580 0571

Elf Audio Visual Ltd, Swinley House, 466 Bath Road, Cippenham, Slough, Bucks. 062-86-5353

Evershed Power-Optics Ltd, 214 Harlequin Avenue, Brentford, Middlesex. 01-560 6151

Hanimex (UK) Ltd, Hanimex House, 15-24 Gt Dover Street, London SE1. 01-407 8161

Johnsons of Hendon Ltd, 335 Hendon Way, London NW4. 01-202 8200

John King Distributors Ltd, Jew Street, Brighton, Sussex. 0273 27674

Rank Audio Visual Ltd & Rank Photographic, PO Box 70, Great West Road, Brentford, Middlesex. 01-568 9222

RCA Great Britain Ltd, Lincoln Way, Windmill Road, Sunbury on Thames, Middlesex. Sunbury on Thames 85511

J J Silber Ltd, 11 Northburgh Street, London EC1. 01-253 8031

Specto Ltd, Vale Road, Windsor, Berks. Windsor 61474

Manufacturers' Addresses — Film Loop Projectors
Fairchild - UK Distributors Gordon Cameras Ltd, 45 Kensington High Street, London W8. 01-937 3481

Taylor Halliday Developments Ltd, THD House, Peacehaven, Sussex. Peacehaven 5791

Technicolor Ltd, Bath Road, Harmondsworth, West Drayton, Middlesex. 01-759 5432

8   Television

There are two main ways in which television is being utilised by educators. In the USA, these are called *educational* television (ETV) and *instructional* television (ITV). The difference is best illustrated by the American situation. Commercial stations do not screen programmes for schools because schools do not advertise. A large number of special broadcasting stations have been set up to fill the gap by screening programmes which have some educational content. This does not necessarily mean that they are designed for certain students on certain courses, such as our own BBC broadcasts for schools. Most of the documentary and discussion programmes we see here at normal viewing times (including the independent networks) would in the USA be screened on the special ETV networks. Our BBC schools broadcasts would in America fall under the heading of instructional television and would probably be screened on a very local network, possibly a local school board's closed circuit system or at most a one-state system. We have now in Britain also a number of such local CCTV systems, for example in Glasgow and the Inner London Education Authority Network. Such local CCTV networks can screen general, broadly educational programmes, or programmes with precise instructional goals aimed at specific types of students.

When discussing the educational merits of TV, it is therefore more helpful to use a classification on the American lines, rather than to talk about open and closed circuit systems. We are not really concerned here with educational programmes in the ETV sense. Of course, such programmes are of immense value, particularly as stimulants of interest and awareness. The imaginative teacher can make good use of them, whether he screens them in the classroom or 'sets them for homework'. Much has been written on the methods of making the best use of such TV programmes. However, such use is always to some extent 'hit and miss' and relies for success on the skill and artistry of the individual teacher. Discussion programmes are seldom screened twice, so the teacher cannot evaluate the content before using them (unless he uses a videotape recorder). They are not supported by any notes for viewers. Nor indeed do they always have clear and precise objectives. Much of their value often depends on spontaneous discussion and a minimum of scripting. Muggeridge's recent series *The Question Why* (BBC1), may well have been an excellent education in how to argue round a point, or monopolise a discussion, and no doubt some viewers might have formed strong opinions on the topics discussed; but the teacher wishing to use such a series has no control over the opinions his students will form. Such programmes fall into the realms of general education. We are concerned here with producing specific learning. We are therefore interested in 'Instructional' or 'Training' uses of TV. The majority of schools broadcasts fall into this category, as do most programmes prepared by teachers or instructors for their own use. The principles of design and selection we would apply will be the same whether the programme is to be screened nationally or locally on a CCTV network.

Research: the instructional effects of TV

There has probably been more recently reported research on the use of television in education, than on any other medium. However, as Peggie Campeau[1] points out, most of it is subjective and poorly designed. Those studies which are properly controlled, generally repeat the pattern of 'no significant difference' found earlier in the bulk of research into film. There are hundreds and hundreds of reported studies comparing TV with traditional methods, but as yet no conclusive results.

For example, Chu and Schramm[2] carried out a review of 207 studies involving 421 separate comparisons. At the college and adult level, results of 235 comparisons indicated that 176 found no significant differences between televised and conventional instruction, 29 favoured television over conventional instruction and 30 favoured conventional methods.

Dubin and others[3] conducted a more rigorous review of studies in which experimental classes taught by television were compared with control classes receiving no televised instruction. They identified 42 studies that could be considered to be comparable on the basis of several criteria, namely, instruction lasted at least one term; identical, written course-content examinations were used for groups being compared; similar methods of instruction were experienced by both groups, etc. First, when teaching methods were matched, face-to-face instruction was only superior to *two*-way instructional television, and then only when the lecture method was used by each medium. ('Two-way' television provided students and lecturer with audio facilities for exchanging questions and initiating discussions, thereby approximating to a 'live' instructional situation.) Second, *one*-way instructional television produced the same amount of learning as face-to-face teaching by lecture, a combination of lecture-discussion-demonstration or discussion alone. Third, instruction by either method yielded no significant differences when the studies were grouped by the broad subject-area headings of humanities, social sciences and science/mathematics. In attempting to explain the odd finding that two-way television was definitely inferior to face-to-face teaching, the authors suggested that the need for students and lecturer to use the fairly complicated technical apparatus necessary for two-way communication may have been the cause.

The trouble with surveys of this nature, and with comparative studies generally, is that in looking at a mass of evidence concerning the 'total course' one may be masking real differences which exist between media for certain aspects of the learning which is taking place. By lumping together the results of a number of studies, one is aggravating this situation. The greater the sample of studies we take, and the more all-inclusive they are, the more likely we are to cancel out any differences which exist and to end up with 'no significant difference'. As Briggs and others[4] point out, we should be classifying studies according to the categories of learning taking place. But the 'traditional' categories as used by Dubin — humanities, science, etc — are not precise enough. We ought to be using such categories as procedures, discriminations, or concepts, as outlined in the opening chapter of this book. We ought also to be investigating learning differences between individuals.

Smith,[5] conducted a series of experiments on the effect of television broadcasts on the attainment and attitudes of students taking City & Guilds 'G' courses at technical colleges in England. The largest experiment involved students in 27 technical colleges watching a BBC television series on engineering science. Some students watched the broadcasts. The control group did not. In all, over 800 students were involved in the study, and were carefully matched for ability. There were no significant differences between groups on the attainment test used to assess the instructional effects of the two treatments. On the other hand, large and significant differences both in ability and attainment were found when the scores for individual colleges were analysed separately. The television broadcasts appeared to have a greater impact on students who were above average in ability and to have more effect on performance in mechanics.

Research of this nature suggests that there may indeed be differences between media which have been obscured in earlier studies. However, much more research at this 'micro' level is still needed before a comprehensive picture emerges.

Research: TV versus film

On the face of it there is little difference, from the audience's point of view, between a television or a cine film presentation. McLuhan[6] argues that the 'here and now' aspects of a TV image, coupled with qualities such as less precise definition, and presence in your own home, make the TV image a much more acceptable, and hence a much more powerful, medium of communication than the cine film.

There is evidence to support this view, particularly from measures of the relative success of advertising on the two media.

However, when both media are removed to the relatively artificial setting of the classroom or workshop, there seems to be very little difference. Mundy[7] compared the effect of television and film presentation of lessons in social studies and geography. He found no difference in the amounts learned through the two media. A similar French study[8] again found no significant differences in the respective effectiveness of TV and film in general, although those students who knew that the TV presentation was live did respond much more favourably to the presentation. They remembered slightly more and were influenced in their attitudes very much more than students who thought they were watching a TV recording. This finding tends to suggest that TV is a more powerful medium than the cinema ever was — not because more people watch television, but because people accept its message more readily, get more involved emotionally and are participants rather than observers.

One major use of instructional television automatically utilises this 'here and now' quality: the use of a CCTV system to increase the size of the audience, by allowing one teacher to address several classrooms or schools at once. We would normally arrange for someone technically competent and gifted as a communicator to deliver a carefully planned and prepared presentation. In addition however, if the speaker is known to the audience either personally or by repute, their level of involvement will be greater. A further personal touch which sometimes pays off is to provide for two-way sound communication between the speaker and the several classrooms, so that members of the audience may take part by question or comment. This is generally appreciated and enjoyed by the audience, though the research quoted earlier casts doubt on the instructional value of such a procedure.

This use of CCTV is valuable for economic reasons. It enables one to make the best use of highly skilled or qualified personnel, cuts down the need for duplication of expensive demonstration apparatus and allows a careful presentation to be viewed by many. The imaginative use of the TV camera can also produce a better presentation. For example, the use of close-ups can focus the audience's attention on particular points, or can blow-up the details of a demonstration so that all can see clearly. One can show an operation from the operator's point of view, or cut-in a pre-recorded sequence from a workshop to illustrate the relevance or importance of the task to be learnt. In short, the principles of design of instructional films, outlined earlier, can be applied to produce an altogether better presentation than would be possible in the 'live' teaching situation.

Any such presentation has, however, instructional limitations — the normal limitations of the large group lecture-cum-demonstration. Opportunity for participation by the audience is limited. It is impossible to diagnose and remedy individual weaknesses (one way of overcoming these problems is discussed later). The success of a CCTV course then, like films, depends very much on the preparation and follow-up carried out by individual teachers and students.

VTR

One further point. We are entering the age of cheap video-tape recorders (VTR's). Some training establishments already make wide use of the VTR to record 'live' lessons for later repetition. Soon the economics of the process will be much cheaper than filming — the technical problems involved much smaller, the time taken negligible.

For example, VTR's are being used very effectively in teacher training. Many establishments have for some time used television to watch in on a lesson, without disturbing the class by the presence of strangers. The teaching methods used can be discussed and the effects of specific techniques observed. We can see how the class begins to mimic a stutter or a nervous twitch on the part of the teacher, or how they are distracted by the way he fiddles with the chalk. 'But of course I never do that sort of thing --'. Now the VTR enables the teacher to see himself and his class immediately after teaching, to see his own distracting mannerism, the weaknesses of his presentation techniques. He can give another lesson at once, attempting to improve specific points. Studies[9] have shown marked improvement in communication techniques after only short exposure to one's own image. D Allen at Stanford University, California,[10] has developed the method into a semi-programmed technique, which he calls 'Micro Teaching'. Each student gives a 5 minute lesson on a prescribed topic (chosen to pose specific problems to the teacher). He then watches and criticises his performance with fellow students. Lessons are repeated till a minimum rating is obtained from the group.

This technique should find a place in many training courses — whenever clear communication is an objective. The video-recording, due to the speed at which it is produced, can be used to supply feedback on sounds and actions in the same way that the language laboratory supplies feedback on sounds only.

The VTR is of course also used for 'canning' lessons — either by the recording of professional programmes such as the BBC schools broadcasts, or the teacher's own productions. It is probably in this way that most of the 10,000 or so VTR's currently in use in education and training are employed. Most of these machines are relatively inexpensive and are capable only of black-and-white pictures. There is little research evidence to suggest that colour adds to the instructional effectiveness of a presentation, unless colour forms an essential part of the learning stimulus.

For example Kanner[11] reported two television studies he conducted to investigate the contribution of colour to learning by American Army trainees. The same televised instruction was presented simultaneously to two groups equated for aptitude. One group saw colour, while the other group saw black-and-white presentations. Immediate post-test results from both studies found no significant differences between treatment in 10 out of 11 comparisons over 11 different subject matters. However, as a spin-off from developments for the consumer industry, there is a drive towards the use of colour TV in education. Many LEA's are now ordering colour TV sets for their schools. Consequently there is an associated drive towards recording colour and this has been associated with the development of the so-called 'Cassette Revolution' and the production of the Video-cassette Recorder (VCR). Much commercial development is currently taking place in this field.

VCR

A recent survey[1 2] listed over 15 world manufacturers or consortia investing in the development of equipment to play back 'canned' or rather 'cassetted' programmes. Many of these projected systems are incompatible with each other and one hopes that they do not all become a reality or chaos will prevail, to the disadvantage of both consumers and manu-facturers. However only a few systems have so far been released onto an unsuspecting market, and there are signs that perhaps a modicum of standardisation around the Philips videocassette may be achieved.

Like the audio-cassette, the videocassette has the advantage of immediate slotting-in or take-out at any point, automatic threading, and therefore less chance of damage. The Philips VCR can play through most domestic TV sets, colour or black and white, with slight modification to the set. For educational purposes Thorn are introducing a VCR compatible machine suitable for use with a TV monitor and monitor-receiver or ordinary video camera, and without tuner. The Philips VCR model N 1500 has a tuner and clock built in for recording off-air and for use with a TV camera. Possibly the cassette will eventually take over from the open reel systems, but only if pre-recorded programmes become available.

Pre-recorded programmes

Although the facility to record off-air or make one's own programmes already exists in education, it is the introduction of pre-recorded videocassettes which will really create sub-stantial demand for the VCR concept. However, there are many problems. The problems most likely to inhibit, or at any rate slow down, the acceptance of the VCR in education are the usual ones of cost (particularly of the programmes, estimated at about £20 per half hour when produced in limited copies), compatibility of equipment, compatibility of objectives between teachers and programme producers and not least agreement among teachers themselves as to what should be 'canned' and how we should 'can' it.

Problems of compatibility

Unfortunately this progress has been marred by a lack of standardisation. All manufacturers now claim that recordings made on one of their machines can be played back on any other of the same model. This hasn't always been the case, and potential purchasers to whom this matters would be well advised to ask for a demonstration so that the claims made can be substantiated. Fewer manufacturers can claim that recordings made on different models in their range are interchangeable. Nobody claims that recordings made on someone else's machines can be re-played on his.

Of course, if you want to record broadcast educational programmes for use at some other time, or if you want to record a student's performance for subsequent analysis and comment, it may not matter at all to you that someone else won't be able to use your recordings. However, this lack of compatibility has inhibited the production of commercial video tapes and the establishment of tape lending libraries.

As a result, a video tape recorder by itself won't get you very far. You will need a programme source. This might be a broadcast receiver, which will probably have to be modified, or a TV camera. You will also need something on which to view any recordings you make. An ordinary receiver can be used with most recorders, but there are specially designed monitors which give better quality pictures. Insist on having a thorough trial under the conditions in which you will have to work, and satisfy yourself that the quality of the pictures you get on playback is sufficient for your purposes.

Running costs

All equipment costs money to run. Video tape recorders cost more money than many other visual aids. Most manufacturers give the life of tape as something like 100 'passes' through the recorder — that is, recording and re-playing 50 programmes or recording one programme and replaying it 99 times, or some equivalent combination. The tape doesn't suddenly wear out, but it does wear and the pictures you get will look as though there is a lot of interference. Tape really becomes expensive, though, when you begin to keep recordings because you think they might be useful in the future. Other consumable items are the recording and replay heads, which may have to be replaced after 500 to 1000 hours. Again, they don't suddenly become worn out — the picture gradually deteriorates.

On all VTR's and VCR's it is possible to record sound as well as pictures. On some of them it is possible to 'dub' or re-record the sound track while re-playing the picture. This makes it possible to add a commentary or to insert additional material. It is not easy to edit the video part of the recording. Generally this requires more expensive equipment and two recorders. On some recorders it is possible, on playback, to stop the tape for a time, to give a still picture effect. On the more expensive machines it may be possible to play back in slow motion.

We may look forward to the widespread use of video-tape recorded lessons in the future. Much of the repetitive teaching at present carried out 'live' will in future be 'canned' for instant retrieval from video-tape libraries.

But we should remember Mr Edison's 1920's forecast on the educational role of cine film, and the reality of today.

Only some of the 'fruits' of learning are suitable for canning and there are different canning processes depending on the desired end product. The effective use of CCTV and video-tape will depend on our knowledge of what to can, how to can it and finally how to serve it.

The research to date, as indicated above, shows little educational difference between TV recordings and cine film. The teacher would therefore apply essentially the same principles to the production or selection of material for TV as he would for film. (These principles are outlined in a previous chapter.)

Again we utilise the systems approach, of defining the problem by its objectives, and then analysing the subject, students and environmental constraints in order to prescribe the most appropriate solution.

CCTV on Indian reservations

As a case study of this approach we might examine the project being carried out by EVCO in Albuquerque, New Mexico.[4] Around Albuquerque there are a number of Indian Reservations. The problem was to run efficient courses on a wide range of subjects such as how to claim benefits, demand your rights or market your produce — one might classify them generally as *citizenship*. The objective stated generally was that the students should be better able to cope with the demands of modern American life.

The students were likely to be of various ages, with a wide range of intelligence and wide differing levels of mastery of basic skills, reading, writing, even speaking English. Furthermore, there were problems of culture and tradition. The reservations are widely scattered and isolated; traditionally, the Indians do not take well to timekeeping, attending classes regularly or leaving the reservations; finally their culture is based on symbolism and signs — picture writing is traditional.

What teaching methods would seem to be ideal for this problem? Consider where the course should be run, what size of groups, what teaching methods, what presentation media.

1 For both geographical and cultural reasons, the course must be on the reservation.

2 Small groups of students all at much the same standard. You cannot afford to bore or mystify anyone, or he will just stop attending classes.

3　Must be geared to continually assessing the progress of each individual, to make sure he is still in the appropriate group.

4　The methods must not be too verbal, relying heavily on illustrations, cartoon techniques, filmed sequences, etc.

Teaching programmes spring to mind at once. They can be used individually, progress is at the rate of the individual and continued assessment of progress is automatic. However, the typical programmed text or machine programme is ruled out, as it relies too heavily on the student's ability to read.

Teachers, supported by a film library, seem appropriate, but this is not a practical solution, as the numbers on any one reservation are not large, and anyway there is a shortage of teachers. Furthermore, the timetable that a teacher can operate is not sufficiently flexible for the Indian character.

Ideally, one needs a system which combines the qualities of a human teacher and visual presentation, with the flexibility and feedback of a teaching machine. A CCTV system, with certain additions, provided the solution. The reservations were equipped with mobile classrooms, capable of receiving one or more lessons at a time from a central studio in Albuquerque. Furthermore, the classrooms were equipped with a remote input (in the form of a card reader) connected to a central computer. At the central studio, there is a comprehensive library of films and video-tape. Each topic can be taught at different levels by choosing the appropriate 'canned' lesson. Each lesson ends with a test, to determine the students' progress. At the end of a lesson, each student sits the test by ticking alternatives on a specially prepared computer card, which he then 'posts' into the card reader. The central computer then marks the test and assesses, on the basis of the student's past record and his present score, the next appropriate lesson he should see. This may be an alternative, easier presentation of the same topic, a more advanced exercise, or a new topic altogether.

The system allows, through TV, the effective use of visual material; through the computer, instant assessment of progress; and through the use of a library of video-recordings, a course which adapts to the needs of the student and is available at any time convenient to him.

This brief description of a teaching system in the full sense, may serve to illustrate the processes of system planning. This is not the only solution possible to the original problem. It was deemed the best in the light of the constraints operating. A similar problem elsewhere, for example Africa, may call for altogether different solutions.

Similarly, a course developed for one industry may need revision before it can be applied to another industry, or even another firm within the same industry. It is well to remember that such revisions may not only be to the content, but equally to the teaching methods or presentation media employed.

CCTV equipment

This is a fast-developing field — probably the fastest of all. New equipment is coming on the market every week. In 1967, for example, the cost of a video tape recorder for educational use was reckoned in terms of thousands of pounds. Now we talk in hundreds. Even the equipment manufacturers have trouble in keeping their literature up to date. The most we can hope to do here is to point out the general trends and the characteristics to look for in equipment, and to list the better known manufacturers who may be contacted for the latest information.

Closed-circuit television involves basically, camera equipment and viewing or monitor equipment, linked by a cable, to give a 'closed circuit'. In practice nowadays, the term is sometimes used to describe systems which are not linked by cable, but by wireless waves over a limited area. The method is employed by a number of American school boards, often using an intermediate transmission station in an aeroplane to give wider coverage. Technically, such systems are really local broadcast or open-circuit systems, and we will not discuss them further, particularly as they are not much used in Britain though presumably the Open University transmissions come into this category. The problems at both ends of the system — camera and monitor — are in any case very similar whatever transmission method is used.

The monitor or receiver

The monitor, or viewer, is essentially a television receiver which picks up its signal from a cable or land-line rather than through an aerial. The signal may be at video frequencies, or at normal VHF frequencies. In the latter case, the monitor is no different from a normal TV, and in fact a standard receiver may be used by simply plugging the land-line into the aerial socket. This of course pre-supposes that the camera is compatible with the receiver. The most common rate of scan employed by closed-circuit cameras is 625 lines. So if you have a TV which receives BBC 2, you could have it modified to receive most CCTV signals. In practice however, it is better to use a special receiver designed for the job. For one thing, it will probably have a 27 inch screen size for classroom viewing. For another, it will give a better picture. Schools or training establishments already equipped with TV receivers for outside broadcasts may, however, find it economically attractive to utilise these as at least an extra or spare viewer in a CCTV system.

In addition to the large receivers, one for each remote classroom, one needs small monitors, one for each camera in use. These show the picture that the camera is focussed on, whether it is being transmitted or not. The producer of the programme may use several cameras in different locations. He will then have several monitors to keep his eye on. He refers to these to see how the programme is progressing and to select appropriate points at which to cut from one camera to another. Hence the name monitor. Further monitors may be used to show the producer the final product as transmitted and to keep other personnel 'in the picture'.

Obviously, the more complex the CCTV system envisaged, the more receivers and monitors are required and the pennies have to be watched.

The camera

Simple TV cameras which give adequate results when used as a visual aid (eg to blow up detail) are not very expensive. For more ambitious work a more versatile camera is required and the cost mounts. The cost of the tube itself may vary from £20 to £200 depending on quality. Also you do not get far without extra lighting, a selection of lenses (or a zoom lens), and at least one monitor. For one thing, the monitor acts as a view finder and check on adjustment combined. If the picture at the monitor is OK, it will be OK at the receiver — that is as long as no faults develop in the receiver or the connecting cables. You can only do without a monitor if you can set the equipment up before the class session, test the picture then and say a prayer. This is only really feasible if you are using the system merely as a visual aid to give the operator's viewpoint, or to show detail of a demonstration. Many modern cameras have built-in monitors.

As soon as more ambitious projects are attempted, you not only need monitors to keep tabs on what is happening, you also need more than one camera. If you wish to change your viewpoint, this can sometimes be accomplished by 'panning' or by coming in closer or by using a zoom lens. Skill is required to perform these actions. A safer way, and sometimes the only way, is to move and adjust one camera while the other is transmitting. When everything is under control, then you can cut to the new camera position. Few training presentations would need more than two cameras, but few would not benefit from the use of more than one.

By the time you have invested in a battery of cameras and monitors, you will need a camera crew, or alternatively, remote control. There is nothing about the system which cannot be adjusted by remote control. The only barrier is cost.

The installation

Many of the recently purchased small CCTV systems do not really warrant the title of an installation. One or two cameras, three or four receivers, and drums of cable are stored in a locked room and are pulled out when required — probably once a year about Easter time, and again on Open Day.

It is a quaint situation when a communication system whose main purpose is instantaneous live communication

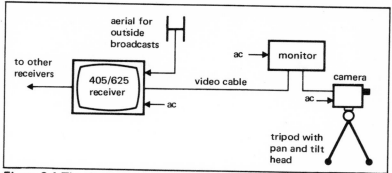

Figure 8.1 The simplest worthwhile CCTV installation

Camera requires setting up before lesson, but you can get away without an operator. Cost about £500 up.

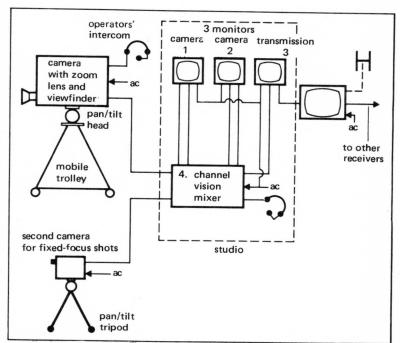

Figure 8.2 A simple studio set-up adequate for most instructional purposes

Requires two operators in addition to the 'actor' teacher, a studio and a certain amount of permanent wiring. Ideally, permanent land lines should be laid between commonly used classrooms. Cost £2,000 up.

between remote points takes several hours, perhaps days, to install for use.

A successful CCTV installation requires permanent land-lines, particularly if the several receivers are very remote from the camera. It also requires careful planning — from where are we likely to transmit, and to where?

Such an installation must be built up around a central studio. Most standard transmission would be screened from the studio, where facilities and equipment are available. Monitoring of programmes is also performed at the studio, preferably from a soundproof booth. Finally the studio acts as a switchboard. Cable from the studio to remote classrooms or workshops may be used as required for the transmission of programmes or for the receiving of signals from cameras 'on location'.

The planning of such systems is a complex operation and specialist help may be needed. Also, it can be expensive. If several remote centres are to be joined by land-lines, the cable costs may exceed the costs of the electronics.

Nevertheless, several CCTV systems are being successfully operated. In America just about every University campus and many a school board have installations. In Britain a pioneer full-scale installation is at Glasgow, where eventually nearly 300 schools and colleges will be linked to a central studio. A similar, more ambitious scheme is under way in the Inner London Education Authority, with the object of linking all establishments of Higher and Further Education within the Authority. The pay-off for the installation will be in terms of the extent and type of use made of it. Economical advantages will arise from the better use of teachers, laboratories and demonstration equipment. But the educational advantages will depend on how we use the system. It is not just a 'Teacher Amplifier'. The new medium calls for new teaching techniques. We see how few of our best professors make it as 'television professors' on the open channels. The secret is partly personality, but largely technique. Education is still learning the techniques which make for effective television communication.

The Open University

Whilst discussing the use of multi-media instruction, particularly instruction by television and radio, one cannot these days omit to mention the Open University.

This is the largest single application of a totally structured, systematically designed, multi-media course in Britain, and possibly in the world. It is a very new development in British higher education, and one which should be, and indeed is intended to be, a base for the systematic research and development of educational methods and media. It is also a very large and complex development, and to date has succeeded in highlighting some of the problems of applying a systematic approach to course design, rather than clarifying some of the answers. However, it is early days yet. The amount of data coming in from thousands of students is in itself a problem. In due course no doubt, some answers will also begin to emerge.

A comprehensive outline of the Open University, its structure, its problems and the way it is attempting to tackle them, was given by Professor Brian Lewis in a series of articles which appeared in the *British Journal of Educational Technology*[14]. The following is a short summary of some of the main points.

1 Course structure and production

The Open University is the newest and most unusual of British universities. It has the same legal status as any other British university being granted a Royal Charter in 1969.

Degrees are obtained by accumulating one or two course credits per year. Each course credit takes about 10 hours of study per week (over a period of about 36 weeks). Six course credits secure a general (BA) degree, and eight course credits an honours (BA) degree. In certain cases, students may be exempted from some of the lower-level courses, and this will reduce the time needed to qualify. In the first year of operation, the University initiated degree courses in the Arts, Sciences, Social Sciences, and Mathematics. In its second year of operation (1972), degree courses also started in Educational Studies and Technology.

In its efforts to offer higher education to as many adults as possible, the University has waived many of the traditional entry requirements. It therefore caters for a large number of people who might otherwise be discouraged (or prevented) from pursuing degree courses.

Study materials are parcelled up and sent through the post to the student, at intervals of about 4-6 weeks. Each package contains a sequence of correspondence and other materials, accompanied by study notes, private exercises, and self-administered tests which the student can take to help satisfy himself that he has understood the main teaching points. Also included are a set of written homework assignments which the student is expected to return, within a specified time period, for marking. So far as is possible, each package is self-contained. Assignments may be marked by tutors or may be computer-marked.

To reinforce and supplement the package study materials, the University is collaborating with the BBC to produce a regular series of radio and television programmes. These appear on Radio 4 and on BBC 2.

When the University was first established, attempts were made to predict the number of academic members of staff that would be required to produce a course within the space of one year. This estimate supposed that each member of staff could produce 4-5 weeks work for the student (out of the 36 weeks work required) and still have enough time to spare for the kind of postgraduate and private research activities in which academics normally engage.

The estimate proved to be wildly optimistic. Just one week's teaching materials can take 12-15 weeks (working 5 days a week) to produce. Experience has shown that it takes at least a dozen academics, working virtually full-time, to produce a complete 36-week course. And, even then, they are too rushed to do a really good job. It would be more realistic to set the estimate at 18-20 academics per one-year course.

In addition to acute time pressure, the Open University is also under severe economic constraints. If money were less important, academic members of staff could afford, for example, to drop the idea of hurriedly concocting a one-volume Reader. They could arrange, instead, for the last-minute inclusion (in the student's correspondence package) of carefully selected offprints. Such an arrangement would give them more time to select the best possible background reading material. But the cost would be very much higher.

Another fact of life is that different academics have different working methods, and different views of the educational enterprise in which they are involved. One member of staff might be enthusiastic about computer-marked objective tests, whereas another might deplore them. One academic might prefer to write in a friendly and egalitarian manner, whereas others might adopt an impersonal approach.

All these differences proliferate if we start to consider the additional problems of television and radio production. Suppose, for example, that an academic agrees to write 4 successive units. This generally means that he has also committed himself to preparing 4 successive television and radio programmes.

In order to plan and produce a complete course of 36 units, it turns out that several hundred quite complicated decisions have to be taken. As an aid to efficient action, special charts are needed to enumerate what these decisions are, and who should take them, and why and when, etc.

However good the home study materials may be (and not all of them are good), it takes a great deal of willpower to work away at these materials, week after week, on one's own. There is consequently a need for special 'support' activities which can spur the student on, and can help to clarify points of difficulty. The regular weekly broadcasts on radio and television about the courses are mainly designed for this purpose. Most of these broadcasts are subject-matter orientated (television demonstrations of scientific equipment, for example) and are usually made several months in advance of transmission. They reinforce and amplify the correspondence materials and provide students with a clearer idea, or a fresh view, of what the correspondence materials are trying to achieve.

A different kind of support activity, but outside the student's home, is provided by the University's system of study centres. About 250 of these are now in existence. All centres are equipped with radio and television receivers. Many of them also contain tape recorders, projectors, a library of the broadcast material in recorded form, and computer terminals for the use of mathematics students. Each centre is regularly visited by specially appointed class tutors and counsellors.

As a further strengthening of its teaching programme, the Open University is currently requiring all first-year (Foundation Course) students to attend a one-week residential Summer School for each course that they are taking.

2 Problems of planning and control

At the present time, the University does not have a 'total systems approach' to its planning and production problems. Moreover, it is not entirely clear where it would be best to begin, in order to develop such an approach. In practice, it is usual to start with those parts of the overall system that are likely to give the most trouble. It also makes sense to focus on the most dominant sub-systems, ie those parts of the overall system to which the remaining parts are obliged to adapt. The planning, control and trouble-shooting within the system is aided by the use of network analysis techniques.

At first glance, the methods of critical path analysis appear to be eminently suitable as a tool for guiding course production. In this method, a complex task is broken down into component subtasks. By attaching a time estimate to each subtask, and by deciding which subtask must of necessity await the completion of which other, and by further investigating the implied demands on resources of various types, it is possible to determine an 'optimal' way of tackling the task as a whole.

For certain kinds of project, especially in the field of engineering, network planning can be very effective indeed. However, it is optimally effective if, and only if, some fairly stringent conditions are satisfied. For example, it must be possible to break down the overall task into subtasks for which accurate time estimates can be obtained. It is also important to be able to specify the relationships and dependencies that exist among the subtasks. And it is important to be certain that each specified subtask will actually occur, and that the persons involved in the project will not have occasion (in the light of ongoing feedback) to revise their plans at any stage. Network planning methods have achieved their greatest success in projects for which conditions of the kind just listed can be satisfied. Unfortunately, very few of these conditions can be satisfied by the average Open University course team. Pending the development of more sophisticated techniques, the Open University is struggling with an assortment of rather conventional tools.

It is also worth bearing in mind that some of the greatest obstacles to course team efficiency are psychological, rather than logistic. In general, course teams are unlikely to feel committed to a planning and scheduling scheme that is imposed upon them from outside.

3 Problems of assessment and evaluation of materials

The Open University, more than any other university, needs a powerful assessment system. The sheer novelty of its teaching methods, and the exceptional nature and size of its geographically-scattered population, makes it imperative to discover (in as much detail and depth as possible) how successful its teaching is.

In recognition of the importance of this problem, the Open University has established an Examinations and Assessments Committee whose main job is to advise and take decisions on the practical handling of the examination and assessment procedures that the University is either using, or proposing to use in the near future. In addition, the Open Univeristy's Institute of Educational Technology (IET) has set up a small working group to examine the problem of assessment in more general terms, and to make recommendations for improving upon current practices in the years to come.

There are several major purposes (and many more minor ones) that a comprehensive system of assessment might reasonably be expected to achieve:

1   From the point of view of *students,* the assessment

system might be expected to tell them how they are getting on.

2 From the point of view of the *University,* the assessment system might be expected to reveal how successful the University's teaching has been. In particular, it might be expected to provide useful guidelines for the future design or revision of courses.

3 From the point of view of the *potential employer,* assessment procedures might be expected to generate a reliable statement of what individual students can be expected to know and to do after completing their courses.

All these expectations are not entirely compatible with one another. Also, evaluation costs money (they have little) and time (they have even less). Thus materials are only sometimes pre-validated before distribution to students. Over the years, however, feedback from·students will be used to revise and improve existing materials.

References

1. Peggie L Campeau, *Selective Review of the Results of Research on the Use of Audiovisual Media to Teach Adults,* Council of Europe, Strasbourg, Publication number CCC/TE(72)5, 1972.

2. G C Chu and W Schramm, *Learning from Television: What the Research Says,* Stanford University Institute for Communication Research, 1967.

3. R Dubin, R A Hedley et al, *The Medium May Be Related to the Message: College Instruction by TV,* University of Oregon, Center for the Advanced Study of Educational Administration, 1969.

4. L J Briggs, P L Campeau, R M Gagné and M A May, *Instructional Media: A Procedure for the Design of Multi-Media Instruction, a Critical Review of Research, and Suggestions for Future Research,* American Institutes for Research, Pittsburgh U S A, 1966.

5. I M Smith, 'Experimental Study of the Effect of Television Broadcasts on the G Courses in Engineering Science' — Parts I and II in *The Vocational Aspect,* Vol 20, nos 45 and 46, 1968.

6. M McLuhan, *Understanding Media: The Extensions of Man,* McGraw-Hill, 1964.

7. P G Munday, *A Comparison of the Use of Television (BBC) Programmes for Schools and Sound Films as a Teaching Aid,* M A Thesis, University of London, 1962.

8. M Tardy, *Live Television and its Pedagogical Implications,* Ecole Normale Superieure de Saint-Cloud, 1963 (French).

9. S Bertran, *Research into the Use of Closed-Circuit Television for the Training of Teachers,* Centre Audio-Visual, Saint-Cloud, 1962 (French).

10. D W Allen and K A Ryan, *Microteachings,* Addison-Wesley, 1969.

11. J H Kanner, *The Instructional Effectiveness of Colour in Television: A Review of the Evidence,* ERIC Clearinghouse on Educational Media and Technology, Stanford University, U S A, 1968.

12. P Hale, 'Summary of Video/Cassette/Disc Systems', pp 386-387 in A J Romiszowski (ed), *APLET Yearbook of Educational and Instructional Technology 1972/73,* Kogan Page, 1972.

13. D A De Kort, *Television in Education and Training,* Phillips, 1967.

14. B N Lewis, 'Course Production at the Open University — I Some Basic Problems; II Activities and Activity Networks; III Planning and Scheduling; IV The Problem of Assessment', four articles in the *British Journal of Educational Technology*, Vol 2, No 1, January 1971; Vol 2, No 2, June 1971; Vol 2, No 3, October 1971; Vol 3, No 2, May 1972.

Further Reading

Raymond S Adams and Bruce J Biddle, *Realities of Teaching: Explorations with Videotape*, Holt, Rinehart, Winston, 1970.

W R Borg et al, *The Mini Course: a Microteaching Approach to Teacher Education*, Far West Laboratory for Educational Research and Development, Collier-Macmillan, Toronto,' 1970.

R M Diamond, *A Guide to Instructional Television in Britain*, McGraw-Hill, 1965.

G N Gordon, *Educational Television*, Prentice Hall,

B Groombridge (ed), *Adult Education and Television*, National Institute of Adult Education and Unesco, 1966.

J D Halloran, *The Effects of Mass Communication with Special Reference to Television*, Leicester University Press, 1964.

H Lynch, *Handbook for Classroom Videotape Recording*, Southeastern Educational Corporation Inc, 3450 International Boulevard, Atlanta, Georgia 30354, 1969.

W R McAleese and D Unwin, 'A Bibliography of Microteaching', *Programmed Learning and Educational Technology*, Vol 10, No 1, January 1973.

NECCTA, *Bulletin*, National Educational Closed Circuit

Television Association, Dean Centre, Belford Road, Edinburgh EH4 3DS. Quarterly.

A Perlberg, 'Microteaching: a New Procedure To Improve Teaching and Training', *Journal of Educational Technology*, Vol 1, No 1, January 1970, pp 35-43.

W Schramm (ed), *Educational Television: The Next Ten Years,* Institute for Communication Research, Stanford, 1962.

J Scupham, *Broadcasting and the Community,* Watts, 1967.

UNESCO, *Television for Higher Technical Education of the Employed,* Mass Communication Report No 55, HMSO,

The Software: Sources of Videotapes

Since videocassettes are still more or less in their early days, details are not at present available of potential sources of pre-recorded programmes. The position as regards videotapes is not much better. No commercial organisations produce videotape programmes for general sale in any large quantities. Two small exceptions:

(1) There is one useful source of information available on videotapes at present. This is the *Helpis* (Higher Education Learning Programmes Information Service) catalogue which is produced by NCET, and is obtainable from Councils and Education Press, Queen Anne Street, London W1. This lists learning materials produced in British Universities and available (often on an exchange basis). Most of the material is on videotape. Of course, one must ensure that one's playback machine is compatible with the original.

(2) The Open University films, mentioned elsewhere in this chapter can also be obtained on videotape 'to order'.

However the VTR remains essentially a device where the user produces his own materials.

The Hardware — Manufacturers' Addresses

Ampex Great Britain Ltd, Acre Road, Reading, Berkshire. 0734 84411

Bell and Howell Ltd, Alperton House, Bridgewater Road, Alperton, Middlesex. 01-902 8812

Dixons Electrical, 3 Soho Square, London W1. 01-437 8811

Grant & Taylor, Arlington House, South Mimms, Potters Bar, Middlesex. 01-766 2288

International Video Corporation, Cheapside, Reading, Berks. Reading 581571

Phillips. Electrical Ltd, Century House, Shaftesbury Avenue, London WC2. 01-437 7777

Pye TVT Ltd, Addlestone Road, Weybridge, Surrey. Weybridge 45511

Shibaden (UK), 61-63 Watford Way, Hendon, London NW4. 01-346 7211

Sony UK Ltd, 11 Ascot Road, Clockhouse Lane, Bedfont, Middlesex. Ashford 50021

Teletape Ltd, 11 Redvers Road, London N22. 01-888 0152

Top Rank Television & Rank Audio Visual, P O Box 70, Great West Road, Brentford, Middlesex. 01-568 9222

9 Teaching Machines and Programmed Instruction

If you followed the correspondence on teaching machines and programmed instruction in the educational press a few years back, you might be excused for forming a conception of a teaching machine as some form of robot teacher which is threatening to take over our schools. As programmed instruction and teaching machines have become more familiar, this fear has subsided and attitudes have swung to the opposite extreme. There has developed the view that teaching machines are a gimmick, a passing fad which will soon die out as the 'laissez-faire' classroom did beforehand. As in most extreme views, there is a grain of truth. After all, in most applications of teaching machines, the teacher does abdicate a certain part of his task to the machine, just as he does when using a film or a radio broadcast. Similarly it is true that much of the early over-enthusiasm and over-promotion of the teaching machine concept has left a bad taste in the mouths of many users who have found that not all the claims made are substantiated.

Much of the initial over-enthusiasm and its associated fears, and much of the present disenchantment have arisen from a basic misunderstanding of teaching machines and their use. Their name has not helped as it suggests a machine which simulates the teacher. In practice, the machine simulates only one function of the teacher — that of presenting material to the student. Other equipment such as film projectors or television also do this. Teaching machines are just another of the many presentation media at the disposal of the teacher, and are just as much under his control. In all cases it is the material presented (the programmes) which determines the effectiveness of the presentation. As we have seen earlier, using different presentation media (eg film versus television) to present the same material only influences results marginally.

The main difference between teaching machines and other media is the structure of the material they present. Teaching machine programmes are structured according to very different principles from the typical film or radio programme. These are the principles of programmed instruction. To understand teaching machines, indeed to be able to define what they are, one must first understand these principles.

Traditional programmed instruction

The first chapter outlined some of the history and research behind programmed instruction. It discussed the main principles and showed how the 'self-correcting systems' approach to course-construction developed. We will now consider some of these principles in greater detail and examine some of the end products.

Basically a teaching programme is a course prepared as a result of an intensive analysis of the learning task. It is generally presented to the student one stage at a time. Each stage presents information and demands a response from the student. He may be required to answer a question, make a decision or practise a procedure. The response that the student makes has two functions. Firstly it ensures that he is actively involved in the learning process and practises the tasks he is to master; secondly it provides a measure of his progress. This measure can be used by the student as knowledge of results, or by the course designer (programmer) to identify and remedy weaknesses in the teaching programme.

The pattern of responses demanded from the student should first and foremost be relevant to the terminal behaviour expected (performance on a job, skill at problem solving etc). Much of the work described in Chapter 1 is concerned with the types of responses most relevant to different types of learning tasks. Task analysis and the systems approach have as their cardinal aim, the design of appropriate relevant training exercises.

37 You have also learnt of two methods of using a lathe to carry out boring operations.

tool post

(1) Work in chuck or on faceplate, boring bar in _____ . (work revolves)

■ ■

saddle

(2) Boring bar in chuck or spindle, work on _____ . (tool revolves)

---

38 Whether the work is mounted on the faceplate or on the saddle depends on the _____ and _____ of the work.

■ ■

size

shape

(either order)!

---

39 Where would you mount the following workpieces for boring the holes marked X?

(A)   faceplate

■ ■

(B)   saddle

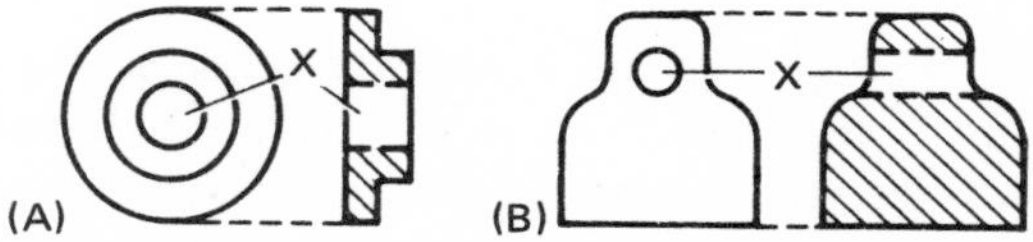

(A)   (B)

---

40 This cube could be mounted either on the chuck or faceplate, or the saddle.
Where would you prefer to mount it if it was
(a) a one inch cube?
(b) a 12 inch cube?

(a) chuck or faceplate

■ ■

(b) saddle

Figure 9.1 A linear programme sequence

This is an excerpt from *Boring Bars and Tools* published by International Tutor Machines.

At this point the trainee revises a previously learnt principle, then applies it to several problems. This programme is used in a Grundymaster teaching machine, which keeps the correct responses hidden until the student has made his own attempt. (© A J Romiszowski, 1967)

However, the response must also be capable of evaluation. The student must be able to judge his response for accuracy; to compare his own effort with a master model. The programmer must be able to judge the responses in order to identify weaknesses in the programme. In the typical programme this may happen in two ways.

Linear programmes

The student may be presented with the correct response immediately after he has made one himself. More often than not, he is obviously correct and proceeds to the next stage (or frame, to use the technical term). If there is a discrepancy, however, he must judge whether his own response is equivalent. If it is not, he must re-read the frame and attempt to resolve the difficulty before proceeding. In either case, he eventually proceeds to the next frame in the sequence — a linear sequence of frames. It is the task of the programmer to ensure that the difficulty of this linear sequence does not increase at a greater pace than the typical student can handle. Otherwise the student will find himself in a situation where he gives a wrong response, and cannot see why it is wrong. The programmer achieves his aim by testing sequences of his programme on sample students. If any response tends to cause difficulty, the reason is investigated and the sequence modified, by adding extra practice material, re-wording, supplying extra help in the form of prompts, etc. The result is the typical linear programme: a large number of relatively small frames, studied in sequence by all students (who rarely make wrong responses).

Branching programmes

Another approach open to the programmer is to present the student with several alternatives. The student may make a response and then compare it with the selection, or he may simply be required to choose the correct response from a selection. If he chooses correctly, he proceeds to new materials. If he chooses incorrectly, he is branched to a remedial frame or sequence of frames. In the branching programme, it is not so important that every student can at every stage respond correctly or indeed judge the accuracy of

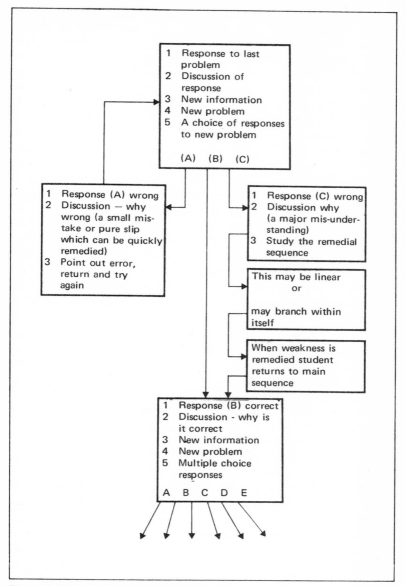

Figure 9.2 Typical branching strategies

The teaching frames may be arranged as scrambled pages in a book or may be filmed for use in a machine, such as the Autotutor.

his responses. Those who cannot, are routed to extra material where they receive alternative explanations and further practice before re-joining the main stream of the lesson. The task of the programmer is to suggest a selection of possible responses which are plausible, which students do occasionally make, and which (if made) point to specific weaknesses or misconceptions on the part of the student. This is not an easy task. To do this he may draw on the logic of the subject, on past teaching experience and, as in the case of linear programmes, on the results of using his programme with sample students.

Programme writers now tend to use both linear and branching techniques. It depends very much on the subject. When learning new words in a foreign language, for example, there are seldom any plausible wrong answers worth following up. Either the student can tell you the meaning of 'plafond' or he cannot. If a student selects a 'plausible' alternative such as 'walls, floor, door' instead of 'ceiling', it tells the programmer little about the student's trouble, except that he is confused. It does not help to produce remedial material. There is some reason to believe that presenting such a choice may in fact help to confuse the student. He may choose incorrectly, and thus practise and perhaps memorise an incorrect response. There are other subjects however, such as fault-finding on machinery, or some types of problem solving, where specific incorrect approaches are well worth following up, and the student may learn much from his mistakes. These are ideal material for a branching programme.

Whatever the technique used to produce the programme, what we end up with is a series of units or 'frames' to be presented to the student. The final structure is always determined by the process of 'trying it out on the dog', ie, it is validated and revised until a sufficiently high level of learning is consistently achieved. Once this final version is produced, it can be used confidently with successive groups of students. It is the fact that the course and the end results can be reproduced which is one great attraction of programmed instruction. Also, it is the characteristic which limits its use to certain applications. Finally, it is the characteristic which makes it feasible to present the programme automatically, by some form of teaching machine.

Types of teaching machine

We see therefore that a teaching machine is simply some form of presentation device which is designed or adapted to present a programme. It may be a simple device which presents one frame at a time whilst keeping the correct response hidden until the student has made his own attempt; or it may be a sophisticated electronic machine which can cope with the presentation of complex branching programmes. Although most teaching machines are akin to projectors, presenting written material and diagrams, our definition does not exclude devices which present audio-programmes, or which communicate through the other senses. Nor does it exclude very simple presentation devices, such as books. It is a functional definition.

1 Linear machines

These are generally simple devices. The programme is printed on a continuous roll of paper, or on separate sheets, and is loaded into the machine, the sole purpose of which is to control the presentation. The student, by winding a handle, can move a fresh frame into view. The correct response to this frame is hidden by a blanked-off portion of the window. The student reads the frame, and writes his response on a roll of paper which is mounted below another window in the machine. He then winds the handle till the correct response appears, and compares it with his own effort which is by then under a transparent perspex window. Thus the learner must commit himself on paper and cannot later alter his response. He can however, if his response is incorrect, re-read the relevant frame (which is still exposed) and resolve his misconceptions before proceeding. This machine therefore differs from text presentation of the same material in the degree of control exercised over the learning process. The student must commit himself in writing, he cannot 'cheat' and he cannot go backwards through the programme by more than one frame. Other linear machines may differ slightly. Some allow the student to wind back to earlier sections at will, others have no synchronised answer roll. In their simplest form they become no more than page-turning devices.

One can of course present a linear programme on film. There are a number of machines which use 35 mm or 16 mm film strips. They have practical advantages of small easily-stored programmes and better colour diagram presentation, somewhat offset by increased machine size and cost. One can also present linear audio-programmes on specially adapted tape recorders, which stop automatically after every unit of presentation. A recent development is to present audio-visual (or multi-media) programmes, by the use of synchronised tape and slide equipment, described earlier, or by special machines in which the tape stops automatically after every instruction to allow the student to respond. The student may take as long as he needs to complete his response and may then proceed by pressing a button, or if he needs to, he may re-wind to hear the instruction again. The audio-visual technique has been found useful particularly in the training of industrial operatives who do not readily learn by reading.

2 Branching machines

One should rather refer to these as machines with facilities for the presentation of branching programmes, as they will all present linear sequences as well. A typical example, the Autotutor, is illustrated on p 253. The programme is stored on 35 mm film. The machine is basically a mammoth film-strip back-projector, capable of storing a film of 1000 or more frames (hence the term 'frame' for a unit of presentation). A series of buttons on the machine coupled to relays and controlled in part by coding on the film, enable the student to proceed to several alternative frames at any one time. Thus students needing remedial material are routed to sub-sequences in the programme, and then automatically return to the main stream. A branching programme can be presented in a textbook, by instructing the student to proceed to alternative pages depending on his choice of response. The machine may exercise more control over the learning by arranging, for example, that once a student finds himself in a remedial sequence, he cannot opt out and return to the main sequence except by following through the prescribed work.

Branching audio-visual programmes are less common, but machines have been devised which can cope with such presentations. They take the form either of modified 4-track tape recorders, using one track of the tape for information and one for control impulses to wind on or back, or a standard type of teaching machine modified to operate tape recorders or loop film projectors by remote control.

3 Adaptive machines

This third category of teaching machines is very different from the previous two. So far our machines have simply presented a programme. The programme was fixed in advance. It was written or selected by the teacher, and the only part of the teaching function entrusted to the machine was that of presentation. An adaptive teaching machine takes over a much bigger slice of the teaching function. SAKI, which we described in the opening chapter, is the classic example of an adaptive machine. The programme is a set of exercises of progressive difficulty, demanding student responses (in this case the punching of the correct data onto cards). The form of these exercises is not fixed however. There are three separate components in the exercise: the speed of presentation, the content, and the amount of visual prompting supplied. Each component is varied by the student's performance. Thus when at a certain stage in his course the student makes a mistake in, for example, punching the number 6, he is subsequently given more practice on 6 than on the other figures; he is given longer whenever 6 appears, and he is given more visual cueing by the position of the 6 lighting up on the simulated keyboard. As the lesson progresses and the 6 is mastered, these learning aids are withdrawn. The exercises a particular student performs are adapted automatically to his needs by his own performance. There is no reason why any two students' lessons should be the same. Such a machine does (for a certain specific learning task) take over all — or nearly all — of the functions of a

Figure 9.3 The Stillitron

A Pressey-type device which can be used to present both training and testing materials. Green and red lights appear to register the selection of correct or incorrect responses. Although using multi-choice questioning, most programmes are basically linear.

Figure 9.4 The Autotutor

Branching machine. Students press the button appropriate to their choice of response.

personal tutor. Indeed, in this particular case the machine performs even more efficiently than a human tutor, in that it identifies and responds to a student's errors much more quickly.

The SAKI machine has been shown to teach most effectively. It is fair to use the word 'teach' in this context, as most of the normal functions of the teacher (presentation, testing evaluation, remedial action) are performed by the machine. However, the credit for the machine's success is not due so much to the electronic complexity of the machine, as to the logic, or teaching strategy, built into it. The success depends on the correct analysis of what makes up the skill of card-punching, and the design of a teaching system which will measure the learner's present level of skill, and select suitable further exercises from a store. At the present moment we know less about the design of such strategies than about the design of the necessary electronics to carry them out. True, the electronics are also a stumbling block. For example, machines similar to SAKI can be built for the training of typewriting skills. The teaching strategy is similar to that in the punching of cards except that many more keys are used. As a result the complexity of the necessary machine makes it too costly to be an economical proposition.

The modern computer has the capacity to store a vast amount of information and to retrieve items at great speed. The capacity of existing computers does not approach the human mind, but the speed and accuracy of retrieval far surpass it. Thus there is reason to suppose that for a limited subject area as, say, physics, a computer could be used to store all relevant data and to retrieve and re-structure it to suit the needs of the individual learner. We can conceive of computers being used as general purpose adaptive teaching machines, capable of handling a variety of subjects at various levels. Then indeed the role of the teacher might be in question. Two problems hold back work in this field. The first is the problem of man-machine communication. How can the learner communicate his exact intentions to the machine? As long as a simple skill is being taught (such as key-pressing) this is simple, but more abstract subjects which rely on verbal communication pose greater problems. There are so many ways of expressing the same idea. The machine can be programmed to use one fixed sentence which is within the student's command of language. The student if allowed to respond freely (as in a human tutorial situation) may reply in any number of ways. The machine must be able to decipher whether he is correct, (or if not, what his error signified), whether he is supplying information or asking for it and so on. This is essentially a language problem. At present the man must learn a computer language, which is restricting. Computer languages are fast developing, becoming easier to use and more versatile in the concepts they can express. The problem of man-machine communication is rapidly being solved.

The second problem facing the designers of adaptive teaching machines is the problem of analysis of the subject matter itself, and the design of appropriate teaching strategies. Here, every task presents a new problem. The strategies for one lesson are only similar to another in as much as the learning tasks are similar. It is in this area that researchers are investigating learning models such as those described in Chapter 1. Such models attempt to explain or to simulate the processes by which learning takes place. Once you have a learning model, you can construct a teaching strategy. The efficiency of the resulting course will depend to a great extent on the accuracy of your learning model.

Such work on adaptive teaching systems is in its infancy, but progress is being made. Successful systems have so far been developed for relatively simple and precisely defined skills — card punching, typing, missile tracking or radar. It is probable, however, that their use will become more widespread, particularly in industrial training.

Computer-assisted instruction

The use of computers in education is increasing, not only as an aid to the administration of education, but also as a presentation medium. Despite the difficulties described above in writing adaptive programmes which attempt to simulate the efficient tutorial situation, computers are already being used to present many programmes of a simpler construction. These are essentially similar to the branching programmes described earlier, in that they can only present a fixed set of exercises. The decision about what exercise the student should study next can, however, be of a much more complex nature. The student will not, for example, be branched to a remedial exercise on the basis of one response only. His pattern of responding over a period of time, or over a lesson, might be taken into account. Such a facility is very useful when a basic skill such as mathematical or reading skills is being learned. One can arrange that an average score over a series of problems will control the student's progress to new material. This approach has been used by Suppes[1] in his 'drill and practice' programmes. Students learn a new mathematical skill, such as, say, long division by the usual classroom methods. They then work for short periods daily, practising the new skill on exercises presented by an automatic typewriter terminal connected to a computer. The exercises are drawn from a store and are graded for difficulty. The performance of the student on an exercise is used by the computer to decide whether the next exercise should be of a similar grade of difficulty, easier or harder. Thus the student's progress and the amount of practice he gets is controlled by his performance. We have an element of adaptability to individual student's needs — more than in the case of a simple branching programme, but less than in continuously adaptive machines such as SAKI.

More ambitious applications of computer-assisted instruction are in use at Stanford and other centres in America. It is but a question of time before they appear in England. The main problem is money. Indeed, one question as yet unanswered is the economic viability of computer-assisted instructional systems. At present they are likely to be applied only experimentally or in highly important areas of training when cost is no object. However, the costs of computer hardware are rapidly falling. It is very probable that it will be economical to install CAI equipment long before we learn how to make the best use of it.

The changing concept of programmed instruction

Few of the characteristics of 'traditional' programmed learning, outlined above, have stood the test of time. Research over the last few years has cast doubt on the general validity of some. Practical experience has shown that others lead to the production of dull, unmotivating learning materials. Much of the recent research has been summarised by George Leith in a pamphlet entitled *Second Thoughts on Programmed Learning*[2]. Among the characteristics which are now criticised are:

1 *Small steps* Over-use of small steps leads to boredom on the part of the students, more often than not. Current practice favours a step size as large as the student can manage. This is generally established by producing first drafts of programmes which are almost sure to be too difficult for the student, and then simplifying those sections which give students difficulty during validation.

2 *Error-free learning* Skinner suggested the maximum permissible error rate on the frames of a linear programme to be in the region of 5%. Subsequent studies have suggested that this figure is not very critical. Current programming practice pays much less attention to error rates within all the frames of a programme, and concentrates instead on analysis of student performance on post-tests and on key criterion frames within the programme.

3 *Overt responding* Again, studies have shown that in most instances, students who do not write down responses to a programme's frames, but simply think them out, do just as well on final post-tests and generally take less time in studying the programme. Leith[3] carried out a series of experiments on this factor, which seem to indicate that less mature students benefit more from responding overtly, and

that the benefit is related to the type of subject being studied — eg learning to spell is improved if students write their responses, learning concepts is not.

4   *Self-paced learning* This was held to be one of the main reasons for the success of early programmes — 'the learner can proceed at his own pace; he is not kept behind by the rest of the class'. Whereas this statement is often true, it has also been found that the learner's own pace — the pace he chooses — is often much slower than the pace he could proceed at if he were given some indication of what was expected of him. Today, programmes are sometimes designed with built-in pacing (a characteristic of some tape-slide programmes.)

5   *Individual learning* Allied to the above point, if self-paced learning is abandoned, one can also abandon individual presentations and revert to group-instruction (with a consequent saving of cost on hardware). Experiments have shown no loss of effectiveness for some programmes when used in the group situation, though this depends largely on the subject and the complexity of student responses demanded. However, even in complex, structured subjects such as mathematics, benefits have sometimes been gained from allowing students to work together in pairs or in small groups.

6   *Programming styles* As already mentioned, programmers now tend to use both linear and branching sequences in the same programme, depending on the learning task they are tackling. There are also other programming styles in use. Some of these have developed their own jargon and sets of techniques. Examples of some notable current techniques (by no means an exclusive list) are:

(a)   *Mathetics* — the creation of Tom Gilbert[4] and

described in some detail in Chapter 1 of this book.

(b) *Information mapping* — the creation of Robert E Horn[5], this attempts to obey all the established principles of good communication, transforming them into a complex set of rules for the layout of information in a book. Features include the titling, sub-titling and cross referencing of all blocks of information in an attempt to make the purpose of the information clear and its retrieval easy. An example of information mapping, describing some of its techniques, is included as Appendix 2 to this book, by kind permission of Mr T Wyant, the author.

(c) *Structural communication* — the creation of Anthony Hodgson[6]. This is a technique based on quite a different approach to learning than the previously described (mainly behaviourist) models. It does not pre-suppose a correct (or even a limited range of correct) answers. Rather, it is designed to enable the student to respond to a block of information presented to him, in as open-ended a manner as is possible in a self-instructional exercise. The student composes a response from a set of 'building blocks' and the structure of this response is used to control the subsequent 'discussion' between author and student. Although textbook presentations in this format exist, it is better suited as a technique for computer-assisted instruction. It has been applied to areas where traditional PI techniques often fail (ie history, literature, management decision-making) and is often used in the group situation rather than by individuals.

In addition to such well worked out and fully documented techniques, there now abound a whole range of individual programme-writing techniques containing some facets of some of the above techniques. The successful programme writer today is eclectic in his choice of techniques rather than a slave to any one. He may be guided in his choice of technique partly by intuition or personal experience, but slowly a pattern is developing which will eventually enable a designer of instructional materials to identify key characteristics of the learning problem and match them to suitable programming techniques.

7   *Presentation styles.* As already mentioned, 'traditional' teaching machines presenting only verbal information (plus occasional diagrams) are on the decline. There is also a decline in the production of 'traditional' programmed texts. However, audio-visual programming is on the increase, and one can also find examples of programmed film sequences. Group presentations are presented by some teachers, frame by frame on an overhead projector. Some of these are linked to feedback classrooms (devices allowing each student to respond to a question, the teacher receiving this information in some easily digestible form — eg percentage choosing each alternative answer). For more detailed accounts of the use of feedback classrooms see Holling[7].

The most significant development is the concept of the instructional 'package'. This is an assembly of instructional materials designed around clearly defined objectives, complete with tests and other necessary controls, teacher notes, etc, and utilising the most appropriate instructional media. It is to the design of such packages that this book is devoted.

8   *Implementation techniques* The idea that programmed instruction might replace the teacher, is as dead as the dodo. True, a good programme may be as effective as most teachers in achieving the limited objectives it sets out to achieve. However there are whole classes of educational objectives which are not suitable for programmed instruction (at any rate, for

'traditional' programmed texts or teaching machines). In the next sections we give a method of assessing the suitability of a topic for programming. Other methods of instruction, such as group discussion, brain-storming, games, individual tutorials, case studies, sensitivity groups and even large-group lectures will always play their part in the total instructional package. Many of these require the presence and active involvement of the teacher. All of them require careful integration and systematic implementation and follow-up if they are to succeed.

9   *The Teacher as manager* It is this role of the teacher which is now being highlighted by developments in programmed learning and in the wider concept of a systems approach. A recent booklet with the above title has recently been published by the National Council for Educational Technology[8] outlining the current trends, the probable changes in the role of the teacher and the necessary changes in both the structure of schools and the structure of teacher training.

10   *From programmed learning to a technology of education* The whole theme of this book supports the above statement. Programmed learning has grown, but in its growth it has shed many of the characteristics by which it was earlier characterised. 'Traditional' programmed instruction still flourishes, though the great revolution forecast by Pressey, Skinner, Crowder and others has not taken place. Or has it? The methods of instruction in the average school have not changed appreciably (but then neither have the teachers in these schools). However, there is a marked degree of activity 'above'. Scientific methods of educational management are gaining acceptance. A growing number of Local Education Authorities are taking an active interest in the work of associations such as the National Council for Educational Technology (NCET) and the Association for Programmed

Learning and Educational Technology (APLET). The National Committee for Audio Visual Aids in Education (NCAVAE) has turned about completely from a 'hardware/how-to-use-it' concept of its role to a 'software/how to develop, implement and evaluate it' concept. This change is shown by an analysis of the main articles in *Visual Education* over the last few years, and by the courses offered by the association as part of its Diploma in Educational Technology. In teacher training, there are also signs of change, promoted by such projects as the 'Colleges of Education Learning Programmes'[9].

The most notable changes have occurred in vocational, military, commercial and industrial training, where the 'instructional package' and 'training by objectives' are now fully established. We have therefore two extreme concepts of programmed instruction:

(a)   'Traditional' programmed instruction, defined in terms of its characteristics as a *presentation medium:* self-study, student paced, active responding, etc. As outlined above, more and more of these characteristics are absent from some currently produced programmes.

(b)   'New' programmed instruction, (otherwise called 'the systems approach' or 'training by objectives' or 'instructional technology'), defined in terms of a basic approach to problem-solving in education and training, involving the stages of *task analysis* leading to course objectives, further detailed *analysis of subject and student* leading to draft exercise design, *validation* leading to possible revision, and finally *controlled implementation* associated with *long-term evaluation.*

When are programmes useful?

We have defined a teaching machine as any device which is used to present a teaching programme. This has embraced equipment using all the communication media discussed earlier. It also includes simple presentation devices such as books or loose sheets. We therefore have a double question to answer. Firstly, when are teaching programmes useful? Secondly, if a programme is to be presented, what sort of device will do it best?

Let's consider the first question. The theme of this book has been that one can design and construct a course by a 'systems approach' which draws heavily on analysis and planning techniques used in the writing of programmes. Firstly, precise objectives have to be drawn up in terms of desired student behaviour. Sometimes this cannot be done with sufficient precision. In English literature, for example, some unexpected behaviour on the part of the student, such as the writing of a poem, may be highly desirable, although it is not necessarily a prime objective. Creativity in the arts, and in science and technology as well, cannot be easily predicted (although one can notice through experience that certain teaching methods tend to be ,more successful in promoting it). It is explained that the particular qualities of the subject (its appeal to the emotions, its creative content) make it impossible to define precise teaching objectives. There is undoubtedly some truth in this, but sometimes it may also be the case that we simply have not given enough thought to how we should teach a subject, or indeed why we teach it at all. Whatever the reason, if we cannot define our objectives, it is futile to attempt to programme the topic. One cannot just construct a presentation based on the belief that something good will come of it. The inability to define objectives implies the inability to test for teaching effectiveness.

If we can define the objectives precisely, it is not necessarily best to produce a programme. We can of course proceed with our systems approach. We can analyse the topic, the target population and the external constraints which limit our choice of alternatives. Considerations which might suggest the use of programmes are as follows:

1   Programmes are fixed in their content and in their method of teaching. Is the subject such that it can be treated in this way? Are students likely to be similar in their background, intelligence and aptitudes? Would anything be gained by including opportunities for discussing personal experiences?

2   Programmes require a capital investment in their production, evaluation and (if machines are used) presentation. Will there be sufficient students to justify this outlay? Will the subject matter remain fixed for some time or will developments render the programme obsolete?

3   Programmes tend to be most effective when used for individual study. In these situations great differences exist between the learning times of individuals. A system which demands a rigid time table has difficulty in using programmes effectively. On the other hand, sporadic groups of students (eg unpredictable labour turnover), individual entrants, shift workers, scattered personnel (eg service engineers, salesmen) can be trained most conveniently by means of programmes.

When such considerations are weighed up, the end product of the systems approach is not necessarily a 'traditional' teaching programme in text or machine. It may be some other teaching method, such as the use of case studies, or on-the-job training, or very often a combination of several methods.

Dr Len Biran has developed a detailed analysis of the factors one should consider before deciding to use 'traditional' programmed instruction. These are classified as characteristics in favour, or against, the use of programmed self-instructional materials, in such a way as to be a useful job aid for the course designer. This analysis was published in the 1972/3 *APLET Yearbook*[10] and is reproduced as Appendix 1 to this book by kind permission of the author.

One recent development in America has been the development and marketing of subject packages or kits. The instructional package may include programmed texts, models, complex training devices or apparatus, slides, films, and always full teacher's notes. This is the ultimate in the multi-media systems approach. Every component in the package is designed to perform a specific teaching purpose, and is evaluated for effectiveness. The package adopts several presentation media not so much to add variety to the lesson (though this is itself valuable) but because analysis of the subject and field testing has indicated that a particular method and medium ensures most efficient learning of a particular concept or task. Do such packages warrant being called programmes? They certainly are designed on the same principles. They are generally produced by or in association with programme writers. It really depends whether one considers that programmed instruction is presentation technique or a philosophy of teaching. It is of course both.

How are programmes used?

As one might expect, programmes are used most to teach subjects which are precise in their objectives, reasonably stable in their content and which have a reasonably large student market. In the schools, the most common subject areas are mathematics, languages and science. Hamer, in a survey of school use of programmes in 1965[11], found that mathematics accounted for more programme applications than all other subjects combined. Programmes have also been successfully applied to teach extra-curricular topics, which the full-time staff are unwilling or unable to teach. Examples are programmes on sex education, computer programming, and the dangers of smoking.

There are several schools and a small number of local authorities who use programmes extensively. The 'Surrey Project'[12] for example, involves a number of schools which teach the major part of their mathematics by programmes on teaching machines. Wiltshire and Gloucestershire Local Education Authorities are among those who have actively encouraged the use of programmes in their schools, to the extent of sponsoring teachers to write and publish material for general use throughout the county.

In general, however, school use of programmes takes the

form of an optional or occasional activity. Many programmes are used only for revision or merely by those who missed the lesson. Other applications rely on the enthusiasm of one teacher who may write and use material despite little encouragement or even active discouragement from above.

The number of programmes on the market is steadily growing, and so is their use, but the well-thought-out, systematically implemented programme-based teaching system is still a rarity. Where teachers, or a group, have set about using programmes systematically, as in Leicestershire[13], results have generally been well worthwhile. Many half-hearted applications have failed, due as much to lack of planning and lack of follow-up as to any weaknesses in the teaching materials.

The situation in industry is somewhat different. For one thing, there is a much wider variety of subject applications. Programmes are used to train managers, technicians, craftsmen and operatives in principles, procedures, skills and good habits. A survey of programmes in industry published by Enfield College of Technology[14], found that in 1966 the most popular area of application for programmes was in craft apprentice training. This was probably due to the large number of published programmes in this field, available as a complete series. Second most popular was management training, followed, a close third, by operative training.

This last area of training is fast expanding however, and programmes are ideal as the subject matter is generally very precisely defined. There is no room for argument or alternative approaches. The aim is that all operatives should use the same tested method. Furthermore, a programmed course solves many practical problems of training operatives: is always available — day or night shift so labour turnover, re-deployment, scattered personnel are no longer problems; it is studied at the student's rate so intellectual level and language difficulties can be overcome; it is presented automatically — the need for training specialists is reduced; embarrassment for older employees needing re-training is eliminated.

It is not surprising therefore that programmed instruction has become established in industry and commerce. The 1966 survey found that of the biggest firms (ie those with over 5000 personnel), over half were using programmes for some part of their training. A further survey, following up the major users in 1967, showed further increases in use of programmes[15]. However, investigations into the ways in which programmes were implemented revealed the same lack of systematic planning and follow-up as in school use. The firms who use programmes as part of a fully worked-out training system, with provision for evaluation of results and correction of weaknesses, are in a minority. In many cases, much of the programme's value is lost due to inadequate follow-up.

There are signs that this situation is slowly improving. Quentin Whitlock, in a recent analysis of developments in the use of programmed learning in industry, notes the tendencies towards more rigorous evaluation, towards systematically designed instructional packages, and towards an application of 'systems approaches'[16]. Whitlock also notes a shift in the main areas of programme application:

'One innovation in the application of self-instructional programmes in industry has been a quite distinct shift in emphasis from the almost total concentration on the target populations of operators, apprentices and craftsmen which characterised programming in the 1960s. Recently many more programmes have been produced for administrative and clerical staff and, significantly, for management personnel up to the highest level. This development may not be entirely coincidental with the relative drop in popularity of the Teaching Machine. Beck reported as late as 1969 that "trainee resistance to using programmes was only mentioned when trainees were of management level. Managers saw the short steps of a programme to be a waste of their intelligence and thought they could learn faster from a textbook"[17].
While more and more trainers have seen how programmed training schemes can be used for training managers, an increasing number of texts have been published on a variety of specific techniques for managers such as Critical Path Analysis and Discounted

Programme Applications

Category of Trainee	No of Firms	No of Programmes
1 Craftsmen; Apprentices	84	1058
2 Managers; Supervisors; Foremen	49	111
3 Operatives	36	115
4 Technicians; Engineers etc	31	56
5 Secretaries; Clerks	21	160
6 Sale Assistants; Representatives	12	41
TOTALS	233	1541

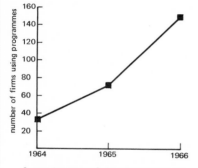

Quoted Advantages Of Programmed Learning

Comment	Number of times mentioned
1 Students proceed at own pace	63
2 Releases instructors, or improves their efficiency	42
3 Uniformity of instruction	35
4 Flexibility of timetable	25
5 Higher retention	13
6 Faster learning	12
7 No supervision necessary	11
8 No social embarrassment (adult trainees)	11
9 Results assessable and controllable	11
10 Stimulates interest & motivation	10
11 No one misses instruction due to absence	8
12 Students are active & involved	6
13 Improves students mental powers/powers of communication	4
14 Integration of theory & practice improved	4
15 Easy to administer a programmed course	4
16 Training can be given where previously impossible	3
17 More students can use same building & facilities due to staggered hours	2
TOTAL	264

Figure 9.5 Some results of the PIC survey on industrial use of programmes

Cash Flow. Training itself and the Principles of Super-
vision are other topics for which many self-instructional
texts have been published over the last two years. In
appearance the pages of these books bear little resemblance to the one frame a page texts on hand tools
for apprentices but conceptually they conform in every
respect to the principles of programmed learning.'

In formal education, there has been perhaps less progress
towards a systems approach than in industry or in the forces.
However, there has been local progress here and there, and
this is most notable where groups of schools, colleges or
universities have jointly cooperated in the preparation of
learning materials. Such projects as the Surrey Schools Maths
Project, the Nuffield Resources for Learning Project and the
Inter-University Biology Teaching Project have brought
teachers from different institutions together to decide on
common learning objectives, and to divide the work of
materials preparation among themselves.

It is interesting that this cooperation has been most
common and has therefore led to the greatest rate of
development, at the two extremes of the educational
spectrum, that is in primary education and in higher
education. In primary education, the Nuffield Resources for
Learning Project materials are now widely accepted. In
particular the Project centred on Coventry College of
Education and Binley Primary School, Coventry, in the
development of a programmed approach to the teaching of
environmental studies, has been most notable. These
materials when used imaginatively by the teacher, enable him
to transform his class into a truly student-directed self-
instructional situation employing a wide variety of learning
materials and a wide variety of media and teacher's aids. The
use of these materials, which are now published by Blandford
Press, is described in a film which has been commissioned by
NCET.

At the other extreme (higher education) we have the
Inter-University Biology Teaching Project which involves
cooperation between 6 universities in the production of

materials to joint objectives. Some of these materials in the form of multi-media programmes in biology are now generally available from Glasgow and Sussex Universities. Furthermore, we have the development of powerful institutes or centres for educational technology in many of the new universities, notably at Surrey, Sussex, Leeds and Liverpool.

A further area of development in higher education has been the area of medical education. It appears that this field of education is highly suitable for the application of planned course packages. The Department of Audio-Visual Communication, set up by the BMA, is doing much to promote production and to disseminate information about available materials.

Thus in all areas of education and training there are signs of perhaps a waning interest in 'traditional' programmed texts and teaching machines, but a growth in the application of the 'new' programmed instruction concept — the 'systems approach'. Also there are signs of more coordination and direction from the top. There are now a number of associations, councils and other groups whose concern is the promotion of programmed instruction and educational technology. Figure 9.6 illustrates the emerging pattern of activity and control. This figure is reproduced from the *1972/73 APLET Yearbook of Educational and Instructional Technology*[18]

What programmes are available commercially?

The *APLET Yearbook* is the most comprehensive source of details about commercially available programmes in the UK. It is in fact compiled every two years, but updating lists appear at intervals in the journal, *Programmed Learning and Educational Technology*. Special subject areas are catered for by some specialist agencies. Medical programmes are listed in a bibliography by Richard Wakeford and Len Biran, 1970[19]: this includes both published and privately available programmes in the field, including some American ones. Since then additions have been regularly reported in the newsletter *Information,* circulated by the Department of

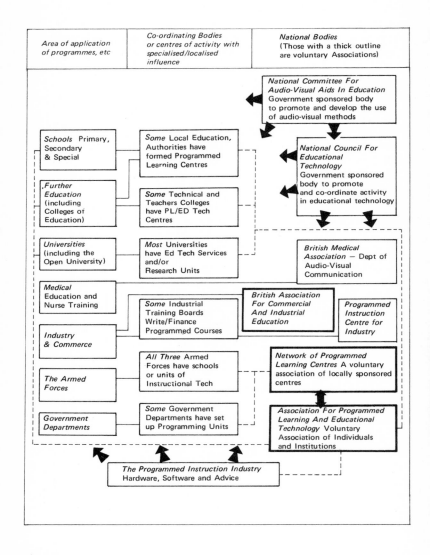

Figure 9.6 The pattern of activity in programmed learning and educational technology in the United Kingdom

Audiovisual Communication of the British Medical Association.

Industrial programmes used to be listed by the British Association for Commercial and Industrial Education, but recently a series of 'mini-registers' of programmes on selected topics has been produced by the Programmed Instruction Centre for Industry at Sheffield University (now moving to Sheffield Polytechnic).

No similar subject lists, giving a full description of content and teaching method used, exist for school programmes, although the National Centre for Programmed Learning (now defunct), did attempt to produce such registers, and the task was later taken over by the Network of Programmed Learning Centres. A few registers have been produced but are not now readily available. However, the membership of the Network (composed of organisations working in the field of educational technology), is pleased to advise individuals on the choice of suitable programmes.

The pattern of programme publishing has varied considerably over the last decade. The compilation of the 1972/73 *APLET Yearbook of Educational and Instructional Technology* provided an opportunity to re-examine the 'State of the Industry' as far as published programmed materials are concerned. Similar analyses were carried out on the basis of data collected for the 1966 edition of *Programmes in Print* and the 1969/70 *Yearbook* The first of these analyses[20] drew five conclusions concerning developing trends in published programmes. The second analysis[21] followed up these same five conclusions, confirming most of them, but noting certain changes as follows:

1   In 1966 there was an increasing number of programmes being marketed by an increasing number of producers. By 1969 there was evidence that a peak had been reached and, although new publishers were still entering the market, total production was declining.

2   The 'growth areas' for programmes in 1966 were mathematics, science, computer science, statistics, etc

(in short the logical, factual subjects). The 1969 figures substantiated this trend.

3   British programmes were still more commonly produced for use on machine, though by 1969 the production of machine programmes was limited to a handful of commercial programme writing firms that also had a machine to sell.

4   Linear programming was more popular than branching, though there was some evidence by 1969 of other approaches as well.

5   American programmes are longer than British programmes.

When compiling the 1972/73 *Yearbook,* we investigated the first four of these conclusions further, and attempted not only to up-date the statistics available, but also to examine any changes in the trends as previously outlined and to suggest possible reasons. The full report appeared in *Aspects of Educational Technology*[22]. Figure 9.7 is reproduced here to show the major finding. Other findings were as follows:

Several trends are noticeable, some of which were identified in the 1970 analysis, some of which are new.

1   Programming effort (as far as published programmes are concerned) has indeed fallen off from the peak in 1967 and now appears steady.

2   Logical and factual subjects are still the most common areas for programming effort. However, the emphasis has moved from the 'formal' subjects — maths, science and languages — to 'problem' subjects. One such a few years back was decimalisation. Currently metrication re-training and medical training seem to be the vogue.

3   Teaching machines are no longer the most common presentation medium for recently produced

programmes. Since 1969, the programmed text has gained popularity. Also a significant growth in the application of programmed methods to audio-visual presentations has been noted.

4   There is little real change in programming styles, although a mixture of linear/branching/etc is more common. It is probable that the techniques of analysis and preparation for programming have undergone more significant changes, but the present study cannot quantify these accurately.

5   The number of producers of programmes continues to increase, but these tend to be organisations with a commitment towards education or training in a particular sphere, rather than commercially orientated publishers. Old-established producers in the field vary from healthy increases in their commitment to programmed learning, to total withdrawal from the market.

6   In the author's opinion, the present picture as presented here, while definitely indicating an end to the boom in programme production of the mid-sixties, does not necessarily present a picture of abject gloom. Activity continues, though in different areas under different systems of sponsorship. Users are developing better skills for the selection of instructional materials. The early 1970's will be a time for producers to re-appraise the situation and to match their production and selection skills to the needs of the market.

When are teaching machines useful?

Assuming that the analysis of a learning task has indicated that a teaching programme may be a useful method of instruction, how does one decide on the particular presentation method or machine to use? The answer is that it is as yet too early to decide. Part of the decision may be taken at this stage — that part which has already been outlined in earlier chapters on media selection. If the subject involves noises, then a device capable of presenting noises must be used. If the study of motion is important to the mastery of certain concepts, then a cine film would probably be indicated. The earlier parts of this chapter indicate that one can present a teaching programme in any of the media. That most programmes tend to be composed almost entirely of words on paper, indicates in part the extent to which we rely on verbal communication and in part the inability or unwillingness of many writers to analyse their topics with a view to systematic media selection.

One might at the initial design stage therefore observe that certain communication media are desirable. Not till the design of the teaching system is near-complete, however, can one finally decide on a presentation device. For example, the decision to incorporate optional remedial material in a programme would indicate the need for a branching machine of some sort. However, one might, on the basis of the subject analysis, or on the basis of expected individual differences in student abilities, plan remedial sub-sequences, and then find that in practice no students use them. The original branches will be removed from the programme during validation. Alternatively a programme originally conceived as purely linear, may 'sprout' branches during evaluation as a result of unforeseen differences in student abilities or background. If the choice of presentation device is made too soon, this may impose unnecessary constraints on the structure of the programme. The selection of a linear machine excludes the use of branching techniques. On the other hand it is quite uneconomical to present purely linear sequences on a sophisticated branching machine. In addition, factors such as maximum frame size or whether motion backwards through the programme is possible, impose further artificial constraints on the programmer. It is therefore best to leave the choice of machine to a later stage in the system design.

There is little danger that one will prescribe a machine which does not exist. Most combinations of branching and audio-visual presentation can now be catered for. Furthermore, one should not overlook the book as a presentation

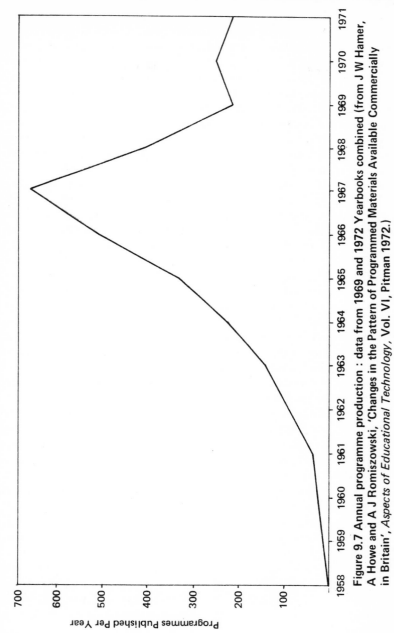

Figure 9.7 Annual programme production : data from 1969 and 1972 Yearbooks combined (from J W Hamer, A Howe and A J Romiszowski, 'Changes in the Pattern of Programmed Materials Available Commercially in Britain', *Aspects of Educational Technology*, Vol. VI, Pitman 1972.)

device. It has many advantages such as a variable frame size and low cost. Nor is the text version of a programme necessarily inferior to the machine version. There is evidence to suggest that there is little to be gained by the use of complex machines. It depends very much on the particular machine and the particular student.

On the whole, mature, motivated students learn just as well from text versions of programmes. This is particularly true of linear or mainly linear programmes. When using linear programmes with apprentices, the author found that there was apparently no difference in the amount of learning produced by text or machine versions of the same programme, in spite of the much greater popularity of the teaching machines[2][3]. Indeed, the machine versions carried a time penalty. It took up to 30% longer to work through them. This may have been due to the mechanics of lining up each frame in the window of the machine, or to 'skipping' of frames in the less strictly controlled text versions. In either case the overall effect was equivalent performance in less time from the text version. Experiments with adults in the same establishment indicated that very simple teaching machines may even arouse hostile reactions by hurting the pride of the students. Results of experiments in schools with relatively young students do not support these results. On the contrary, linear machines have been found in some cases to improve learning efficiency.

This is much more the case with branching machines. For one thing, these machines present material clearly and efficiently. The pressing of buttons has a peculiar fascination for some. For others, the alternative text presentation in a 'scrambled' book form tends to be difficult in use and is almost designed to arouse hostility. The student is required to jump sometimes forward, sometimes back, by a variable number of pages. He spends almost as long finding his page as he does reading it. He soon develops the habit of keeping one finger in the previous page, so that if his choice of response is wrong, he can quickly refer back. He soon runs out of fingers, drops the book and loses his place completely. Even if this does not happen, there is a strong temptation, when routed to a set of remedial pages, to justify one's error as a mere slip and omit the tedious subsequence. This may of course have an adverse effect on learning. The experiences of the Royal Navy in their early experiments on programmed instruction[24] indicated that scrambled books were not as effective as Autotutor versions of the same programme.

In conclusion therefore, before considering teaching machines as a presentation medium, one should first establish that programmes are a suitable and desirable method of instruction for the topic. Secondly, one should actually write and develop the programmed material. Only then can one make a balanced decision on presentation method.

The considerations to be taken into account are first, which communication media are indicated by the subject matter; and second, what is the simplest device which will present the type of programme produced.

References

1. P Suppes, 'The Use of Computers in Education', *Scientific American,* September 1966.

2. G O M Leith, *Second Thoughts on Programmed Learning,* National Council for Educational Technology, Occasional Paper No 1, 1969.

3. G O M Leith, *A Handbook of Programmed Learning,* University of Birmingham, 2nd ed 1966.

4. T F Gilbert, 'Mathetics: The Technology of Education', *Journal of Mathetics,* No 1 and 2 1962. Since reprinted as a booklet by Longmac, 13 Wisteria Rd, London, SE13.

5. R E Horn, Elizabeth Nicol, J C Kleinman, *Information Mapping for Learning and Reference,* Electronic Systems Division, US Air Force, Bedford, Mass, 1969.

6. A Hodgson, 'Structural Communication — A New Automation Aid', in I K Davis and J Hartley (eds), *Contribution*

to an Educational Technology, Butterworth, 1972. See also *Systematics,* Vol 5, No 3, December 1967 and 'An Experiment in Computer Guided Seminar for Management' in *Aspects of Educational Technology,* Vol V, Pitman, 1971.

7. K Holling, 'The Feedback Classroom' in D Unwin (ed), *Media and Methods Instructional Technology in Higher Education,* McGraw-Hill, 1969.

8. G Taylor (ed), *The Teacher as Manager — a Symposium,* National Council for Educational Technology, 1970.

9. G Collier (ed), *Colleges of Education Learning Programmes,* National Council for Educational Technology, Working Paper No 5, 1971.

10. L A Biran, 'The Role and Limitations of Programmed Instruction in A J Romiszowski (ed), *APLET Yearbook of Educational and Instructional Technology 1972/73,* Kogan Page, 1972.

11. J Hamer, *The Use of Programmed Learning in England 1964-65,* PIC Publication, Enfield College of Technology, 1966.

12. Surrey County Council, *A Systems Approach to Secondary School Mathematics — The Surrey Auto Tutor Project 1965-1970,* Surrey County Council Education Department, 1970.

13. J Leedham and D Unwin, *Programmed Learning in the Schools,* Longmans, 1965.

14. A J Romiszowski, 'A Survey of the Use of Programmed Learning by Industry in England in 1966', *Programmed Learning and Educational Technology,* July 1967. Also in M J Tobin (ed), *Problems and Methods in Programmed Learning,* School of Education, Birmingham University, 1967.

15. A J Romiszowski, 'Trends in the Use of Programmed

Learning by Industry', *Aspects of Educational Technology*, Vol 2, Methuen, 1969.

16. Q A Whitlock, 'Programmed Learning and Educational Technology in Industry', in *APLET Yearbook of Educational and Instructional Technology 1972/73*, ed A J Romiszowski, Kogan Page, 1972.

17. J E Beck, 'A Survey of the Problems Encountered by a Number of Industrial and Commercial Users of Programmed Instruction', *Aspects of Educational Technology*, Vol 3, Pitman, 1969.

18. A J Romiszowski (ed), *APLET Yearbook of Educational and Instructional Technology 1972/73*, Kogan Page, 1972.

19. R E Wakeford and L A Biran, *Programmes in the Health Sciences*, NCPL British Life Assurance Trust/British Medical Association, 1970.

20. C K Basu, P Cavanagh, C Jones, 'Trends in Programmes in Print in the United Kingdom', in *Problems and Methods in Programmed Learning*, ed M J Tobin, NCPL Birmingham University, 1967.

21. P Cavanagh and C Jones, 'Further Trends in Programmes in Print in the United Kingdom', *Programmed Learning and Educational Technology*, Vol 7, No 1, Sweet and Maxwell, 1970.

22. J W Hamer, A Howe and A J Romiszowski, 'Changes in the Pattern of Programmed Materials Available Commercially in Britain,' in *Aspects of Educational Technology*, Vol VI, Pitman, 1972.

23. A J Romiszowski, 'Living with Programmed Instruction', *Technical Education and Industrial Training*, August 1965.

24. R Wicks, 'The Royal Navy Study', in *Programmed Learning*, Vol 1, No 1, May 1914

Further Reading

Books Specifically Concerned with the Principles and Applications of Programmed Learning

B Dodd, *Programmed Instruction for Industrial Training,* Heinemann, 1967. 92pp.

W R Dunn and C Holroyd (eds), *Aspects of Educational Technology,* Vol 2. Proceedings of the 1968 APL Conference, Methuen, 1969. 671pp.

R Glaser, (ed), *Teaching Machines and Programmed Learning 2 — Data and Directions,* National Education Association, Washington, 1965, 831pp.

H Kay, B Dodd, M Sime, *Teaching Machines and Programmed Learning,* Penguin, 1968. 173pp.

J F Leedham and A Bajpai, (eds), *Aspects of Educational Technology,* Vol 4, Proceedings of the 1970 APLET Conference, Pitman, London, 1970.

A P Mann and C K Brunstrom (eds), *Aspects of Educational Technology,* Vol 3, Proceedings of the 1969 APL Conference Pitman, London, 1969. 104pp.

National Centre for Programmed Learning, *Programmed Learning — A Symposium,* NCAVAE, 1969.

National Society for the Study of Education, *Programmed Instruction — 66th Yearbook of NSSE,* University of Chicago Press, 1967. 400pp.

G D Ofeish and W C Meierhenry, *Trends in Programmed Instruction,* Department of Audio-Visual Instruction, National Education Association, USA, 1964. 290pp.

Derek Packham, Alan Cleary, Terry Mayes (eds), *Aspects of Educational Technology,* Vol 5, Proceedings of the 1971

Teaching Machines and Programmed Instruction
APLET Conference, Pitman, London, 1971. 488pp.

M J Tobin (ed), *Problems and Methods in Programmed Learning.* Proceedings of the 1967 APL Conference School of Education, University of Birmingham, 1967. Part 1 — 122pp, Part 2 — 109pp. Part 3 — 104pp. Part 4 — 123pp. Part 5 — 61pp.

D Unwin and J Leedham (eds), *Aspects of Educational Technology,* Vol 1. Proceedings of the 1966 APL Conference Methuen, London, 1967. 545pp.

Programme Writing
D M Brethower, S Markle, et al, *Programmed Learning, A Practicum,* Anne Arbor Publishers, USA, 1964.

I E Espich and W Williams, *Developing Programmed Instructional Materials,* Pitman, 1967. 136pp.

B N Lewis and P J Woolfenden, *Algorithms and Logical Trees. A Self-instructional Course,* Algorithms Press, 1969. 56pp.

S Markle, *Good Frames and Bad — A Grammar of Frame Writing,* Wiley, 2nd ed, 1969. 308pp.

P Pipe, *Practical Programming,* Holt, Rinehart, Winston, 1966. 70pp.

Applications in Schools
M Brown and N Precious, *The Integrated Day in the Primary School,* Ward, Lock, 1969. 157pp.

K Bung, *Programmed Learning and the Language Laboratory,* Longmans, 1968. 243pp.

J Leedham and D Unwin, *Programmed Learning in Schools,* Longmans, 1965. 140pp.

L G W Sealey and V Gibbon, *Communication and Learning in the Primary School,* Blackwell, 1964. 168pp.

Application in Higher and Further Education

Joan D Browne, The Development of Educational Technology in Colleges of Education, Councils and Education Press, 1970.

N Mackenzie, M R Eraut and H C Jones, *Teaching and Learning — an Introduction to New Methods and Resources in Higher Education,* UNESCO and the International Association of Universities, Paris, 1970. 209pp.

D Unwin (ed), *Media and Methods — Instructional Technology in Higher Education,* McGraw-Hill, 1969. 219pp.

Applications in Industry and Commerce

Bacie Bibliography (British Association for Commercial and Industrial Education, London). Vol 1 1960-62 100pp, Vol II 1963-67. 132pp.

R W Lyne (ed), *Programmed Instruction in Industry.* A reference series of case histories. Pergamon, from 1967 to 1969. Several issues each year.

10   Simulators and Games

The field of simulation and training games has expanded over the last few years to a point where it is often treated as a major training technique in its own right. Of course, simulation has for a long time been used in certain aspects of education. In primary schools in particular, the idea of learning through a game or dramatisation (eg playing shop) is as old as education itself. Over the last fifty years or so, we have seen developments at the other extreme. Complex simulators are used to teach pilots to fly aircraft, starting from the wartime 'Link' trainers through to devices which simulate weightlessness or high gravity loadings, for the training of astronauts. We have also seen the birth of a variety of business games and simulations, ranging from role-playing in typical sales or interview situations to games which enable the players to take all the decisions necessary to run a complex business empire, in competition with other players (other companies) and under the control of a simulated 'economy' (often computer-based) which feeds in the elements of chance and change.

But only recently have we seen the use of these techniques in secondary and further education. In technical training, special training exercises for psychomotor skills have been developed which often use simulated 'off the job' training situations. Much pioneering work in this field is due to Seymour's work on skills analysis training[1] . In secondary and further education, there has been a rash of simulation and training games exercises which aim at developing social skills or understanding of complex problems. Examples of the first type include simulations of job-interviews, classroom-discipline situations, boy-meets-girl situations, where the participants play out the roles which will actually be expected of them in later life. Examples of the second type include role-playing of others' roles to gain greater under-standing of their problems (eg the Shelter simulation which investigates the problems of seven groups sharing an over-crowded house), or 'real' games (involving boards, cards or dice etc) which, somewhat like the game of Monopoly, allow participants to make decisions within a system and 'see the system at work'. However, the game of Monopoly may be seen as a not-too-good example of simulation when we examine it more closely later in this chapter.

What are simulation and gaming?

Simulation has been defined as an attempt to 'give the appearance and/or to give the effect of something else'[2]. This somewhat wide definition would seem to cover such things as play-acting, disguise, models, even photographs and paintings. Certainly a photograph gives the appearance of the real object and in some limited way it may also give the effect (otherwise how do we account for the sales of girlie magazines and posters). A computer-based model of the economy on the other hand, certainly reproduces the effects of certain decisions, but the way it does this (paper print-out of data) has little resemblance to the appearance of these effects in a real economy (new jobs, rising prices, industrial action etc).

There is one further aspect of simulation which our definition should include. All the examples we have so far mentioned have one thing in common. They actively involve the learners in making decisions, playing roles, adopting attitudes or operating the simulator. The learner learns by 'manipulating the model'. If we use the word 'model' here in the wide sense (ie a model of an object, or of a process, or of a complex system) then simulators are models which can be manipulated or operated in some way or other. We might therefore extend our definition of simulation as follows: An educational simulation;

1 Requires a model (something giving the appearance and/or the effect of something else).

2 Requires that the learners operate or manipulate the model, in order to learn.

The model is usually a simplified version of the real object, process or system under study. However, the extent to which one can simplify the model depends very much on the learning objectives. Those aspects of reality under study must be reproduced as faithfully as possible in the model; aspects not under study may be omitted from it. Thus when learners operate the model the effects of certain actions or decisions are similar to the effects one would obtain in reality.

Educational gaming is sometimes considered as a branch of educational simulation. However there are some differences. Certainly the well-publicised 'war games' (in which army officers play out strategic moves against each other and a computer), or 'management games' (which pit executives against each other in similar battles concerned with production or sales) are examples of simulation. The participants make decisions and follow rules very similar to those in reality. The computer (or sometimes a human 'adjudicator') acts as a store of the sort of data which could normally be available in reality and sometimes also as a generator of the type of 'chance' events which again may occur in reality. The value of such games to the participant is in direct relation to how well the games simulate the decisions that have to be taken in real wars or in the real business world.

The main difference between these games and other simulations (such as computer simulations of a business structure or of an economy) is the element of competition which is introduced. Indeed this is perhaps the main discriminating factor between games and simulations. Some games may be simulations, others may not, but all games have an element of competition. This element of competition may be natural to the reality being studied as in the two examples above, or it may be purposely introduced into the learning to make it into a game.

For example, during the period leading up to decimalisation, or 'D' day in Britain, several organisations used a card game similar to 'Snap'. Some cards were labelled with various amounts in old currency, others with their equivalents in the new decimal currency. Players simply shouted 'snap' when two cards of equivalent value were turned up. The objective was to improve trainees' ability at identifying equivalent values in the two currencies. The game certainly worked. Trainees became quicker in their responses to such a degree that it was obvious that they were identifying the equivalents 'on sight' rather than by mental arithmetic. Similar games have been used for learning basic multiplication as an alternative to swotting up tables, or for learning foreign vocabularies. It is doubtful whether many readers would classify these games as simulations. However, they could conceivably be considered as partial simulations, based on very simplified models of reality. The decimal currency game, for example, deals with one skill that presumably was felt to be required for transition to the new currency. Whoever devised the game presumably had formed a model of how people would behave when the new currency was introduced. Rather than attempting a total simulation (such as playing 'shop') which would involve participants in practising a range of skills, he singled out one skill and devised a training exercise for it. Because his exercise contains an element of competition and scoring, we call it a game.

This digression into decimalisation might serve to make several points:

1   Simulation and the design of special-purpose training exercises may be thought to lie upon a continuum. At one end we have reality, or a perfect simulation of reality. At the other end we have exercises designed to develop specific skills or sub-skills which are required in order to perform in the real-life situation. In between we have exercises based on progressively more

and more simplified models of the reality we are studying.

2   The benefit of a 'realistic' simulation is that the learner gets an overall impression of the object, process or system under study. He may come to an 'overall understanding of the problem' or he may practise 'the whole job'. However, the complexity of the whole may be such that he learns little about the component parts. In some circumstances this may not matter. In others, it would be beneficial to simplify the model and concentrate on simulating only those parts of reality which are relevant at this time. In still other circumstances, particularly where one component of the whole is particularly difficult to understand or to master, it may be beneficial to single out this component and design a training exercise for it.

3   There is no reason why a particular course of training should not include both special skill exercises and relatively realistic simulations of the whole job. A detailed analysis of the learning task is needed to decide on the best course structure.

4   If they contain an element of competitive fun, both training exercises and simulations tend to be called games. Sometimes the competitive element appears as a natural consequence of the reality we are studying. However, there is no harm in injecting an artificial competitive element, provided it does not destroy the 'realism' of the simulation.

5   Simulation requires an adequately realistic model of the reality under study (training exercises may be considered as dealing with only some part of this model). They will only be useful as training aids to the extent to which the model is correct. For example, those readers who were involved in decimalisation training may have doubted the validity of the example quoted above. You may remember the debate which

raged at the time between those who believed that 'learning the equivalents' was an essential part of the proposed training, and those who said it was quite unnecessary, indeed harmful, to engage in such practice. These people said 'let the trainees work only in the new system — encouraging them to contrast old and new will only prolong the transition'. They would obviously have rejected the 'Snap' game described, as it did not fit into their model of how people should behave during the transition.

At this point we might revert to considering the game of Monopoly. Is this a simulation? Is it an educational game? On face value it seems to give the appearance and some of the effects of property deals in the City. Also one can certainly become involved and 'operate' the model. One can, for example, take losses now in order to reap profits later, or one can make decisions to specialise in, say, 'commercial' property or to build up a 'balanced' portfolio. However, even the most superficial analysis reveals that the rules and possibilities in Monopoly are very different from reality. Monopoly is a very poor simulation of the real property game: poor not in the sense that it is simplified to concentrate on certain aspects, but in the sense that it diverges from reality in many respects. It is doubtful how much a building property speculator would increase his skills by the playing of Monopoly. However, one might possibly expect enthusiastic players of Monopoly to be more likely to develop a desire for real property speculation. There may be a motivational effect. One particular weakness of the game (considered as a simulator) is the disproportionate part that chance plays in the transactions. If we were to consider the educational merits of the game, we might therefore discount its value as a training device for property tycoons, but consider its value as a training device for gamblers.

The benefits of simulations and games

Among the usually quoted benefits of the use of simulation and gaming exercises are:

1 They can provide the student with experiences and practice which are much closer to the real-life situations he will encounter, than might otherwise be possible in a training course. In particular they can reproduce the pressures and stresses under which students will have to work.

2 They can therefore be useful as methods of measuring how well students are able to apply previously learnt facts, concepts, or principles to real-life situations.

3 They allow one to simplify reality, controlling which aspects of a real-life situation a student should attend and respond to.

4 They are often economically justified as a substitute for on-the-job practice when it would be difficult to arrange this, eg expensive, easily broken equipment (medical simulators), remote situations (space-travel simulators or school geography games), equipment used for production day and night (industrial process simulators) etc.

5 They are often justified on safety grounds, in that they enable students to practise dangerous or threatening jobs without any danger (pilot-training simulators, simulations of highly-stressed personal situations such as dealing with discipline problems in the classroom, war games etc).

6 A well-designed simulation or game is generally found to involve students in the learning task more than other available techniques, both intellectually and emotionally.

7 As a result of 6 (and also of 3) they have been found to be an extremely effective way of measuring, changing and reinforcing student attitudes.

8 Finally, simulation can of course be used as a research technique. The model being used in the simulation should reflect reality. If we understand the real-life phenomenon under study sufficiently, we should be able to construct a valid model. If however we do not fully understand the real problem, we construct a 'tentative' model — a model which reflects our hypotheses about the problem. We then operate the model and observe the effects, comparing them with the effects we obtain in reality. Any discrepancies are analysed and the model is re-designed, our hypotheses changed, if necessary. The study of complex systems such as political systems, nervous systems, sophisticated electronic systems (ie the science of cybernetics) relies heavily on simulation as a research technique. In the instructional situation we shall also be using simulation in this way for two reasons: (a) the designer of the simulation exercise should evaluate it and to do this he must compare the effects of operating the model with the effects of similar actions in reality; (b) the learners participating in the simulation, if it is intended that they should gain 'understanding' of the real phenomenon, should compare the simulation with reality. In this way both teacher and learner may gain insight into both the phenomenon under study and also their reactions to the phenomenon.

This last point emphasises the importance that should be placed on a 'post-mortem' discussion after any simulation exercise. Usually, it is only then possible to judge how much transfer of learning one can expect from the simulation or game to the real-life situation. The only other alternative is to place the learner in the real-life situation and observe what happens. However this may often be an expensive, impractical, dangerous or downright fatal procedure.

Planning simulations and games

Earlier on we illustrated the importance of analysing a learning problem most carefully before designing a simulation or game. Two types of analysis were mentioned — analysis of the real phenomenon so that we can design a valid model, and analysis of the learning tasks and difficulties so that we can determine how much simplification of the model or break-down into special exercises would be appropriate. In the last section we emphasised the need to evaluate the simulation exercise and to feedback the results of this evaluation either to improve the design of the exercise, or even to revise the model and the hypotheses upon which it is based.

Thus we see that the design of simulation and gaming exercises follows (in broad outline) the systems approach which we have been plugging all the way through this book from Chapter 1:

1   *Analysis* — of the system, the students, the learning tasks.
2   *Synthesis* — of appropriate exercises and test instruments.
3   *Evaluation* — leading to revision of earlier stages.

The exact steps one would follow may differ depending on the type and purpose of simulation one is planning. Using Bloom's three main categories of objectives, we can distinguish between purposes of simulation and games:

(a)   Those aiming at *Cognitive objectives.* Students should demonstrate an understanding of the phenomenon being simulated. In particular they might be applying previously learnt knowledge in problem-solving situations (Bloom's categories of analysis, synthesis and evaluation).

(b) Those aiming at *Affective objectives*. Students should emerge with a changed attitude to the phenomenon under study. They may achieve this by observing and discussing how their own actions affect others or how they are affected by the actions of other people.

(c) Those aiming at *Psychomotor objectives*. Such objectives usually involve mastering chains of SR—links (with occasional discriminations thrown in). Any well-designed 'off-the-job' exercise must in fact be either a simulation or a specific exercise for a component sub-skill. Gagné's conditions for learning suggest this. Seymour puts the same thing in different words as a principle of skills analysis training.

We can see therefore that, depending on the category of objectives, different approaches may be necessary to the structure of simulation exercises.

Tansey[3] suggests that there are three basic techniques used in simulation:

1 the case study
2 role playing
3 gaming

He argues that although the plain case study would not be considered by some as an example of simulation, it does in fact present the learners with a model of a real-life situation. He also suggests that some form of case study is usually implied in the instructions for a role-play exercise.

Experience would seem to bear out that cognitive objectives of a simple nature do not necessarily need simulation exercises at all. Cognitive objectives at the concept, or principle level, and particularly at the problem-solving level, can be tackled effectively by case studies. Role-playing or gaming would not necessarily be essential, but may nevertheless be included to add interest and motivation to the exercise. Some cognitive objectives, such as learning to apply a particular interview procedure, may demand role-playing by their very nature.

Affective objectives, on the other hand, are most likely to be achieved by realistic role-play exercises, coupled to a detailed discussion at the end. How much value there would be in trying to inject an element of gaming (an artificial element) is debatable. In the author's opinion, anything interfering with the realism of the simulation might have an adverse effect on the attainment of affective objectives.

Finally, for psychomotor skills, some form of simulation is dictated, if learning 'on the job' is impractical or too difficult. Role-playing is used in the sense that the learner is playing his own future role (there is no point in learning a psychomotor skill if one is not going to use it). Gaming is rarely used, though 'against the clock' or 'against the target' exercises which simulate the piecework situation in industry have been found to be very effective (these however are examples of competitive elements that exist naturally in the real-life situation).

To complete this chapter let us look at the way that some practitioners set about planning role-playing and gaming exercises, and finally conclude with a detailed consideration of psychomotor skill training.

Role-playing exercises

Peter McPhail[4] suggests six factors which one should consider when planning a role-play exercise:

A good role-play exercise should (a) have a clear purpose or purposes relevant to the needs of the participants; (b) use a situation which is real to those participants; (c) include only the number of people who can actively contribute; (d) be conducted in physical conditions which make it easy for those role-playing to accept the reality of the situation and identify with it; (e) have enough time allowed to let it run as long as the motivation lasts; and above all (f) be non-authoritarian in organisation and practice.

He then contrasts the procedures which one would use to

build role-play exercises depending on whether one was attempting to establish a particular skill such as selling a car (cognitive objectives), or to help people to take into consideration others' needs, feelings or interests (affective objectives).

In brief the procedure he suggests for the *cognitive* domain runs as follows:

1 The organiser states what the skill is which the role-play is designed to improve. He may expand his introduction by showing a film or video-tape to demonstrate skilled or unskilled performances.

2 The situation or situations to be role-played are selected for their relevance to acquiring the skill in question, preferably in consultation with the course members.

3 The course is divided up into role-play groups. For most situations small groups of 5 to 10 are best.

4 The amount of detailed information required by participants before they can respond to a situation will vary according to their experience and the particular situation. Nevertheless, classical role-play allows maximum freedom to those taking part and it reaps great motivational and learning benefit from doing so.

5 The participants play out their roles. Those who cannot have active parts are asked to observe the principal's solution, evaluate it and decide what they would do in his position.

6 As long as the participants are interested, and there is time, other members of the group can be asked to play out what they would do rather than just talk about others' performances.

7 The organiser of the role-play discusses in detail with

the participants their approach to the problem posed and the role-play solutions to it. If he has a tape recorder or, better still, a video-tape recorder, a record of the proceedings will clarify exactly what individuals said and did.

8 When the role-play situations are simple dyadic (one to one) encounters, for example, where interview technique is practised by A interviewing B, a valuable feedback technique is to reverse the roles and try the whole exercise over again before further discussion.

9 Towards the conclusion of the course it is valuable to hold a plenary session where course members are encouraged to give their impressions of the course — to be uninhibited in their criticism.

10 After the plenary session some role-play organisers talk to the whole course about the insights which have been gained and learning which has taken place.

For *affective* objectives, particularly ones associated with teaching people to get on with others, he suggests:

1 A conflict situation is chosen for role-play, preferably by the game members themselves.

2 The situation described, with support from cartoon, straight drawing or photograph, is read and seen by the group. To make the impact even more vivid it can be acted.

3 Two participants naturally inclined towards the points of view in conflict are asked to play out what they would do, while the other group members watch and decide how they would react.

4 The conflict roles are reversed and the participants

take the place of the other and play out what they would do.

5   Both participants then revert to their original roles and play out their 'final' responses. Wide experience suggests that the final responses are more considerate than the behaviour originally suggested and that this experience can, in many cases, affect people's life styles.

6   Other members of the group should be encouraged to criticise what they have seen and play out their solutions as long as they are interested.

Examples of role-play simulations aiming mainly at cognitive objectives are the Oxfam simulations. The Oxfam Education programme includes two simulations designed to teach young people about developing countries. In the *Aid Committee Game* the players study the problems of one developing country, examine six projects and decide which projects deserve financial help. In the Development Game the students divide into groups representing the government of a particular country and each group prepares a development plan for presentation to a committee which decides which plan merits aid.

An example of a role-play exercise aiming primarily at affective objectives is the Shelter simulation *Tenement*. This deals with the problems of families living in a multi-occupied house.

Further examples of available simulations may be found at the end of the chapter[5].

Games
Rex Walford[6] suggests that before deciding to use or design a game one should consider at least three points:

1   Is this the place in my classes where I really need a

game? Is the game going to teach about a process or represent a decision-making situation more effectively than other teaching modes? Do I know why I am choosing to use a game?

2   Is the game that I choose to use, or adapt, or build from scratch, one that is a reasonable representation of reality? The game may be well-built, and good fun and exciting — but is it 'real'? (In this sense, an educational game may have different objectives from a commercial, entertainment game.) If the game is not founded on some kind of reality, it may be a pleasant interlude in class but a source of misconceptions at the same time.

3   Have I learnt enough about this game to run it properly? Do I understand the basic intentions of the game, and can I manage it reasonably in my own class situation? Games require a different kind of teaching technique, and the teacher who uses them needs a degree of managerial expertise.

He goes on to outline a procedure for the design of educational games as follows:

1   What is the basic idea of the game?

2   What is the context of the game?

3   What style of game will be most suitable?
     Style can refer to the type of equipment needed (board? counters? or just talk?). The development of groups within the game — Individuals? Groups of five or six? Larger groups? The amount of competitiveness desired: games can be entirely co-operative if required.

4   Who will the players represent?

5   Are there to be defined objectives for the players?

Sometimes such definition gives the game urgency and purpose. At other times, it is instructive to let groups work towards the definition of their own objectives — which may differ.

6 What do the players do to make the game work? What interaction is needed to move the game on? Talk? Or the throwing of a dice? Or a planned move on a board?

7 How does this become a game reality?

8 What limiting constraints are needed to make the game playable?

9 What are the operating instructions for the players? At this stage, comes a self-testing device. Is it possible to set out rules in a 'How to play' framework, and make sense of them? The cooperation of someone so far uninvolved in the game is invaluable here. The rules, however, are not necessarily those which are given to players; better that their substance is explained in the classroom.

10 Does the game match up to reality? At this final stage, the model is held up to its source. It may be possible to have a playable, exciting game but one which is not a replica of the factors that actually exist. In the desire to motivate or to be 'fair to all', rules and interactions may have become detached from real-life sources. However good this game may be, it is not a simulation. Back to the drawing-board and start again . . .

Games may again be sub-classified into those which aim mainly at cognitive objectives and those which are concerned with affective objectives.

Examples of available games in the *cognitive* domain include: *Man in His Environment,* a game devised to help students understand some major ecological principles. This is produced by the Coca-Cola Export Corporation. The Sellotape *Airline Adventure Game* (produced by Sellotape) is a game about the operation of airlines along international air routes.

Examples of games which at least in part aim at *affective* objectives are *Streets Ahead,* a game designed to help children face and understand the problems of city life, by the Humanities Curriculum Project, and *Crisis in Lagia* — a simulation on aspects of war and society. Further examples may be found in references 4 and 5 at the end of the chapter.

Psychomotor skills

In the remainder of this chapter we will be specially concerned with devices which communicate through the sense of touch and the kinaesthetic sense. Such concepts as hard and soft, hot and cold, rigid and flexible are established (at an early age) by confronting the learner with a series of objects, some hard, some soft, and identifying them as such. The child learns to discriminate first between very hard objects (like the floor he falls on) and very soft ones (like the porridge he spreads over the floor). In time he learns to classify objects as hard or soft with increasing precision.

At a later stage of the learner's development, when he can understand a certain amount of verbal communications, one can cut corners. One might for example succeed in establishing the concepts flexible and rigid at that stage by simply saying: 'Flexible objects bend easily; rigid ones do not.' The intelligent student (or rather the one who is sufficiently prepared verbally) will probably straight away be able to classify the broomstick as rigid and the broom's bristles as flexible. He may still need quite a bit of practice however to classify different bristles according to flexibility.

Whereas he may even distinguish visually between the flexibility of a broom handle and the bristles, the fine discrimination between different bristle types may require a highly developed sense of touch, or a kinaesthetic sense, or both. Such precise discrimination skills often form part of industrial tasks. The training of such skills is often aided by special devices or simulators.

Another class of skills which rely on the kinaesthetic senses are skills of coordination — either the coordination of the position of the limbs (as in panel beating) or of movements as in many sports, driving or high-speed industrial operations. Again the learning of such skills is often aided by the use of specially designed devices.

We have seen the extent to which man relies on verbal communication. Visual and audio-visual methods tend to act as aids to the basic process of verbal communication. We did see, however, that certain information can only be effectively communicated by the use of non-verbal methods: characteristic noises or postures of mating birds for example. We are now about to consider information which can only be communicated by the feel of the subject, or the feel of a certain action pattern.

Information used in learning a skill

Generally, one performs an action in order to achieve a specific result. A golfer's drive has the objective of getting the golf ball to move a precise distance in a precise direction. The novice soon learns this. He may then practise driving a golf ball down the fairway. Where the golf ball actually goes gives him an idea of his progress. Thus we have two forms of information in use; information on the purpose of an action (objectives if you like) and information of the results (knowledge of results, or feedback).

This is still insufficient for efficient learning. The novice may note that one attempt was better than another, but will learn little unless he takes note of information about his actual movements. This may come either from some outside source, such as guidance from a trainer, or it can come from inside the learner. He may note the 'feel' of making a stroke which produces good results. A man may learn to drive a ball accurately without formal training. His technique may turn out to be unorthodox, but the results may nevertheless be quite good. Instruction and guidance by an expert may improve results or reduce learning time, but are not absolutely essential to the mastery of the skill. What is essential, however, are the two forms of information feedback — knowledge of results (or *external feedback*) and knowledge of the 'feel' of the action (*internal feedback*). If either is removed or impaired, learning is inefficient. People who 'lack coordination' do not generally develop any high level of motor skill. If through illness they are completely lacking in the use of their kinaesthetic sense they have difficulty in walking or in performing any controlled movement. They rely on visual information exclusively to control the position of their limbs. Similarly, learning to drive a golf ball in the dark, without knowledge of results, is not very effective. One might expect the learner to develop and practise a bad habit to perfection in these circumstances. The perfect slice!

There is strong evidence for the need for these two types of feedback. We mentioned earlier the experiments of Thorndike[7] with groups of blindfolded people drawing lines on paper. Knowledge or results, in the form of saying 'right' or 'wrong' improved accuracy. Groups without knowledge of results lost accuracy. Further experiments on these lines indicated that the type of feedback supplied also affected accuracy. Feedback on the size of error was better than just 'right' or 'wrong'. Inconsistent feedback was worse than no information at all. Finally, persistent practice with no feedback resulted in progressively more consistent errors from the desired length. A 'bad habit' was being efficiently learned.

This illustrates an important change that occurs in the learning of a skill. In the early stages the learner relies heavily on external stimuli. He must look down to find the gear lever. He must observe the ball in flight. As skill develops, internal, kinaesthetic stimuli increasingly take over control. He finds the gear lever 'instinctively' whatever gear he is in. He can tell whether his drive is successful almost before his swing is complete, just by the feel of it.

How to teach skills

Thorndike's experiments indicate one way of improving the conditions of learning a skill. If knowledge of results is not actually present in a particular task, some way of supplying it might be devised. For example, when tapping a screw thread in a hole, it is important not to put too much pressure on the tap. If you push too hard, the tap will break. The problem is to learn just how hard is too hard. One method is by trial and error which takes a long time and may be costly in replacement taps. If one can arrange for the tap to 'cry out' just before breaking point, then one might expect learning to be more efficient. One would certainly cut down on breakages.

Another method might be by guidance. The instructor may guide the student's hand while performing a job, or give him hints on what to watch for. In teaching a student to use a file, the instructor first imparts the correct stance and the correct way to hold the file. He may demonstrate the motions and then supervise, correct and even guide the student's motions. The golfer's swing is sometimes taught by strapping the novice in a harness, which controls the extent and direction of his motions.

When designing training tasks both the factors of feedback and guidance should be considered. They are not as simple as they appear at first sight. Any feedback won't do. Some guidance methods are better than others.

Types of feedback

There are two types of feedback which may be present in a task. One tells the learner how well he has peformed — *knowledge of results*. The other tells him how he is performing right now — *knowledge of performance*. This second (termed *action feedback*) is of importance in continuous adjustment skills, like steering a car along a road. One is continuously using the visual feedback from the road to adjust one's actions. However skilled the driver, he is technically out of control if all his lights fail on a dark night. Knowledge of results, on the other hand, only becomes apparent once the action is complete. Steering into a skid produces (generally) desirable results. Action feedback (in the form of visual and kinaesthetic information) tells us we are skidding. Previous learning tells us to steer into the skid. A comparison of the extent of our corrective action with the result it produces constitutes the basis for learning skid correction. Knowledge of results is therefore sometimes called learning feedback.

Learning feedback is vital for efficient learning. Action feedback does not help much at all. This was demonstrated by an experiment performed by Annett and Kay[8]. Subjects were told to press down with a certain pressure on a spring balance. If they were allowed to see the scale while pressing (action feedback) they of course performed perfectly. If they were only allowed to see the scale after they had applied pressure (learning feedback) they initially made errors, but improved with practice. When after an equal number of trials all feedback was removed, the group that received learning feedback performed adequately for some time, but the group who had received continuous action feedback immediately deteriorated. They had not learnt the 'feel' of the correct pressure. The learning feedback group's performace also tends to deteriorate in time if the feedback is withheld, but this happens slower. We might say that the group is 'forgetting' the feel of a two-pound pressure. This finding is important as well, as it indicates the limitations which some training devices may suffer from.

If the knowledge of results a training device supplies is quite different in form from that found 'on the job' the learning may not be permanent. Goldstein and Rittenhouse[9] found that in training aeroplane gunners to aim on a simulator, performance could be vastly improved by supplying knowledge of results in the form of a buzzer whenever the gun was on target. When the aid was removed, however, performance rapidly deteriorated until it was much the same as people trained by normal direct methods. There seemed to be no long-term benefit whatever from using the extra artificial feedback.

Seymour[10] on the other hand, used training devices successfully to teach the amount of pressure permissible in picking up fragile electrical insulators. He used dummy insulators which were spring loaded against micro switches and wired so that too much pressure gave a red light, the correct amount gave a white light and insufficient pressure gave no light at all. Other experiments have also given good results from the use of not normally available or 'artificial' knowledge of results during training. The evidence is conflicting and more research is needed, but it seems that success may depend on what sort of artificial feedback one uses, and how one uses it. How similar is the artificial feedback to that actually present in the task? How is the 'transfer of control' from the artificial feedback to the natural feedback effected?

For example, Annett's experiment with the spring balance gives better long-term learning if the subject is allowed to check his results only at alternative trials. Thus he follows each trial with artificial feedback by a trial when he must rely on the natural feedback present in the task. Seymour's work shows similar results. Artificial feedback is supplied at progressively longer intervals till the learner does not need to rely on it at all.

The gun-aiming experiment described did not support this view. Intermittent supply of feedback was no better in achieving long-term learning. Perhaps the difference lies in the type of feedback and the information it gives. Gun aiming is a skill where there are degrees of error. One must recognise these degrees of error to apply appropriate degrees of correction. A buzzer is either on or off. It does not inform of the degree of error.

The scale reading in Annett's experiment does inform of the degree of error, and appropriate adjustments of pressure result in appropriate reductions of error. The artificial and natural feedback — although received through different senses — give the same sort of information.

Seymour's experiment is not so clear. The white light indicates a range of pressure which is safe. The learner may experiment for himself in adjusting pressure throughout the safe range. Perhaps, as in Annett's experiment he can practise adjustments in pressure, and therefore the natural kinaesthetic feedback plays more of a part in the learning right from the start. It may on the other hand all boil down to the fact that most kinaesthetic skills are poorly developed and so show marked response to training, whereas the visual skill of gunners may be less prone to improvement.

These last observations are conjectures which could act as the subject for experimentation. However one may make several practical suggestions on the basis of work so far completed:

1   When training a skill, examine whether the normal method of training provides satisfactory knowledge of results.

2   When doing this do not confuse action feedback, with knowledge of results.

3   If the naturally present knowledge of results is not easily observable by the student (ie it uses undeveloped kinaesthetic or tactile senses), consider the possibilities of a training device which supplies more obvious feedback.

4   Try to arrange that the artificial feedback supplies information of a similar nature to that supplied by the natural feedback.

5   Try to arrange training so that the trainees occasionally rely on natural feedback alone, and progressively withdraw the artificial aids.

This last process is akin to the fading of prompts in a programme. It can probably be most efficiently done by some means of adaptive control, responsive to the learner's performance, as in SAKI.

Types of guidance

We might guide the student in a learning task in a number of ways. We may give verbal guidance — 'Use your body weight!' We may demonstrate an action visually. We may actively guide the physical responses of the student.

The first two types of guidance are really supplying pre-knowledge; what to do and how to do it. The techniques are those discussed in the earlier sections. For example, when demonstrating an action it is best to demonstrate it as seen from the learner's viewpoint. Hence one value of film or television in training skills. The decisions on what verbal knowledge is required to perform a task and how it should be taught spring from the task analysis.

It is the third type of guidance, actual physical control that can be built into training devices or simulators, that is our concern here. This can be achieved in two ways. One can physically 'force' the correct movements out of the learner (forced response), or one can allow the learner to make his own motions, but restrict the direction or extent of these motions (physical restriction). Both methods are used in training devices. We have already mentioned the harness used for training a golfer's swing. This is an example of physical restriction of the learner's movements. The learner makes his swing but he cannot deviate from the correct path. Of course, he may still produce a poor swing. He may not follow through as far as he should. His movements may be even more restricted than the harness allows. Many golfing coaches therefore employ the forced response techniques, by standing immediately behind the learner, holding the learner's wrists or club, and physically guiding the stroke every inch of the way. Such methods are of application to motor responses, where the extent of a movement or its exact path are critical. Physical restriction is often employed in training devices and simulators, by the use of stops at the end of a machine bed, for example. Forced response techniques are more often employed by instructors. They are rarely employed in training devices as it is difficult to construct a mechanism that would adequately simulate the required complexity of movement.

Both methods of guidance do produce training results. They have been employed for simple tasks such as the pencil tracing of mazes, and have been found to reduce training time appreciably. Holding[11] describes an interesting series of experiments on the use of physical guidance. These are an adaptation of Thorndike's earlier line-drawing exercises. In this case a knob had to be moved a distance of four inches along a rod. One group acted as control, receiving no guidance or feedback. Another received forced guidance by means of a spring that towed the learner's hand through the appropriate distance. A third received a mixture of forced guidance and free practice. The fourth group practised in a physically restricted set-up — a stop was fixed at the 4-inch point. The last two groups received no guidance, but did receive knowledge of results 'a la Thorndike'. Group 5 had 'yes-no' feedback, and group 6 had feedback on the magnitude and direction of their errors. The restricted response method using a stop, gave most effective learning. Then came: full knowledge of results, yes-no feedback, and finally forced response and the mixed method about equal last (but still producing an appreciable amount of learning). Holding argues that the relatively poor results of the forced response in this case was because the simulation was inappropriate. Instead of pushing the knob, the learner's hand was being pulled by the spring. A modified experiment where the final task involved the pulling of a handle, produced much better results for the forced response technique — superior in fact to the restricted guidance method.

The lessons for the training officer or instructor therefore are:

1 Restricting the possibilities for motion or forcing the correct movement can produce effective learning.

2 Restricting the extent or direction of motion (eg by stops or grooves) is easier to apply appropriately and can be expected to train as effectively as methods based on the supply of knowledge of results.

3 Forcing the response is more difficult to arrange, (except by direct human effort) due to difficulties in simulating the exact condition. It can be as effective as restriction or feedback if applied well, but inappropriate forcing (eg pulling instead of pushing) reduces effectiveness drastically.

Some simple training devices and simulators
Training devices need not be complex electronically

controlled simulators, such as the RAF flight trainers, or the SAKI machine described earlier. The complexity of a training device will naturally be a reflection of the complexity of the task being trained. The object of a flight simulator is to give the pilot every possible experience of flying without risking valuable lives and equipment. One therefore arranges for every possible relevant stimulus to be fed to the pilot. The ideal flight simulator would react to the pilot's responses in every detail — instrument reading, noise, vision through cockpit and the feeling of gravity changes through the seat of his pants. Simulators of such complexity are used in the training of astronauts, but the cost precludes their more general use. For many purposes a partial simulation suffices.

When a full task analysis is carried out, certain skill elements are often found to be particularly difficult to master. Such elements should be isolated and trained separately, irrespective of whether a progressive-parts training technique is being used for the whole task, or whether it is being practised all at once. Very often, simulation can help in training these elements.

The learning problems associated with the difficult element must be identified. This may involve detailed observation and questioning of skilled performers *and learners*. The questions to consider are:

1   How is the element learnt? What sort of a task is it? What senses are involved and how?

2   What is making the learning difficult? Lack of aptitude? Underdeveloped motor skills? Conflict with previous learning? Fear of equipment?

If the difficulty is due to certain defects of perception or muscular coordination, then the possibility of a special training exercise should be considered. This may take the form of eye-focussing exercises for inspection skills, or a special bit of equipment for sensory-motor skills. As an example of the design of training devices, let us consider an area of training which will be familiar to most readers — the beginnings of a craft apprenticeship course or a metalwork course in school.

One of the first objectives is that students should master the use of the basic hand tools. In the good old craft days, it was said that a boy needed several months of practice in order to learn to file flat. Now we don't spend so much time on this skill, mainly because the use of machine tools has reduced the need. Trainees spend considerably less time, and reach a slightly lower standard of skill. It is probable however, that a systematically designed training aid would be capable of training to the high standard that used to take weeks or months to achieve, in a matter of days or even hours. Let us look at a few examples of training aids in this area.

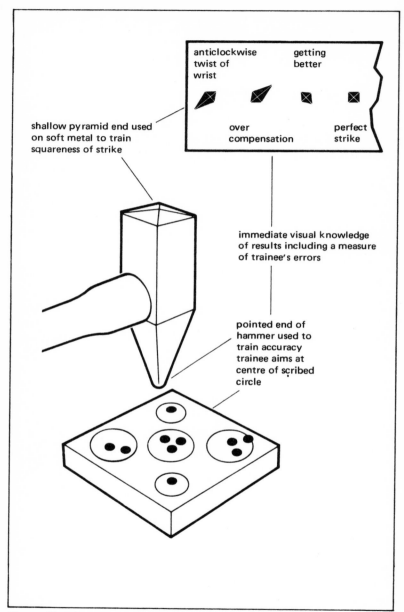

anticlockwise twist of wrist

getting better

shallow pyramid end used on soft metal to train squareness of strike

over compensation

perfect strike

immediate visual knowledge of results including a measure of trainee's errors

pointed end of hammer used to train accuracy trainee aims at centre of scribed circle

Figure 10.1 Special training hammer

1 Use of the hammer

<u>Objective:</u> To strike accurately and squarely.

<u>Analysis:</u> Points of difficulty to learner — no obvious feedback either on accuracy or squareness, as hammer rebounds too quickly. Only difficult-to-interpret feedback such as sideways jump of hammer is present naturally.

<u>Training design:</u> (a) Accuracy: soft workpiece, pointed hammer. Mark circles of decreasing size as targets. Aim for centre.
(b) Squareness: soft workpiece; shallow pyramid point on hammer. Strike at a series of targets (eg along a line)

<u>Evaluation:</u> (a) Student self-judges progress by position of marks relative to centre of circle (knowledge of error).
(b) Square strike leaves a square indented pyramid. Any irregularities in indent point to specific errors in strike. Student refers to sample errors (knowledge of error) or instructor corrects strike (forced response).

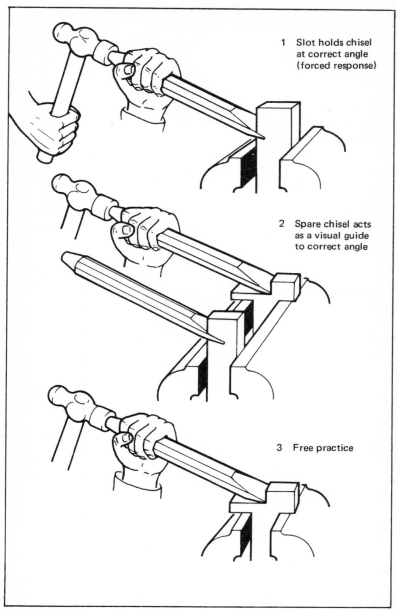

1 Slot holds chisel at correct angle (forced response)

2 Spare chisel acts as a visual guide to correct angle

3 Free practice

Figure 10.2 Use of the cold chisel

2 Use of the chisel

Objective: To use chisel at the correct cutting angle.

Analysis: Points of difficulty — keeping angle constant and correct while hammering. Control of chisel angle is part visual and part kinaesthetic.

Training design: (a) First stage — guidance (by forced response). Chisel held in groove, fixed at correct angle. It cannot wander. Student concentrates on hammering.
(b) Second stage (visual guidance only). Correct angle is demonstrated by one chisel in slot while the student uses another freely alongside.
(c) Third stage — free practice.

Evaluation: First stage: No chance of error. Student learns 'feel'.
Second stage: Self-evaluation against a visual guide.
Third stage: Instructor must evaluate both method and resultant quality of work.

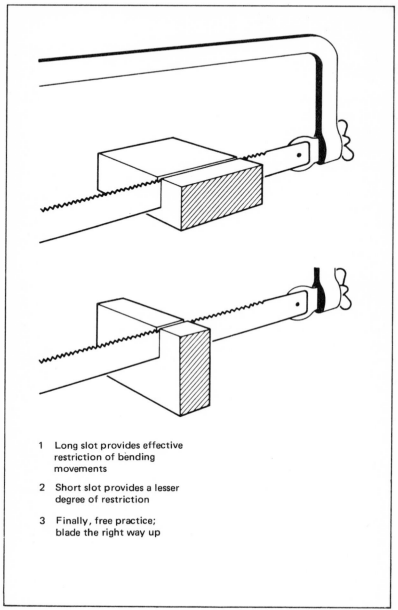

1 Long slot provides effective
restriction of bending
movements

2 Short slot provides a lesser
degree of restriction

3 Finally, free practice;
blade the right way up

Figure 10.3 Training device for use of the hacksaw

3 Use of the hacksaw

Objective: To cut straight, vertical slots accurately.

Analysis: Student must learn new skill of moving hands in one plane. There is action feedback present in the job (eg the bending or bowing of the blade) but the strongest control comes from the kinaesthetic sense (ie student must learn the feel).

Training design: (a) First stage (physical restriction). Use a hacksaw with blade wrong way up, in an accurately pre-formed saw cut along the wide edge of workpiece.
(b) Repeat in another cut along narrow edge. (Less physical restriction.)

Evaluation: Bending of blade produces noise of teeth on sides. This artificial action feedback brings to student's attention his error and the less obvious 'natural' action feedback of the blade bending.
Progressive reduction of length of slot reduces guidance. Instructor must judge when to change slots. One weakness — device does not simulate the need to press harder on forward stroke than on back stroke.

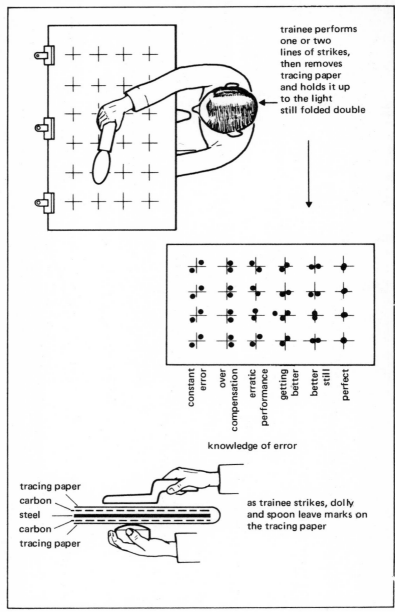

Figure 10.4 Use of dolly and spoon

4 Use of dolly and spoon

Objective: To beat out small dents in metal sheet.

Analysis: Difficulty in learning to strike so that dolly and spoon are exactly at the right spot. Slight discrepancies can make the dent worse. This knowledge of error cannot be relied on in training as only several wrong strikes (ie practising errors) will make new dent appear obvious.

Training design: Sheet of steel for practice has carbon paper and tracing paper interleaved as shown. Target crosses marked on top sheet of tracing paper.

Student strikes with spoon at a series of crosses in turn, holding the dolly below.

Evaluation: After exercise (say 8 strikes) complete, tracing paper is removed. Student can see the relative positions of cross, upper impact and lower impact (knowledge of error). He can attempt to correct error on next exercise. Several characteristic types of error exist (eg dolly always to left, or lines of motion of dolly and spoon always at a fixed angle.)

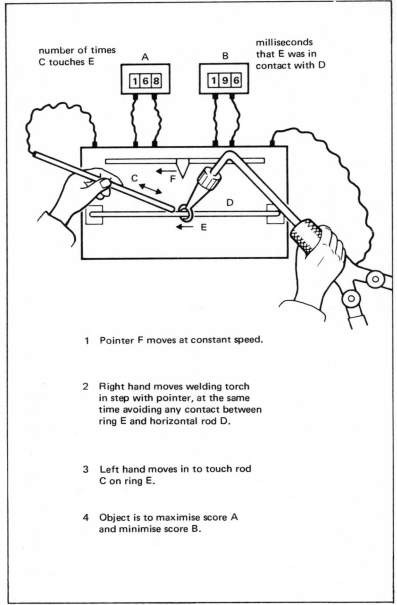

number of times
C touches E

milliseconds
that E was in
contact with D

1   Pointer F moves at constant speed.

2   Right hand moves welding torch
    in step with pointer, at the same
    time avoiding any contact between
    ring E and horizontal rod D.

3   Left hand moves in to touch rod
    C on ring E.

4   Object is to maximise score A
    and minimise score B.

Figure 10.5 Gas welding simulator

5 Use of welding torch

<u>Objective</u>: To move torch smoothly at constant speed along seam, while other hand is irregularly feeding in welding rod.

<u>Analysis</u>: Coordination of uniform movement of right hand and jerky movement of left hand difficult to learn. Both speed of progress and distance from metal of the welding flame are critical.

<u>Training design</u>: As in diagram. Welding torch is moved right to left in step with the clockwork pointer. Loop on torch nozzle must not touch horizontal wire. The other hand feeds in the rod to touch the loop as often as possible. Each touch of welding rod on loop registers 1 on counter A. Time of contact between loop and horizontal wire registers on counter B.

<u>Evaluation</u>: Object is to maximise score A and minimise score B. Scores act as terminal knowledge of results, and as a measure of progress against pre-set standards.

This device is more of a full simulator than the earlier examples, as several skills are practised in coordination. One can in training break this down and first practise the right hand alone, then add the left. The scores can be used with some degree of objectivity, as a measure of the skill. Although the lowest scores on counter B did not necessarily make the best welders, it was found in practice that scores above a certain maximum ceiling indicated the futility of attempting to train the individual as a welder. The device has been used to aid selection as well as training.

The first three examples have been developed by the French Michelin Tyre Company[1][2] the last two are from the author's own experience in industry.

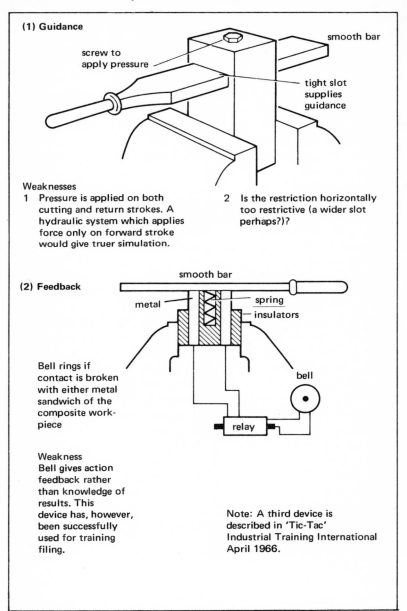

(1) Guidance

smooth bar

screw to
apply pressure

tight slot
supplies
guidance

Weaknesses
1   Pressure is applied on both
cutting and return strokes. A
hydraulic system which applies
force only on forward stroke
would give truer simulation.

2   Is the restriction horizontally
too restrictive (a wider slot
perhaps?)?

(2) Feedback

smooth bar

metal

spring

insulators

Bell rings if
contact is broken
with either metal
sandwich of the
composite work-
piece

bell

relay

Weakness
Bell gives action
feedback rather
than knowledge of
results. This
device has, however,
been successfully
used for training
filing.

Note: A third device is
described in 'Tic-Tac'
Industrial Training International
April 1966.

Figure 10.6 Filing flat — some possible solutions

Exercise on simulator design

Figure 10.6 illustrates two hypothetical attempts to design a simulated exercise for the skill of filing flat. This skill, you may recall, was practiced 'on the job' in the old days, and it was traditional to expect the new apprentice to spend up to several months doing precious little else other than filing bits of scrap metal to odd configurations to a high standard of accuracy. One often heard the seasoned craftsman say 'it takes 3 to 6 months to learn to file flat'. Nowadays apprentices spend much less time, not because training has improved but because in this machine age, the need for hand-fitting of components to high tolerance levels has diminished.

Nevertheless engineering apprentices still usually spend the equivalent of several days work on filing exercises, in order to reach a tolerable standard for today's needs.

The reader may like to consider the two suggested exercises, and related criticisms, shown in Figure 10.6. Perhaps other criticisms may spring to mind. He may find it interesting to attempt to design an improved exercise.

To the author's knowledge, neither of these examples has been extensively used, though the second one was used experimentally by the author giving promising results. There was however a commercially produced filing simulator put on the market in 1966, which does overcome some of the weaknesses of the two shown here. Readers who come up with a design of their own, may like to compare it with 'Tic-Tac' which was described fully in an article in *Industrial Training International* of April 1966.

Conclusion

The design principles of complex simulators are no different from the principles outlined above. Difficulties may arise with very complex tasks, either in (a) the analysis stages (eg how does the 'good' manager differ from the mediocre — the analysis of management skills is at present only a partly completed task, hence the variety of approaches to management development and the generally poor transfer to the job of skills learnt on courses), or in (b) the design (synthesis) stages (eg the design may call for the simulator to incorporate sophisticated electronics or computerised data stores as on flight simulators or in business games etc.)

It is outside the scope of this book to deal exhaustively with more complex games and simulators. Readers may refer to the suggested further reading for descriptions of practical applications. We have tried here to illustrate only the general underlying principles of simulation and gaming.

Simulation emerges not as a panacea for training ills, but as a set of techniques of exercise design with particular advantages in particular situations. We have also tried to show that the decision process for the selection of a particular type of simulation can be considered as part of a general systems approach to training design. Stimulus-response approaches (eg Skinner, Gilbert), hierarchical approaches to learning tasks (eg Bloom, Gagné), skills-analysis approaches (eg Seymour), programmed instruction, and finally simulation and gaming are seen to be quite complementary sets of techniques. Indeed they are seen to depend in the main on the same basic set of questions that the training designer must answer. They are merely alternative ways of seeking the answers to these questions.

The lesson to carry away from this book is that as far as training design is concerned 'it's not what you do, but the way that you *set about deciding how to* do it — that's what gets results'.

References

1. W D Seymour, *Industrial Skills,* Pitman, 1966.

2. R F Barton, *A Primer in Simulation and Gaming,* Prentice Hall, 1970. See also D R Cruickshank, 'The Notions of Simulations and Games: A Preliminary Enquiry', *Educational Technology,* July 1972.

3. P J Tansey, 'An Introduction to Simulation and Gaming', in *Games and Simulations,* BBC Publications, 1972.

4. P McPhail, 'Building a Role-Playing Exercise', in *Games and Simulations*, BBC, 1972.

5. P J Tansey and D Unwin, *Simulation and Gaming in Education*, Methuen, 1969.

6. R Walford, 'Using, Adapting and Building Games', in *Games and Simulations*, BBC, 1972.

7. E L Thorndike, 'The Law of Effect', *American Journal of Psychology*, Vol 39, 1927.

8. J Annett and H Kay, 'Knowledge of Results and Skilled Performance', *Occupational Psychology*, Vol 31, 1957.

9. M Goldstein and C H Rittenhouse, 'Knowledge of Results in the Acquisition and Transfer of a Gunnery Skill', *Journal of Experimental Psychology*, Vol 48, 1954.

10. W D Seymour, *Industrial Training for Manual Operations*, Pitman, 1954.

11. D H Holding, *Principles of Training*, Pergamon, 1965.

12. J Wellens, 'Teaching the "Feel" at Michelin', *Technical Education and Industrial Training*, August 1965.

Further reading

W D Seymour, *Skills Analysis Training*, Pitman, 1968.

P J Tansey, *Educational Aspects of Simulation*, McGraw-Hill, 1971.

R A Walford, *Games in Geography*, Longman, 1970.

Appendix 1

The Limitations of Programmed Instruction by Dr L A Biran

This article is reproduced by kind permission of the author, and should be read in conjunction with Chapter 9 (page 269). It may also serve as a useful job aid later.

1 Programmed Instruction in the narrow and wide sense

In considering the limits of applicability of programmed instruction one must bear in mind the different levels on which this term is used. At the more general level of 'a systematic strategy of teaching, aided by technological aids and psychological tactics', programmed instruction merges into modern teaching methodology, and a separate discussion of its limitations becomes meaningless. At the most restricted level of *'structured, individual self-instruction'*, programmed instruction is a teaching technique in competition with others, such as independent learning in small groups, teacher-led instruction, project work etc. Each of these has advantages, disadvantages and pre-requisites on which a decision about the usefulness of a particular technique in particular circumstances can be based.

2 Difficulties in evaluating single teaching methods

The human being is an adaptable animal, and the more able of the species will learn *something,* however taught (which is why educational innovation is possible). Hence, in considering the choice of teaching methods one is rarely faced with alternatives which are absolutely 'good' or 'bad'. Rather one has to divine the optimum, taking into account the characteristics of the learning task, as well as those of each proposed method, and the availability of other solutions. (Drill teaching of the 3R's may be far from ideal education, but in a remote village school may be a big advance over no education.) One should also bear in mind that it is often possible to use a 'bouquet' of teaching methods, rather than a single one. Research suggests that for long periods of instruction, such a bouquet (self- and teacher-led instruction, individual and group instruction, reception and discovery learning), provided it is well arranged, is preferable to any single method. This further qualifies any generalisations about the limitations of individual methods.

3 Limitations of programmed instruction in the narrow sense

Despite the above reservations, an example is given below of factors which influence the usefulness of a particular teaching technique. The discussion will concern programmed instruction in the restricted sense of *individual self-instruction through textual materials*. This example is chosen for two reasons: it represents an extreme in the continuum of individual-centered versus group-centered learning (hence the issues are clearer than in other cases) and it is a case of practical importance, being the standard situation in which a 'classical' programmed text stands in for the unavailable human teacher. To sum up, therefore, the limitations will be considered for the following method:

Programmed self-instruction

— for individual use: only small teacher involvement, eg to deal with difficulties, mark tests, etc.

— mainly through textual materials.

— it will be further assumed that the materials will have to be specially produced (or extensively adapted), rather than being available off the shelf.

Some of the factors determining the ease and value of adopting this type of programmed instruction are discussed in the Tables on the following pages. It should be remembered that following none of the factors rules programmed instruction absolutely 'in' or 'out', but they should be considered in a cumulative manner, their relative importance being determined by the specific situation under study. The Tables should not be regarded as an exhaustive decision tree. Rather, it is hoped that the examples and their discussion will stimulate the reader to delve into his own experience for the factors which are really of importance to the particular educational problem he is called upon to solve.

Factor	Column 1 Characteristics in Favour of programmed self-instruction	Column 2 Characteristics Against programmed self-instruction	Reasons and Remarks
Subject matter	Symbolic Mathematical	Descriptive	There may be no point in programming Column 2 material.
	Tightly logical, but difficult to follow (eg derivation of formulae)	Easy to follow	
	Retention important	Retention not essential	
	Invariable, basic knowledge	Rapidly changing, advanced knowledge	
	Problems with unique answers (eg elementary physics)	Problems with variety of answers (eg human relations)	It is difficult to deal in a self-instructional programme with a variety of responses, unless one has a teacher, a computer or sophisticated students. The unexpected response clearly calls for evaluation by a human being.
	Sensory discrimination skills	Psychomotor skills (difficult but *not* impossible to programme)	It is easy to *present* the required variety of stimuli but difficult to *evaluate* a variety of responses. Simulators may help here.

Table 1

Factor	Column 1 Characteristics in Favour	Column 2 Characteristics Against	Reasons and Remarks
Objectives: General	Short term Clear and distinct Easy to test	Long term Diffuse and interdependent Difficult to test	Attempts to 'programme' sections of academic syllabi at school or university level have often led to a general increase in the precision of definition and testing of objectives, and to supplementing long-term objectives by short-term ones.
Objectives: Cognitive (in terms of Bloom's taxonomy, see Chapter 1)	Knowledge and 'discrimination' skills (comprehension, analysis, evaluation) Algorithmic strategies of solving problems	'Production' skills (application, synthesis) Heuristic strategies of solving problems	In addition to this division, the higher levels of the taxonomy (analysis, synthesis, evaluation) are more difficult to treat in a programme than lower ones. Difficulties with evaluation of response in case of heuristic problem solving.
Objectives: Attitudes	Situations where change of attitude likely to result from achievement of cognitive objectives ('understanding' in everyday language)	Situations where change of attitude likely to require social interaction, making other methods more suitable (group discussion, games, role playing)	The neo-behaviourist theories of Skinner, on which linear programming is based, have also resulted in successful systems for changing attitudes and habits by means of conditioning, using positive and negative reinforcement, and punishment.

Table 2

Factor	Column 1 Characteristics in Favour	Column 2 Characteristics Against	Reasons and Remarks
Student population: Numbers and location	Numerous Dispersed The case of dispersed students is one where efficient and effective self-instruction may be especially helpful. Group of at least 30, easily available for testing materials during production.	Scarce In a single group Student population too small or too dispersed to provide a test population.	A programme for a small group is relatively very expensive to produce, and may be difficult to revise, due to lack of 'human guinea pigs' on which to test it.
Student population: Knowledge and academic sophistication.	Beginners in subject, general interest.	Advanced students, specialised interests.	In addition to 'subject matter variables', it may not be worthwhile to structure very closely the learning of advanced students, because their network of connecting ideas facilitates comprehension of any new communication in their field. Further, the advanced students' existing knowledge is likely to be very heterogeneous, making a uniform approach for everyone uneconomic.

Table 3

Factor	Column 1 Characteristics in Favour	Column 2 Characteristics Against	Reasons and Remarks
	Students without well developed and currently used study skills (eg early school leavers, adults long out of school etc.)	Students undergoing 'academic' education, with recent practice of studying, abstracting, note taking etc.	The groups in Column 1 often particularly welcome a programmed approach. Groups in Column 2 may resent a closely structured programme, and do better with just guide lines and questions to check progress.

Table 3 (continued)

Factor	Column 1 Characteristics in Favour	Column 2 Characteristics Against	Reasons and Remarks
Student population: Age range, for students in schools, colleges, etc.	Ages 13 onwards in secondary and technical education.	Advanced post-graduate work REPRESENTS A CONTINUUM OF IN-BETWEEN STAGES Beginning of primary school.	This is a rough summary which applies to conceptual subject matter and takes into account students' background knowledge and sophistication, the characteristics of the subject matter normally taught at different ages, as well as objectives which tend to be loaded on the affective side in early years. The summary does not apply to psychomotor or discrimination skills or to rote learning ('drill'). Here programmed self-instruction may be the best method at any stage.
Resources: Teachers	Not available, or not yet recruited.	Plentiful, in permanent posts.	In an educational system well endowed with entrenched teachers programmed self-instruction is expensive, since its adoption cannot lead to significant economies. (continued)

Table 4

Factor	Column 1 Characteristics in Favour	Column 2 Characteristics Against	Reasons and Remarks
(continued) *Resources:* Teachers	(continued) Not available, or not yet recruited.	(continued) Plentiful, in permanent posts.	The reverse applies where teachers are not available, or where a *new* education system is being designed, and the complementary roles of teacher- and self-instruction can be taken into account in preparing staffing estimates and job descriptions.

Table 4 (continued)

Factor	Column 1 Characteristics in Favour	Column 2 Characteristics Against	Reasons and Remarks
(continued) *Resources:* Teachers	Available and interested	Hostile and apathetic	Hostility and apathy have killed many a promising innovation. Since the use of self-instruction changes the teacher's role, rejection is common. Some ways of overcoming it: Present and organise self-instruction so that teacher's authority is not undermined. Involve teachers in production of materials and in testing. Maintain and support 'centres of excellence' using programmed instruction effectively and over a long period of time. On the other hand, avoid formation of weak little programmed instruction activities, which fizzle out and leave an aura of failure. In a centralised system exert pressure for large scale adoption rather than small pilot projects.

Table 4 (continued)

Factor	Column 1 Characteristics in Favour	Column 2 Characteristics Against	Reasons and Remarks
Resources: Capital for development, and hence: Teachers' time for production of materials. Financing of an effective presentation of materials. Ability to use audio-visual presentation where appropriate. Re-training of teacher-users and establishing a system for revision and up-dating, with the help of teacher-users in rotation.	Available	Not available	Programmed instruction can be used in a way permitting useful economies (eg in staff/student ratio), but it requires a considerable initial investment, unless published materials happen to fit the needs of a particular project. Hence, re-allocation of resources may need to be the first step in adopting programmed instruction methods.

Table 5

341

Appendix 2

Extract from Simplified Information Mapping, by T G Wyant

This extract is reproduced by kind permission of the author. It should be read in conjunction with Chapter 9 (pages 264-271 in particular.)

Notes
1   This is an extract of only a few pages, but it forms a useful and understandable study. One feature of information mapping is the ability to extract only relevant material, without losing the sense of the whole.

2   The maps included are:
1-2 Overview. . . Listing the origins and application of information mapping.
2-5 Information Network Diagram . . . Like a contents page, but illustrating the inter-dependence that exists between the maps. Note which maps have been included and which excluded in this extract.
5-10 Information Map Layout . . . Note the standardisation and ability to cross-reference between maps.
10-12 Map Types . . . Note the eclectic nature of the technique, drawing on a variety of other techniques.
10-13 Block Types . . . Note that each block of information is put in the map for a carefully considered purpose.

Introduction Simplified Information Mapping is an elementary version of Information Mapping as designed by Roberı E Horn of Massachusets, United States of America.

Description Information mapping procedures have been designed to assist in information retrieval, logical development of related pieces of information, reduction of reading material when acquiring information.

The information maps, which will all consist of single pages, may also be used for:

- A method of revising knowledge and its structure.

- As a method of filing information when in the process of compiling a book, instruction manual, programmed instruction etc.

- As a quickly assimilated method of learning new concepts, principles, procedures, etc.

- Obtaining a quick overview and thought organising device.

- Establishing the position of a piece of information in cognitive hierarchy.

Procedure When making use of the information maps in the following pages, use the information network to establish those maps to which you wish to refer and your sequence of reading and studying same.

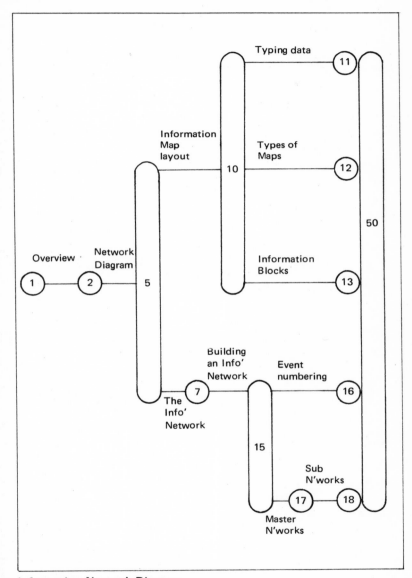

Information Network Diagram

Introduction Each Information Map will have the same basic format.

Diagram

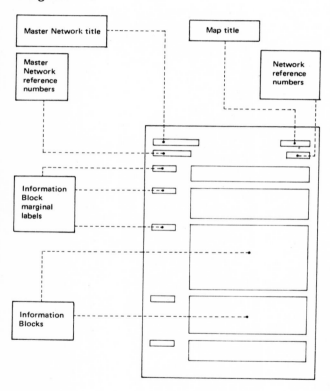

Paper Size: A4

Information Map Layout

Introduction Simplified Information maps will be mainly used to give information, guidance, revision and outlines with regard to subjects and their topics in a syllabus.

Description The maps used will fall into the following categories:

- Overviews
- Objectives
- Review
- Procedure
- Decision
- Diagram
- WHIF chart
- Input/Output
- Parts/Function
- Summary
- Feedback
- Exercises
- Networks
- Parent Networks
- Sub-networks

Reference   See Map Types Information network for map references

Introduction Information Maps will consist of information blocks of varying sizes and types. Each information block will be complete in itself.

Description Information blocks on each Information Map will fall into the following categories:

- Parent network identification
- Map title
- Map reference numbers
- Introduction
- Description (or definition)
- Example
- Formula
- Use
- Comment
- Notation
- Rule
- Synonym
- Diagram
- Illustration
- Analogy
- Reference
- Cross-reference
- Procedure

Reference See Information Block Types network for map references

Index